Luther P. Jackson and a Life for Civil Rights

New Perspectives on the History of the South

Florida A&M University, Tallahassee
Florida Atlantic University, Boca Raton
Florida Gulf Coast University, Ft. Myers
Florida International University, Miami
Florida State University, Tallahassee
University of Central Florida, Orlando
University of Florida, Gainesville
University of North Florida, Jacksonville
University of South Florida, Tampa
University of West Florida, Pensacola

New Perspectives on the History of the South

Luther P. Jackson
and a Life for Civil Rights

Michael Dennis

University Press of Florida

Gainesville · Tallahassee · Tampa · Boca Raton
Pensacola · Orlando · Miami · Jacksonville · Ft. Myers

Library of Congress Cataloging-in-Publication Data
Dennis, Michael, 1967–
Luther P. Jackson and a life for civil rights / Michael Dennis.
p. cm. – (New perspectives on the history of the South)
Includes bibliographical references and index.
ISBN 0-8130-2727-6 (cloth : alk. paper)
1. Jackson, Luther Porter, 1892–1950. 2. African American civil rights
workers–Biography. 3. Civil rights workers–United States–Biography. 4. Civil
rights movements–United States–History–20th century. 5. African Americans–
Civil rights–History–20th century. 6. African Americans–History–1877–1964.
7. Southern States–Race relations–History–20th century. I. Title. II. Series.
E185.97.J26D46   2004
323'.092–dc22
[B]   2004042554

The University Press of Florida is the scholarly publishing agency for the State
University System of Florida, comprising Florida A&M University, Florida Atlantic
University, Florida Gulf Coast University, Florida International University, Florida
State University, University of Central Florida, University of Florida, University
of North Florida, University of South Florida, and University of West Florida.

University Press of Florida
15 Northwest 15th Street
Gainesville, FL 32611-2079
http://www.upf.com

To my mother

and to the memory of Gerald Stortz

Contents

Illustrations

(Following page 96)

1. Luther P. Jackson on his graduation from Fisk University
2. Johnella Frazer
3. Luther and Johnella on their wedding day in 1922
4. Mattie Jackson, Johnella, and "Mama Laura"
5. Jackson and the Virginia State chapter of Omega Psi Phi
6. Luther P. Jackson, circa 1942
7. Jackson and the ever-present suit, hat, and smile
8. The faculty at Virginia State University, ca. 1946
9. Watercolor of Jackson

Foreword

Recent scholarship on the civil rights movement underscores the broad and important role that members of the black middle class played in battling Jim Crow and racial proscription. Michael Dennis's carefully researched, elegantly written, and thoughtfully argued *Luther P. Jackson and a Life for Civil Rights* is a superb case study of a professor who plowed the fields of racial change in Virginia before, during, and following World War II. "More than a chronicler of events," Dennis explains, "Jackson was an author of change in the early civil rights era."

Joining the worlds of academics and social activism, Jackson was a revisionist historian, a persuasive and spellbinding public speaker, a powerful promoter of racial reform at the community level, and, above all, a tenacious optimist. He cajoled, implored, and lobbied black Virginians to vote. Dennis positions Jackson at the center of the black middle-class initiative that challenged Jim Crow long before the 1954 *Brown v. Board of Education* decision. A respected historian and educator, he urged students and teachers throughout Virginia to "claim the political equality implied by their social accomplishments and extend it to all African Americans." "More than anything else," Dennis concludes, Jackson's life "was a life for civil rights."

Descended from ex-slaves, Jackson was born in 1892, attended school in Lexington, Kentucky, and received bachelor's and master's degrees in 1914 and 1916 respectively from Fisk University. In 1922, after teaching assignments in South Carolina and Kansas, Jackson joined the faculty of Virginia Normal and Industrial Institute (later Virginia State College, then Virginia State University) in Petersburg, where he taught until his death in 1950. While in South Carolina, Jackson conducted research on African American education under slavery and during Reconstruction. He published pathbreaking articles based on this work in the *Journal of Negro History*. In 1937, Jackson received his Ph.D. in history from the University of Chicago. His dissertation, "Free Negro Labor and Property Holding in Virginia, 1830–1860," argued that free blacks in that state held considerably more land than previous historians had assumed. Jackson published this study in 1942, and it remains the definitive work on the subject. History provided Jackson with a window through which to examine and illuminate past racial injustices and to celebrate contemporary Negro accomplishment and humanity.

Influenced strongly by the famed historian Carter G. Woodson, founder of the Association for the Study of Negro Life and History, Jackson also emphasized race pride and self-confidence, reminding his audiences that African Americans had made major contributions to world history. Woodson and Jackson differed over history's utility, Dennis explains: "While Woodson championed scholarship as the route to overturning racial oppression, Jackson favored community building and political engagement as the means for widening the cracks in the wall of Jim Crow. The two men crafted distinctive and often competing notions of black historical inquiry." Over many years Jackson blended the study of black history with political mobilization and local business regeneration. In contrast to Woodson, Jackson "recognized that the relationship between historical inquiry and public consciousness was too vital to sever by academic obfuscation. He understood that the analysis of the past should not be carried on within the boundaries of an exclusive professional caste."

Jackson's foremost legacy, according to Dennis, was his persistent advocacy of black voting rights. "By publishing, organizing, and proselytizing on behalf of voting, he helped stimulate a political awakening among black Virginians." Pragmatic, not theoretical, Jackson wrote little about the meaning of race and racial identity. Rather, he preached that black suffrage would open doors to better schools and to more services for Depression-era Afro-Virginians: "It provided a tool for achieving genuine equality, a society freed of racial discrimination, and the space in which black cultural pride could evolve into racial self-determination."

Specifically, Jackson studied voting patterns, organized voting leagues, wrote articles, and mobilized members of the Virginia Teachers Association to pay their poll taxes and vote. He espoused a moderate, biracial, liberal ethos—one that accentuated moral suasion and civility over the direct action and confrontation practiced by later civil rights activists.

Undeterred by the failure of antisegregation legislation, Jackson had an undying faith in the political process. "As a historian," Dennis notes, "he took the long view, recognizing that failed legislative maneuvers did not render conventional methods of change useless."

While mindful of the limits of Jackson's middle-class interracial reform strategy, Dennis nonetheless credits him with helping to lay the foundation for the modern civil rights revolution: "His was a protest born of tremendous optimism about the potential for change through conventional institutions." Convinced that the future of race depended on political action, Jackson worked at the grassroots level to build organizations that helped to implement integration in the post-1954 period. His greatest contribution, according to Dennis, was the "example of political responsibility for those accustomed to indifference." Jackson rooted his activism "in steady resistance to racial discrimination and an abiding confidence that blacks had it within their power to take control over their lives. At a time when African Americans lacked visible leadership, his work lent authority and a voice to the struggle for equality in Virginia and the South."

Dennis's book rescues from obscurity a talented pioneer scholar who successfully redefined the historian's public role. "Jackson believed that the past was not a museum of curiosities but a repository of lessons and alternatives for the present," Dennis explains. Jackson's determined and indefatigable voting rights crusade helped blacks move from the past to the present, from the indignities of Jim Crow to the new freedoms and responsibilities of full citizenship.

John David Smith
Series Editor

Acknowledgments

Countless people have helped to shape what was originally a nebulous idea into its present form, and it is my pleasure to acknowledge them here. This project began through conversations with Fitz Brundage, whose erudition and guidance have proved indispensable since I was a student of his at Queen's University, Kingston, Ontario. It was Fitz who introduced me to Luther P. Jackson and who offered constructive criticism throughout, and I am once again grateful for his support. As I worked through the Jackson Collection, trying to knit together the strands of his personal and public life, I benefited enormously from the assistance of Lucious Edwards, archivist at Virginia State. His encyclopedic knowledge of the collections was invaluable, and so too was his insight into African American and Virginia history. I am grateful for both. At Virginia State, I was fortunate to receive the professional assistance of several librarians and assistants, most of whose patience I tested with questions sublime and ridiculous. Their expertise helped me out of more than one bind. I would also like to thank professors Edgar Toppin and Joe Goldenberg, the former, for his knowledge of Jackson and for a sightseeing tour that helped me better understand him, and the latter, for his hospitality and kindness during my extended stay. My major research trip would not have happened, though, without the assistance of the Canada–U.S. Fulbright program and the financial assistance of the Office of Research and Graduate Studies at Acadia University.

Special mention must be made of the Jackson family for their remarkable support and encouragement. Their willingness to provide recollections of Jackson, along with valuable research materials and cherished photographs, was simply astonishing. They lent me their time and memories while respecting the need for scholarly detachment, and I am grateful to them for both. In particular, I would like to thank Edward Jackson, DeLoris Lightfoot Jackson, Luther P. Jackson Jr., Nettie Jackson, Luther P. Jackson III, Onaje Jackson, and Dorothy

Hodge Davis Johnson, all of whom made this project not only possible but rewarding. All of the photographs included here appear courtesy of Luther and Nettie Jackson and family. Quotations from the Luther P. Jackson Papers, including the administrative and personal collection at Virginia State University in Petersburg, are reprinted with the kind permission of the Jackson family.

For their critical and constructive reading of the manuscript, I wish to thank Peter Wallenstein and the anonymous reader, both courtesy of the University Press of Florida. John David Smith, Meredith Morris-Babb, Deidre Bryan, and Jenny Ward skillfully guided this manuscript through the publishing process at UPF. Larrisa Smith offered important research leads and her own expertise in Virginia's civil rights movement. Had Dita Zemanek not wielded her organizational skills in codifying research materials and hunting down sources early on in the project, I might still be at it. Karen Kapteyn and Lindsay Taylor also provided vital assistance in the last stages of research. Pat Mac-Nutt, the administrative assistant in the history and classics department at Acadia, poured hours of simply invaluable editorial labor into this project and completed a multitude of miscellaneous tasks that ultimately made my job easier and this book better. I am particularly indebted to her for this. Finally, my wife, Melanie, who accompanied me on the first trip to Petersburg, read drafts of the chapters, discussed the ideas and the issues, and endured everything that came with it, deserves more gratitude than I can express.

Chapter 1

—————••—————

That the Hope Might Become a Reality

In the early Virginia spring of 1950, Dr. Luther P. Jackson addressed the State Conference of the Future Teachers of America at the Hampton Institute, Booker T. Washington's alma mater. It was a routine address, one of any number of lectures an academic was expected to deliver as part of his or her contribution to university service. The address meant an additional drain on his limited time, filled as it was by departmental responsibilities at Virginia State College and multiple commitments to various reform organizations. But Jackson did not disappoint. In a formal lecture to a group of students who offered little in the way of career advancement or professional prestige, Jackson, as Palmer noted, "bore [them] all along on the wave which his infectious enthusiasm generated," Hampton teacher L. F. Palmer reported, "in his usual dynamic fashion."

Yet his address had little to do with pedagogical technique, still less to do with career management, course development, or academic administration. Instead, he focused on "Civil Rights for Negroes." The message was simple, direct, and powerful: voting and litigation would produce equality. Instead of platitudes about educating students for a challenging workforce, the assembly heard Jackson speak "eloquently and learnedly about first-class citizenship for Negroes in the American democracy." But more than this, they encountered "a Negro man who had dedicated his life to hasten the day when that hope would become a reality." Here was an academic "who not only talked about this all-important topic, but also one who did things in this vital area." Following the address, Jackson buoyantly shared with Palmer his plans for future research, addresses, and conferences. Two weeks later, at the age of fifty-seven, he died in his sleep from heart failure.[1]

If there was a representative moment in the life of this professor, historian, activist, and musician, the address at Hampton was it. It illustrated his struggle to combine academics and action, his commitment to education as the wellspring of social change, and his conviction that political influence would produce black liberation. At the same time, it encapsulated his belief that altering African American perceptions of the world and its political structures was the prerequisite for meaningful change. Yet as resourceful, energetic, and relentless as Luther P. Jackson was, he was no anomaly. He belonged to that group of African American activists—a good many of whom were teachers—who fostered the ideas and organizations that would blossom in the later civil rights movement. They were part of the black "bourgeoisie" that staffed the allegedly legalistic NAACP while filling the ranks of the fraternity lodges that supposedly fiddled while black America burned. Of course, this historiographical depiction has become a little weary, as scholars of the postmovement period have uncovered the critical contributions of the NAACP and its middle-class activists to the movement as early as the 1920s.[2]

Even so, few have paid attention to the civil rights struggle in the Upper South, particularly Virginia. Here, race relations followed a tradition of genteel paternalism that avoided the routine brutalities that accompanied the defense of white dominance in the Deep South. Yet aristocratic paternalism was no less effective in denying African Americans political power and economic opportunity. The Virginia tradition of white noblesse oblige offered little relief from the ignominy of segregation. If anything, a relatively hospitable atmosphere—a velvet glove approach to racial management—neutralized African American protest under the cloying weight of white benevolence. Virginia's ruling class fashioned a political system built on an extremely restricted electorate, powerful machine rule, and the conviction that only the better sort should govern. Understanding the resilience of Virginia's political and social traditions, Jackson called on African Americans to vote and litigate for change. Tirelessly he appealed to people to vote, believing that conventional avenues of political expression offered the best hope for gaining control over their lives. First, however, their conceptual framework had to change, and the way to change ideas was through education.[3]

Luther Jackson's experience is important, then, not only because it illuminates a largely forgotten chapter in the civil rights movement, but also because it underlines the pivotal role that educators played in advancing racial equality. Building his political program on the foundation of Virginia State College, the school at which he taught for more than twenty-five years, Jackson spun his web of political activism across black colleges throughout the state and the region. He built a network of college professors committed to using their classrooms and the resources at their disposal to spark political engagement. Through his initiative, the network embraced teachers in training at Virginia State, at other colleges, in elementary and high schools, at Rosenwald training schools—at institutions where activists could influence young African Americans. Jackson, Rupert Picott, LuTrelle Palmer, and a host of other reformers integrated the Virginia Teachers Association into an expanding reform alliance, forging it into a conduit of information and ideas. Jackson's story is also the story of these teachers, people who grappled with larger issues at the same time that they confronted the limits of their power, the tenuousness of their jobs, and the often-appalling conditions of black schooling in the South. Jackson and the teachers struggled to transform schools into arenas of self-determination against the crushing indignity of Jim Crow.

But Luther Jackson was more than an exemplar of some abstract group of black, middle-class activists. If there is one point of consensus among historians plumbing the early civil rights movement, it is the recognition that protest did not follow a uniform pattern and schedule featuring easily recognized stock characters.[4] Yes, voting rights activists could be found throughout the South, and an effort has been made to link Jackson's experience to people such as Harry T. Moore and Osceola McKaine. But Jackson did not simply fit into a generic mold for civil rights workers. The sheer range of his activities sets him apart from many. At any one time between 1937 and 1950, he was simultaneously leading NAACP voting and organization drives, the Virginia Voters League, the Negro Organization Societies, the Virginia chapter of the Association for the Study of Negro Life and History (ASNLH), the Virginia Teachers Association, and the fraternal order of the Elks. This does not include his work for the Virginia History Commission, the Southern Conference for Human Welfare, the Southern Regional Council, and the Virginia Civil Rights Organization. This ceaseless determination to use overlapping constituencies to achieve political regeneration distinguished his public career from those of many others who channeled their energies into one group. By coordinating disparate and potentially influential groups, including teachers, educational administrators, and students, Jackson achieved political synergy. More than this, he wove political action into his teaching, scholarship, and college administration, subverting education as an instrument for reproducing class and race distinctions.

In the broadest perspective, he fashioned organizations and strategies that would guide a later civil rights movement.[5]

Yet not all of these groups survived, and some played only a marginal role in the later struggle. Activists of the Martin Luther King generation replicated some of Jackson's protest strategies, particularly in the area of voter education and registration, but they adopted techniques of direct action that reflected their own pressing circumstances. What did persist was an ethos of political engagement that provided the kindling of civil rights militancy. What clearly continued was the conviction that local activism and community mobilization was essential to any effective assault on segregation. What later activists *did* embrace was the notion that social reform would not come through white paternalism but through African American protest. Did Jackson achieve mass mobilization? Did he reach the rural proletariat that saw voting as a "white man's business"? Yes and no. Falling short of achieving a collective uprising— as did later civil rights activists, it should be noted—he stirred the embers of political awareness that burned very low in Virginia. He did not mobilize all of the teachers, nor did he activate all of their students or their impoverished or simply disinterested parents. But he did reach many, and it was these who carried the cognitive reorientation foreword. Teachers didn't throw off the posture of racial deference to white authorities and launch mass protest, but many came to a political awakening during the period, a development that can be attributed at least in part to Jackson's indefatigable work. Political consciousness—indeed, a changed perspective on racial possibilities—is not easily quantified, although readers will find numbers to support the claims advanced for Jackson. But a changing worldview, a new understanding of the nexus between race and class, an altered conception of the racial order and the place of African Americans in the United States can be documented. In fact, Luther Jackson spent a considerable part of his career doing precisely this.

Individual efforts did matter, and in Virginia, Luther Jackson's mattered more than most. His life's work should not be ignored because he did not achieve the prominence of John Lewis, Stokely Carmichael, Robert Moses, or Martin Luther King. If recent historiography is correct, we have done a considerable disservice to local activists by privileging only those who captured the headlines and the attention of a media-conscious president. Of course, we also do an injustice to Jackson and his counterparts by dismissing him as another local activist, another obscure figure belonging to an anonymous group of forerunners to the *real* civil rights movement. If there is a key presupposition pervading this work, it is this: the period between 1933 and 19549–the period encompassing the New Deal, the Second World War, and the nascent Cold War—witnessed the flourishing of the civil rights movement. It was not, as some would like to parse it, simply a preamble to what would come later. Activists at this time could not look into a crystal ball and expect their work to produce protests, marches, and sit-ins. For people like Jackson, the civil rights movement *was* unfolding in a dramatic and surprising way in places as unlikely as Petersburg and Farmville, Virginia.[6]

This is not to suggest that historians should abandon analytical distinctions between periods or diminish the momentous achievements of the 1960s. Without the bold leadership and innovative tactics of that generation of civil rights organizers, legal barriers to racial equality would not have been dismantled and the efforts of an earlier generation would have meant little. But there is a danger in freezing these periods as discrete chronological morsels for convenient retrospective consumption. Considering the negligible amount of time between the *Brown v. Board of Education* decision and the sit-ins at Greensboro, it makes little sense to separate them as if they were a world apart, two dramatically different historical epochs that have little in common. This movement gained momentum, narrowed its objectives, and shifted focus between 1950 and 1960, but it followed a continuum stretching back to the litigation and voter registration drives of the early 1940s. The search for racial justice that Jackson and countless others pursued was the same search that SNCC activists would take up, albeit under decidedly different circumstances.[7]

Historical contingencies are critical in explaining the intensification of voting rights activity, labor organization, and litigation in the 1940s. Jackson's circumstances were not of his own choosing, although the choices he made suggest the range of opportunities that were open to those who rejected the status quo. As the New Deal and mobilization for the Second World War increased the prospects for black advancement, Luther Jackson became more uncompromising in his thought and strategy. He never accepted political disfranchisement, but he operated within the parameters of segregation when few whites questioned it and even fewer southern blacks dared challenge it *openly*. This changed quickly in the following decade, as southern liberals, union organizers, and African American activists expanded the fissures that had developed in the Solid South during the 1930s. Infused with the kinetic energy of wartime change, Jackson began to believe that black enfranchisement belonged to a larger movement to rehabilitate the feudal and oppressive South. This movement, he believed, depended on a working-class alliance that stretched across the racial barrier. His intellectual odyssey was inextricably tied to forces that churned up the barren soil of southern political life in the New Deal era. If the story of biracial southern liberalism is inseparable from a regional and national narrative, then Luther Jackson's experience is as well.

His experience is also entangled in this larger story because he made it that way. As much as he focused on developments in Virginia, he found a political and scholarly voice that resonated well beyond the Commonwealth. Through his voting surveys, his study of free blacks during slavery, his support for inter-racial reform organizations, and his contributions to political strategy, Jackson joined a swirling debate on race and reform that irrevocably altered the structure of southern society. Luther Jackson was not a harmless proponent of inter-racial goodwill, but a resolute though flawed and sometimes shortsighted advocate for democratic reform. His struggle for voting rights—the centerpiece of his political worldview and his public career—paralleled the work of activists across the South. Voting rights activists were not part of a moderate or, even worse, conservative, movement for token change. Some, such as Harry T. Moore and later Medgar Evers, paid with their lives for challenging the southern prohibition on black citizenship.[8]

Along with other Virginia activists, Jackson adopted a pragmatic approach to negotiating between segregation and civil rights.[9] Recognizing expanded opportunities for black political action in a caste-based society, he focused on avenues that promised the greatest results and the least likelihood of reprisals, the latter of which few could afford. The momentum of war and the ideological contradictions it exposed encouraged activists to attack segregation directly. For Jackson and others, this meant a shift in expectations, not ideology. If he subscribed to a "racial uplift ideology" that sought to "rehabilitate the image of black people through class distinctions" and racial hierarchies, it never governed his thinking about political reform, and it faded into obscurity in the late 1930s.[10] Instead, he premised his political thought on the republican egalitarianism of the Reconstruction era. Instead of racial transformation, he advocated black civic consciousness in the movement for full citizenship.

Jackson was above all a public figure whose organizing and scholarship converged in the drive for political consciousness. Yet, in elucidating his public activity, we are invariably drawn to the private domain, not simply because the two are logically inseparable, but because it was in the private world of personal study, social encounters, family relations, friendship, menial jobs, and companionate affection that Jackson fostered notions of social change and his place in the movement. It was in the private realm that he first struggled with the questions of race, power, democracy, and the prospects for African American freedom. Here he encountered the irrationality and callous indignity of segregation. Here too he struggled with his identity—the Washingtonian and Du-Boisian polarities, if you will—in a society that made middle-class virtues the portal to social entitlement, except for blacks. Yet family, music, friends, social clubs, and church gatherings bound Jackson and others together in collective defiance of the insult of segregation. It is here that an understanding of Luther Jackson should begin.

A final caveat is necessary. This book is not in the strict sense a biography (a denial that historians now regularly make for fear of being censured for writing something as prosaic as a biography). I have not tried to present a comprehensive account of Jackson's life. A thorough account would double the pages but obscure the issues to which Jackson gave priority over the course of his career. This analysis focuses on those critical years when economic upheaval, political realignment, military intervention, labor conflict, and international struggles for power seemed to throw everything into question, including the American tradition of racial inequality. What I have tried to do is offer a sense of Jackson's place in a larger, changing social panorama without reducing him to the expression of a historical era that disfigures him. What I have discovered is that Jackson profoundly shaped the organizations that he joined, but that they in turn left their imprint on him, altering his worldview and raising in some cases his hopes for change. In more ways than this book can capture, the 1940s—at least for Americans—were a time of hope, and not simply because the Second World War converted the country into the industrial and military superpower that banished fears of economic desolation to the past. It was a time of hope for the common people that Franklin D. Roosevelt so famously remembered, since for them, it promised an America in which they would not be forgotten again. Jackson responded to these broad social forces, but he played a part in directing them against the "American Dilemma" that sociologist Gunnar Myrdal identified at the center of the nation's soul. In other words, the time made the person, but the person molded the time and the environment in which he lived. If that were not the case, we would not be reading and writing about Jackson at all.

Origins

Born in Lexington, Kentucky, in 1892, Luther Porter Jackson was the son of former slaves. Some uncorroborated reports have it that his grandfather, Jordan Jackson, who was born into slavery, was a brother to Mary Todd Lincoln. He was the sixth boy in a family of twelve headed by a father, Edward Williams Jackson, who operated a dairy farm on the margins of penury. Luther Jackson probably absorbed his political sensibilities from his father, Edward, a devoted newspaper reader and follower of political affairs. Delilah Culverson, Jackson's mother and a teacher by profession, ensured that her children attended school. She enrolled each of them at the Chandler Normal School, which the American Missionary Society constructed as part of the great wave of northern educational philanthropy for African Americans in the early postwar South. The children supported the family by taking janitorial jobs at the school and helping out on the farm. Family solidarity was not enough: Edward Jackson lost the farm to bankruptcy in 1908, when Jackson was a high school senior. He died the following year.[11]

On finishing high school in Lexington, Kentucky, Luther Jackson enrolled at Fisk University and graduated in 1914. A coronet player with ambitions to lead a band, he was drawn to Fisk by the Jubilee Singers and its reputation for musical training. But other interests soon competed with his musical proclivities. Historian George Edmund Haynes—former executive director of the National Urban League and a founding member of the NAACP—sowed the seeds of Jackson's historical consciousness. He decided to pursue a career in teaching, probably imagining that he could combine his passion for music with his newfound interest in history. Jackson absorbed more than an affinity for history and fine music from Fisk. He also imbibed the tradition of social service espoused by the university's missionary founders and by George Edmund Haynes. "This worthy Fisk man," Jackson noted in an address to Fisk graduates in 1939, "was so thoroughly imbued with the notion of service to others that we can safely say that the department which he founded, sociology, was cradled in service." From his years in Nashville, Jackson internalized the notion that education was above all an exercise in social service and the educator a leader for change.[12]

After a brief sojourn at the University of Kansas, Jackson enrolled at City College of New York in 1920 to pursue teaching credentials. Universities wielded a polite form of racial discrimination against black candidates, often questioning the merit of their degrees from black colleges. Columbia rejected most of the credits Jackson had earned for his master's degree at Fisk. He made up lost ground by attending a year of classes at City College of New York and then enrolled at Columbia University Teachers College, where he earned a master of arts degree on the strength of a thesis on "The Educational Activities of the Freedmen's Bureau and Freedmen's Aid Societies in South Carolina, 1862–1872." The paper had its genesis during Jackson's first and perhaps most formative teaching assignment as director of the academic department at the Voorhees Industrial School in Denmark, South Carolina. The paper later found its way into the *Journal of Negro History*, Carter G. Woodson's pathbreaking outlet for black historical research. By 1922, the budding historian and dedicated teacher had made his way to the Virginia Normal and Industrial Institute, the school that would harbor him for the rest of his career.[13]

That year represented another milestone: his marriage to Johnella Frazer. A companion and fellow musician since their days at Fisk, Frazer had arrived first at Virginia Normal, teaching piano to students who invariably admired and emulated her. As much as Jackson would range beyond the campus in pursuit of black political mobilization and historical data, Frazer provided the anchor against insecurity and uncertainty. Sacrificing her own career, she became a resolute supporter of Jackson's career and a dedicated mother to their four children. It is in chapter 2 that we meet Johnella, a fascinating person in her own right. It is through their relationship that we see Jackson's ideas and convictions emerge. More than this, their relationship provides a window on black middle-class life in the Depression era. It offers a glimpse of how black professionals understood the struggle for equality and managed the world of Jim Crow. No less important, it illustrates the efforts of black men and women to establish a sense of cultural independence that balanced the search for democratic inclusion. Understanding Luther and Johnella is essential for understanding Jackson's place in the movement.

History influenced Jackson's perception of the black experience and his vision of the civil rights movement. Chapter 3 uncovers Jackson's intellectual awakening as a graduate student at the University of Chicago, where he studied with the likes of Avery O. Craven and William E. Dodd. As much as Chicago molded him professionally, Carter G. Woodson and his Association for the Study of Negro Life and History shaped his conception of black history's place in the struggle for equality. The conviction that black dignity and political reform lay in an encounter with the past flowed through his major works, which included the acclaimed *Free Negro Labor and Property Holding in Virginia,*

1830–1860; Negro Office-Holders in Virginia, 1865–1895; and *Virginia Negro Sailors and Soldiers in the American Revolution.* This chapter also explores the fruitful but often acrimonious relationship between Woodson the ascetic scholar and Jackson the activist intellectual. While Woodson mentored the Chicago graduate, it was Jackson who made the association a presence in Virginia. Through the ASNLH, he tilled the seeds of popular black historical consciousness, built the organization into a powerhouse for independent black action, and fused it to other organizations committed to racial equality. At the same time, he redefined the role of the scholar in American public life. Each phase sheds light on Luther Jackson, the movement in Virginia, and the flowering of political awareness in the South.

At Virginia State College, the school at which he would teach from 1922 until his death in 1950, Jackson crafted a life that combined scholarship, study, and social activism. As a professor at an institution that produced black teachers, he invariably linked education and racial reform. Teaching offered him an avenue for recovering the black historical experience, but it also connected him to the teachers who understood precisely what role education played in racial amelioration. Chapters 5 and 6 explore Jackson's growing conviction that teachers and their professional organizations, schools, and colleges offered the staging ground for the movement against racial exclusion. Classrooms would provide the space in which notions of racial equality could be fostered, but teachers' organizations could become the conduits for transmitting the message of change through political education. As civic education secretary for the Virginia Teachers Association, he disseminated the program that would govern his thinking about civil rights until his death. But he also discovered that many teachers had already awakened to the possibilities of change through political instruction and participation. A symbiotic relationship developed between Jackson and the teachers, one that galvanized the conviction that equality was possible. In stimulating political consciousness among teachers and students, he established the groundwork for the challenge to segregation in the 1950s.

It was the Second World War, though, that shook the foundations of the racial caste system in the South, and Jackson did much of the shaking. During the war, the NAACP grew exponentially, black political consciousness and voting activity escalated, hidden antipathies toward segregation became public, and racial justice fused with working-class determination to make the Four Freedoms a reality at home. Jackson immersed himself in each of these developments. He evolved at this time into a vigorous, uncompromising proponent of racial change. Solidifying the political networks he had established earlier while joining leading progressive groups throughout the decade, he participated in the wider southern movement for democratic revitalization. The frustrations and accomplishments of that movement, which swept up national elites along with African American and white local activists, constitute the story of beleaguered New Deal liberalism in the dawning hours of the Cold War. That story unfolds in chapter 7.

And yet Jackson still had considerable fight in him, and some of his most remarkable accomplishments would come only at the end of the 1940s. Generating support for a civil rights conference at Monticello, organizing opposition to segregation in Richmond, fanning the flames of black discontent over inequitable education, and heralding Supreme Court decisions against segregated interstate travel—all of these came after the war. Chapter 8 sketches these developments, but it also tries to establish a sense of Jackson's legacy in the 1950s, the period when blacks enjoyed their greatest victory through the courts and faced their strongest opposition from southern elites committed to "massive resistance." By that time, the notion that blacks could permanently be excluded from American political life had been irrevocably eroded. The story of how that happened follows the story of Luther P. Jackson. If anyone can claim that they gave their life to a cause, it was this ebullient, charming, determined, sometimes intemperate, and ultimately dangerous professor. More than anything else, his was a life for civil rights.

Chapter 2

———•———

Jubilee Days

Luther Jackson, Johnella Frazer, and African American Life

Educated, employed, and active in community life, Luther Jackson and Johnella Frazer were typical middle-class African Americans. They placed education at the center of their mental universe; they scrimped and saved to rent a modest house on the campus of Virginia State University; they joined community organizations, attended church, and spent next to nothing on personal frivolities. Jackson himself was noted for wearing the same rumpled suits day in and day out. But he wore his suit regardless of the circumstances—he was, after all, middle class.

Luther and Johnella struggled with typically middle-class concerns, but their status failed to shield them from the racial realities of the Jim Crow South. If anything, it mediated their understanding of the black experience in America, governing their attitudes about leadership, social responsibility, and personal behavior. They inhabited a world patterned after southern fears, but the grip of white dominance was susceptible to black resistance and social change.[1]

Jackson, Frazer, and others built an internal life that shielded them from many of the indignities of segregation. Like the African American community in Norfolk that historian Earl Lewis has studied, they transformed segregation into "congregation," achieving a measure of independence that mitigated the injuries of racial exclusion. The "congregation" they built reflected their middle-class outlook, one that placed a heavy premium on family and companionship in the larger struggle for equality. If we are to understand Luther Jackson, we need to explore his relationship with his wife and his family, since it is through them that he molded his ideas on the racial struggle, defined the place of education and history in the drive for equality, and framed the vision of democratic community that would guide his thought throughout his public life. In that relationship, we see the possibilities and limits of racial self-determination not as an abstraction but as a living reality. The relationship between Luther and Johnella provides a window on the professor's intellectual development, but it also reflects on the black middle-class experience in the interwar years. By examining their lives, we examine the experience of the southern black middle-class on the precipice of change.[2]

Up from Fisk

By the time that Johnella Frazer arrived in Nashville in 1911, Fisk University had become one of the leading African American colleges in the South. Assisted by the Freedmen's Bureau, Fisk combined elements of the classical tradition favored by northern missionaries and the industrial education that Booker T. Washington championed. The university had already produced illustrious graduates. In 1889, W.E.B. DuBois graduated from Fisk with a bachelor of arts degree but was burdened with a poignant awareness of racial inequality and the importance of education for black advancement. In 1930, Harlem Renaissance writer James Weldon Johnson brought distinction to the university when he left the NAACP to join its faculty. There, he wrote the probing *Negro Americans, What Now?* which called for black solidarity in support of full integration. Sociologist Charles Johnson, an advisor on New Deal programs, added to Fisk's luster. He was also a vital force in the Commission on Interracial Cooperation and the Southern Regional Council, as well as a consultant to national education associations. In 1944, Johnson established the controversial Race Relations Institute at the university, a summer seminar that brought white and black activists together.[3]

In the years before the First World War, though, when Jackson and Johnella attended the school, Fisk was best known for its Jubilee Singers. To relieve financial distress, Treasurer George White assembled the group in 1875 to perform traditional African American spirituals for paying northern audiences. After wildly successful performances throughout the Northeast, the group toured England, Germany, and other continental destinations. After only a few years of performing, the group had raised $150,000, a percentage of which the students used to finance Jubilee Hall on the Fisk Campus.[4]

If students at Fisk considered the Jubilees an expression of their African American heritage, some whites saw it differently. Fisk's president, J. G. Merril, supported the group's "negro music" for its supposedly uplifting qualities. Writing to Wallace Buttrick of the General Education Board, Merril claimed: "They are born musicians. They are bound to sing. . . . No surer way of toning up the pulpit end of the church can be found than by elevating the music end."[5] Like much of African American culture in the era of segregation, the Fisk singers testified to the multiple meanings of black self-expression. While students considered the songs an expression of religious faith and cultural pride, whites filtered them through the screen of racial caste. They sifted through them in search of features that confirmed familiar stereotypes of black behavior. In this case, Merril combined assumptions about black musicianship and spirituality in a program for civilizing blacks. Few whites escaped the tendency to ascribe racial stereotypes to black literature and music.

For Johnella Frazer, Fisk University meant the opportunity to study and perform music, her passion since childhood. Born in 1896, Johnella was the daughter of two teachers. Her father, P. T. Frazer, had been dean of Eckstein-Norton University in Cane Springs, Kentucky, and president of the M. & F. College in Hopkinsville, Kentucky. We know little about her mother, but it seems that she cultivated Johnella's musical sensibilities. Frazer's mother— affectionately referred to as "Mama Laura"—took over many of the household responsibilities on the campus of Virginia State when Jackson and Frazer held simultaneous teaching appointments. In keeping with the family's musical proclivities, Frazer's parents named her brother Mozart. He lived up to his namesake, taking up the violin and accompanying his sister during choral performances. In 1911, she enrolled in a three-year music program at Fisk. There she also joined the Fisk Jubilee Singers, an experience that had a lasting impact on her musical consciousness.[6]

In 1916, Frazer accepted a position at the Virginia Normal and Industrial Institute in Petersburg. Established during Reconstruction as a liberal arts college for blacks, the institution suffered a humiliating setback when the state government reduced it to a high school, as part of a larger attack on black civil rights, in 1902. Through the efforts of President John M. Gandy, the state restored the institution to collegiate status in the 1920s. As a product of Fisk, Gandy became a consistent supporter of its graduates. When given a chance, he hired Fisk alumni for faculty positions at Virginia Normal and Industrial Institute. Along with Frazer, Gandy brought Felicia D. Anderson to the school to teach drama and English. In a later search for a solid historian and social science teacher, the president would net Luther Porter Jackson.

As a piano instructor at Virginia State, Frazer left a lasting impression on her students. Matie Wilkerson remembered her as a uniformly calm and patient teacher who expected her students to absorb daily Bible lessons alongside arpeggios and scales. John Lee recalled a "superb" teacher who encouraged struggling students and made them want to please her through practice and improvement. India Taylor Johnson described her as a "superb" person who loved her family and her students. Evelyn Spaights recalled that Frazer became a mother to her as she suffered the pangs of homesickness in her early years at Virginia State. On occasion, Frazer would invite her to breakfast to enjoy the splendid offerings that issued from "Mama Laura's" busy skillet. Spaights also noted that Frazer was "nobody's fool"; her kindly demeanor hid a stern determination to make her students excel. Each recalled her abundant talent and graceful mastery of the ivories.[7]

Few things mattered to Johnella Frazer as much as perfecting her craft. Along with teaching responsibilities, she accompanied the school choir and a host of soloists, organized a choral club in Petersburg, tutored local children in music, and performed privately for local families. She often included selections from the Jubilees in her repertoire, but her students were not always eager to perform traditional spiritual songs. As Frazer complained of one Sunday school class, "These children here have little respect for the melodies—don't get the right spirit into them."[8] Their reluctance to sing the spirituals may have reflected the growing African American discomfort with the legacy of slavery, but the uneasiness barely registered in the minds of Johnella Frazer. Nor did it have much of an impact on Luther Jackson, who also found it difficult to teach the Jubilees, particularly in cases when the "past tradition" was "lacking." More disturbing, however, was his discovery that some objected to "singing the songs of our people." If some considered them the reminder of a painful past, Frazer and Jackson believed them the purest expression of racial authenticity.[9]

Autumns in New York—and Petersburg

Friends during their days at Fisk, Frazer and Jackson began to correspond regularly after the war. Music and the Jubilees brought them together, and it would continue to bind them closely throughout their years together. Their relationship intensified during Jackson's years at City College of New York. By then, both wrote to each other weekly, Jackson routinely putting pen to paper on Saturday nights. In September 1920, Johnella signed her letters "Sincerely

Yours," while Jackson responded with a restrained "Most faithfully." By April, Jackson was no longer "My dear Lute," but "My own Lute," the apostrophes now gone from a term of affection that felt comfortable. She now ended her letters with variations such as "With a *whole* lot of love always" or "Lovingly your own John." Jackson, too, had grown warmer in his salutations, leaving behind "My dear girl" for the more emphatic "My Own Sweetheart."[10]

Strained by a long-distance liaison, Luther assured Johnella that their friendship was anything but "ephemeral." He intimated at marriage by suggesting that he "done some cataloguing as regards you and me which I shall bring up for consideration at our near approaching 'conference.'" Anything but sentimental, he claimed that the basis of his affection for her was the "solid material" that formed her "immaculate character." Frazer waxed more eloquently about her betrothed. Anticipating a visit after a separation of several months, she saw her feelings reflected in nature: "But everything is so *beautiful*—just as tho' nature itself were preparing for my Boy—I haven't been out to our woods yet, but I know they are 'be-decking' themselves for the great event." Jackson was never much of a romantic, but he remained complimentary and affectionate toward Frazer throughout their marriage. Responding to Johnella's account of a performance she had given in Chicago, Luther assured her that he knew she "would give perfect satisfaction in your accompanying. I know you are hard to beat in this field."[11] Despite prolonged separations, family illness, and ever-present financial stress, that mutual respect never dissipated.

Frazer was not pining away, however. In addition to teaching and conducting several ensembles, she enjoyed an active social life that included travel and entertainment. Like many African American southerners, she found the church a source of both social stimulation and spiritual comfort. Often noted as the central institution in the black community, the church offered a public space to exchange stories, solidify friendships, and build social cohesion free from the scrutiny of white southerners. In August 1921, she attended church services followed by a barbecue, an event she described as a "Kentucky Basket Meeting." The day featured "a fairly good sermon, terrible singing by the choir, but several melodious jubilee songs," and, of equal note, "loads of eatables." The selection included "chicken, hamcake, and pie until you were 'truly to [sic] full for utterance.'" The festivities continued into Sunday night as "Charles," "Harriette," "Bertie," and "so on up the line" regaled Frazer and her friend, Dell Green, with "their many and varied experiences."[12]

She also took regular car trips to visit neighboring friends in Low Moor,

Covington, Clifton Forge, and Caroline.[13] Like any tourist, Frazer visited the "historic" sites in Virginia, including the birthplace of George Washington and—in evidence of a public history designed by white defenders of the Lost Cause—the birthplace of General Robert E. Lee. Frazer enjoyed the excitement of travel, but it was an experience that invariably reminded her and other African Americans of the limits of their freedom. After one of her many trips to Clifton Forge, Johnella returned by train to Virginia State via Fredericksburg. Unlike the usual noise and discomfort of travel on the segregated line, on this occasion she enjoyed "a *whole* coach" and a "quiet crowd." The enticing landscapes and the company of a "good magazine" made for a "pleasant ride in a Jim Crow Car." Frazer's comments reflect her class sensitivities, since a "quiet crowd" probably meant the absence of the working-class African Americans who normally mixed indiscriminately with middle-class blacks. They certainly suggest her ability to defend against the indignities of segregation.

Yet Frazer lived in a state where leading whites believed that aristocratic benevolence had made it into a model of racial harmony. Lulled by images of enlightened plantation grandees indulging their faithful slaves, Virginia's elites imagined themselves the benefactors of an appreciative, downtrodden race. Providing minimal social services, second-class employment, and paternalistic assurances of the rewards of hard work, white elites insisted in return that blacks submit unconditionally to their authority. The myth had its basis in a fragment of reality: racial violence was much less common in the Commonwealth than in states due south, where the prevalence of one-crop, labor-intensive agriculture supported by the coercive crop-lien system made the Deep South fertile soil for the "strange fruit" of Billie Holliday's song about the lynching of blacks. In addition, as Jackson himself would discover, antebellum Virginia and Maryland held half of all the free blacks living in the slave states, which meant that the transition to freedom was less jarring than in places like Mississippi and Alabama. Since Virginia's whites lived in closer proximity to slaves and on smaller plantations, they worked out relationships based less on physical coercion than on subtle forms of control. Virginia also fostered a more complex economy that depended on a fairly skilled labor force, again setting it apart from the serflike conditions that prevailed in Deep South states. Underlying economic and demographic factors influenced race relations more than did white benevolence.[14]

But the myth of white benevolence also prevented Virginia's elites from understanding that blacks did not gratefully acquiesce to white paternalism. As

Johnella hinted, and as Jackson and others would clearly announce, segregation was an affront to human dignity, an obstacle to social advancement, and a bulwark against racial equality. When Richmond, Norfolk, and other cities began adopting segregation ordinances on common carriers, some black residents boycotted, while others launched suit against the new disfranchising constitution of 1902. When Jackson, Lutrelle Palmer, and the NAACP's Lester Banks challenged segregation in the 1940s, they followed in the footsteps of people like John Mitchell, fiery editor of the *Richmond Daily Planet*. Condemning segregated streetcars, Mitchell claimed that "those who willingly accept discrimination and submit uncomplainingly to outrage are not sufficiently advanced to be entitled to the liberties of a free people." Protests, library sit-down strikes, court challenges to segregated higher education, and demands for teacher salary equalization reminded Virginia's whites of the chimera of paternalism. Through daily acts of quiet resistance, through periodic episodes of noisy protest, and through organized opposition to political exclusion in the years before the Second World War, African Americans challenged the assumption that segregation was anything but a policy of control.[15]

Rhapsodies in Black and White

Frazer and Jackson shared a common cultural heritage that included an affective religion, extended family networks, a commitment to social mobility through education, and traditional African American hymns. Both active musicians at Fisk, they continued to enjoy traditional spirituals, comparing favorites and commenting on memorable performances. Writing to Johnella after they had married, Luther regaled her with the details of a concert he had directed in Petersburg after joining the Virginia Normal and Industrial Institute faculty in 1922.[16] On another occasion, Frazer was pleased to report that her YWCA choral club would perform "Arise, Shine," "I'm Going to Do All I Can," "Every Time I Feel the Spirit," and a handful of other spirituals at a Jubilee program. While they performed independently—Jackson on the coronet and Frazer playing the piano—they also enjoyed singing together. As Johnella wrote to Luther during one of their many separations: "Won't it be great to play and sing together again? It seems a mighty long time since the spring of '17."[17]

But performing black spirituals before white audiences forced musicians to confront the troubling issue of black cultural autonomy. As Robert Moton, principal of the Tuskegee Institute, once explained to philanthropist George

Foster Peabody, blacks often "looked with suspicion on Negro melodies." Many considered it a degrading form of Uncle Tomism to perform traditional black songs for expectant white audiences.[18] In February 1922, Frazer accompanied the choral society of Virginia Normal and Industrial Institute in a performance for the Virginia General Assembly. The contrast between the newspaper report and Frazer's account of the event illustrates how racial consciousness informed white representations of black behavior in the New South. The *Richmond Times-Dispatch* reported that "Colored" musicians had entertained Virginia's House of Delegates with "Negro melodies, hymns, songs by negro composers," and opera numbers. Each piece, the reporter added with customary condescension, had been handled with "equal facility and skill." Most pleasing to the audience was the chorus's rousing version of "Dixie," which met with throaty cheers of approval. No doubt the House also approved of President John Gandy's remarks, which cast the school's musical mission in the unthreatening terms of racial uplift.[19]

Johnella Frazer was equally pleased with the performance, but for different reasons. She was gratified by the "very enthusiastic" applause and the legislators' and spectators' "complimentary" remarks. Most satisfying, however, was the rapt attention the audience paid her piano solo, since "Southern whites often draw the line on Negroes playing the piano." By displaying technical prowess and ethereal artistry in the legislative assembly that had disfranchised black Virginians, Frazer subtly subverted the racial code of southern life. While performing piano concertos that suggested black absorption of Anglo-Saxon cultural norms, Frazer demonstrated that culture is malleable. Her performance effectively detached European chamber music from a framework of racial hierarchy. In her hands, Bach, Chopin, and Beethoven soared above white presumptions about the universality and supremacy of Anglo-Saxon civilization. By Frazer's era, civilization and Anglo-Saxon cultural norms had become virtually indistinguishable in the transatlantic lexicon of white dominance. Instead of anthems to white superiority, she crafted a musical performance that captured a sense of timelessness and transcendence, qualities that remained for the most part foreign to the southern white mind. She was acutely aware of the contrast between a white audience that applauded the choral performance and a newspaper report that refused to apply courtesy titles to blacks, standard practice when the subjects were white. She complained about the newspaper's objectionable failure to use capital "N" to refer to "Negroes." And yet, as much as Frazer's solo performance reclaimed the baroque concertos from a thicket of convictions about whiteness and civilization, racial boundaries delineated the choir's performance. The group was concerned that a performance by educated blacks before an audience of Virginia's powerful might aggravate white anxieties about "social equality." In deference to southern sensibilities, the group decided to play "Dixie." As Frazer tried to explain, the decision was purely "diplomatic," not an endorsement of the song's ideological message. Ideological or not, the performance of "Dixie" starkly illustrated the limits of black cultural autonomy in the interwar years.[20]

The concert can be read in a number of ways. For Johnella Frazer, it was a grand occasion, a personal triumph, and a stunning transgression of traditional racial lines. Entertained and impressed, Virginia's elite acknowledged at least momentarily black dignity and talent. From the newspaper's perspective, the performance was a surprising exhibition of "facility and skill" by students of a "negro institution," rather than the racially neutral "school" or "college." Placing racial distinctions front and center, the newspaper identified the chorus as "Colored Musicians." Lest any readers infer that by skillfully rendering piano concertos and motets the students had escaped their proper racial place, the account emphasized the group's crowd-pleasing performance of "Dixie." What remains at the edges, though, is the tension inherent in black performers rendering "Negro melodies" before an audience of white legislators committed to a racially stratified social order. We can only speculate what the performance meant to its white audience members, but it is not difficult to imagine that it comforted them in the assumption that state-sponsored education could both "civilize" and subordinate African Americans. If "Dixie" and the spirituals soothed white sensibilities, they probably also raised questions of racial accommodation that were invisible to most whites but which discomfited Frazer and the others that February evening.

Racial dualism was never more apparent to Frazer than during a visit of the governor to Virginia State College. Inviting governors for campus visits gave historically black colleges an opportunity to strengthen links with the state government, solicit additional funds, and showcase academic accomplishments for those altogether skeptical about black education. It also gave state authorities the opportunity to investigate black institutions and exhibit their own sense of noblesse oblige. Yet, in a curious illustration of Heisenberg's uncertainty principle, the very act of staging a governor's visit replete with formal addresses and attentive assemblies distorted the outcome, confirming racial stereotypes and deflecting genuine dialogue. Frazer was sensitive to the dynamic, commenting to Jackson that the governor and his entourage of twenty had turned "everything topsey-turvey." Of course, in the context of segregated education and official black political exclusion, little more could be expected of such formalities. Black college officials stood to gain from hat-in-hand submissiveness, placating white expectations of black deference in the hope of maintaining institutional autonomy and support.[21]

The ritual included an "elaborate dinner" thrown by the domestic science department and accompanied by a musical review from the choral society. The "entire student body and faculty" then dutifully assembled to greet "His Excellency," Governor E. Lee Trinkle. Standing six feet tall with an "enormous bay window" of a gut, Trinkle possessed, in Frazer's estimation, a "good-natured politician-y looking face." The beneficiary of a "barely average education," he exuded a "sort of father-y attitude toward us colored folk (I'm white and you're colored—both know our places and must stay in 'em.)" For Frazer and probably most of the students and faculty of Virginia State, Trinkle was no anomaly, but "all one could possibly expect a Virginia Governor to be." The formal assembly and the rest of the day's events followed a pattern of mutual banalities: "the students applauded him, President was courtesy itself, so I'm sure Gov. E. Lee went away *thinking he had made a marvelous impression*" [my emphasis], having offered platitudes about "the appearance of things here, the type of work etc. etc." Typical of cross-racial exchanges in the Jim Crow South, the governor's visit operated on a level of masquerade and self-deception that reinforced unexamined racial assumptions. Innumerable interracial encounters followed a script dictated by the region's racial etiquette, featuring the paternalistic and condescending white power broker and the grateful, well-mannered, and obsequious black retainer. Entertaining their white benefactors, the Virginia State community reassured the authorities that the college harbored only "good" blacks, not subversives. At the same time, Gandy and others donned racial masks that purchased African Americans mental and physical space as well as tangible resources. A time-honored strategy for black southerners, the charade of black subservience was remarkably effective at manipulating the white mind.[22]

Although African Americans understood the paternalism that infused the white perspective, some continued to seek their approval of black culture. By 1925, Jackson was directing a college choir that performed for black and white audiences throughout Petersburg. He and Johnella routinely swapped stories of memorable performances. After one such occasion, Jackson wrote that his choir had "made a home run." The "practically all white" audience packed the hall in anticipation of Jackson's mixed vocal and orchestral performance. His group did not disappoint: "They were bubbling over with enthusiasm at times, even reaching heights of ecstasy. Their applause was so generous that we enjoyed giving every single number." Again, Jackson delivered the Jubilees, rounding the numbers out with "lots of peps and snakes at the end," driving the predominantly white audience "simply . . . wild." He was at pains to add that the performance showcased black skill for white listeners: "We could all tell that those white people were simply dumbfounded over the quality of program we gave." For Jackson, as for Frazer, the performance offered another opportunity to prove African American character before the bar of white opinion. This conviction underlay countless African American efforts in college sports and academics; if anything, it reflected the basic assumptions of Washingtonian conservatism, that blacks would achieve civil rights and racial equality when they met white expectations and internalized white middle-class values.[23]

While Jackson believed that lively performances of black spirituals could erode racial inequalities, he also realized that they could paradoxically confirm white stereotypes about blacks. As Jackson wrote of another choral performance before Governor Trinkle, "Of course white people like just anything that Negroes attempt in jubilees."[24] White audiences applauded black performances as long as they conformed to popular images of the emotionally religious African American. Rather than racial schizophrenia, Jackson—like most of his contemporaries—suffered from an acute ambivalence about the cultural interstices where southern blacks and whites met. Any cross-racial meeting in the segregated South carried multiple meanings, and the performance of the Jubilees for enthusiastic white audiences was no different. On the one hand, they expressed African American independence, created at least the promise of racial dialogue, and allowed blacks to define the terms of that discussion. At the same time, they followed the familiar pattern of black entertainer and white audience, fitting into the time-worn grooves of white paternalism and black deference. It is not difficult to imagine that the audience at Jackson's show and Frazer's recital left entertained, even impressed, but content in the belief that African Americans were a uniquely talented, spiritual people who also knew their "place."

Both savored traditional African American hymns, but Frazer expanded their musical horizons by sharing with Jackson her deep appreciation for classical music. Her letters are laced with vivid descriptions of piano concertos that she was either perfecting or performing. At a private recital, Frazer treated the assembled to Roger's *March Militaire*, Lasson's *Crescendo*, the finale from Schumann's *Symphonie Etudes*, as well as a variety of other piano arrangements. During a summer session at Virginia Normal and Industrial Insitute, she cherished the opportunity to practice selections from Grieg's *E Minor Sonata*, and Schult's *Reverie in A.*[25] In her letters to Jackson, she regularly included critiques of musical performances. After a show at the Metropolitan Community Center, Frazer wrote to Jackson about George Garner, who, according to another music expert, was "the Race's greatest tenor." Unconvinced by that adulation, Frazer offered her own commentary. He was "very, very good. A splendid voice,—well trained, excellent stage presence," she noted. On his performance of "Thank God for a Garden," though, she observed, "I liked George Leon Johnson's interpretation of the latter much better than Mr. Garners, however." Frazer's discerning approach to classical music reflected the conviction that art should engage the mind as much as much as the senses.[26]

In lavish portraits of musical performances, Frazer's technical proficiency shone through. Reporting to Jackson on an annual recital at which she was the accompanist, Frazer noted that the program had started with "the De Beriot 'Concerto' in G, a big, gripping thing." The conductor then began Hayden's *Sonata in D Major* with "a dignified, stately theme, the second allegro, with a quick little motive brought in first by the violin and then answered by the piano." The third movement, the "Larghetto," was "a broad massive theme, with ringing octaves in the left hand, a kind of secondary motive to the violin." The fourth piece, she breathlessly related, was "another fast, brilliant movement." Frazer also recommended recordings and provided accompanying critiques, praising in one letter the "rich, full 'Kreisler tone'" of Heifetz playing "de Sarasate's 'Introduction and Tarantelle.'" Anything but a dilettante, Fraser was a gifted professional with an infectious enthusiasm for exquisite music.[27]

While Frazer introduced Jackson to the world of European chamber music, he shared with her his affinity for choral music history. She once asked him to send a copy of a paper he had written on Richard Wagner to her parents in Chicago, which she was sure her musically inclined father would enjoy.[28] While many whites considered European and African American cultures diametrically opposed, they considered both part of the fabric of a common, middle-class American culture. Although Fraser and others at schools such as Fisk first encountered classical music as part of a deliberate program for civilizing black southerners, they transplanted it into a mental universe that included the works of black spiritual and folk music.

Johnella felt no compulsion to fit her musical expertise into a framework of racial uplift like the one evident in the newspaper account of the recital for the legislators. Invisible to southern paternalists, she and other African Americans created a world that was bracketed by segregation but flourished on aesthetic principles untouched by white antagonism. Describing the performance of one of Bach's fugues in a music history class, Jackson wrote, "these fugues he played in that organ were simply beautiful—really I have never had my aesthetic nature affected more."[29] And in these early days, Johnella Frazer played accomplished professional to Luther Jackson's struggling student. If black women as a whole suffered the double burden of gender and racial discrimination, some like Johnella Frazer demonstrated their capacity to shrug them off on occasion. Surrounded by likeminded women pursuing intellectual and professional ambitions in an environment that suspended judgments based on race, Frazer and others glimpsed a more complete identity than Jim Crow often allowed. Only in child rearing would she sacrifice the free-spirited independence of her early years at Virginia Normal and Industrial Institute.

Listening to the choral and orchestral classics, Jackson and many others of the middle separated themselves from working-class African Americans. Frazer extolled the virtues of Roland Hayes, the Fisk graduate who performed for British royalty, and Marian Anderson, the famous contralto who sang with the New York Philharmonic but did not sing when the Daughters of the American Revolution notoriously barred her from Constitution Hall.[30] But Hayes and Anderson appealed primarily to the black middle class, not the working class, who sought out Mamie Smith and W. C. Handy for a treatment of the blues and jazz.[31]

Musical tastes reflected the influence of their middle-class sensibilities. Jackson and Frazer fused the values of hard work, economic self-reliance, and respectability to the cultural expressions that anchored the middle-class perspective. Molded by their education, they considered themselves privileged and cultivated. When Jackson notified Frazer that he would attend a performance of Wagner's *Lohengrin* in New York City, she proclaimed, "Isn't it wonderful to be so blessed, and to know how to appreciate it thoroly [sic]?"[32] Frazer was surprised and disappointed to learn that a pianist who she believed "never played anything but the very best of music and *that* in the finest style" also played ragtime. For that matter, she also confessed that she "did not appreciate the *art* in Ragtime."[33] Commenting on a piano recital by a guest performer at Virginia State in 1933, Frazer noted that the faculty enjoyed the Beethoven sonatas, but they were "too heavy for 8/10ths of the student body," who sat in sullen silence while the teachers at the back of the auditorium politely applauded. Frazer never seemed to consider the merits of a revised musical program, one that might have expressed the students' own strategy of opposing white cultural ideals through alternative music. She was convinced that the faculty should have expounded on the musical styles of the various composers, "preparing them for it all."[34]

In the longer view, Frazer's and Jackson's perspective reflected the black middle-class ethos that coalesced in the years following Reconstruction. Emboldened by Booker T. Washington's philosophy of racial self-help and economic independence, southern blacks expanded the business and professional class in the late nineteenth century, transforming themselves according to the Christian, middle-class ideals imbued by northern missionaries and their Union army counterparts. Afflicted by neither the insecurity attributed to them by E. Franklin Frazier nor the unapologetic elitism of their upper-class betters, the middle class believed—as Glenda Gilmore has suggested in her analysis of the black middle class of New Bern, North Carolina—that "they were setting the best example for other African Americans to follow, and they aimed to help the less fortunate along." Embracing middle-class virtues of thrift, sobriety, industriousness, and piety, they challenged white presumptions of racial superiority. Engaged in business and professional activities that brought them a measure of social distinction, they undermined the southern white program to reduce blacks to subservient field hands. They acquired property, clothing, and social graces that threatened white notions of race and class alignment. Education was central to this program of social mobility, imparting not only the skills necessary for competitive survival but also the liberal humanist ideals that lit the way toward a more egalitarian society.[35]

This cultural worldview continued to shape the black middle class through the civil rights era. The world of the Odd Fellows, the Elks, and the Masons; of the Eastern Star and the National Association of Colored Women; of the mutual aid societies such as the Beneficial Association of Petersburg and the Young Mutual Society of Augusta; of black-owned insurance companies and struggling storefront businesses; of local choirs and church bazaars; of hard-won diplomas from historically black colleges and training schools; of persistent efforts to unify against the opponent through the NAACP: this was the world of the black middle class, the world of Jackson and Frazer, and the world of the teachers, lawyers, physicians, doctors, and business owners who challenged Jim Crow from Greenwood, Mississippi, to Norfolk, Virginia.

Of course, middle-class sensibilities are not enough to explain the paths taken by early activists. When Aaron Henry, Amzie Moore, and Medgar Evers launched voter registration campaigns in Mississippi in the 1950s, they did so out of the belief that responsible political action would generate the least resistance and produce the greatest social change. As John Dittmer explains, "White repression made direct action projects more dangerous, and endemic black poverty meant that the right to spend the night at the Heidelberg Hotel was not a high priority for most black citizens."[36] White hostility quickly proved them wrong on the first assumption—that voter mobilization would not antagonize whites—but right on the second, that political action threatened the racial hierarchy that ordered the southern white cosmos. Yet this belief that political and legal institutions were susceptible to change, this confidence that educated people of middling means had an obligation to social leadership and moral example, animated people like Moore, Henry, and Evers.

These beliefs animated the leaders who cultivated the movement in Jackson's own Virginia. In Farmville, where a student strike at Robert Moton High School would propel the state into the foreground of the judicial assault on segregation, people such as Reverend L. Francis Green, president of the NAACP chapter and PTA leader, and M. Boyd Jones, principal of Moton High, exemplified the middle-class ethos. It was Griffin, a World War II veteran and graduate of Shaw University, who launched the NAACP in Farmville, a village lodged in the Black Belt of southern Virginia and in the state's tobacco-stained history. He crystallized the alliance with Spottswood Robinson and Oliver Hill—the NAACP lawyers engaged in litigating the equalization of school facilities in Virginia—forging the kinds of networks that Jackson and others created, breaking down the isolation that preserved the racial status quo. Griffin found support among other ministers, but also from Moton's cautious but committed principal, M. Boyd Jones, who, in the words of historian Richard Kluger, "came full of self-confidence and the conviction that a good Negro high school should equip its students to cope with the realities of the outside world and not settle for a disguised form of serfdom."[37] This is not to suggest that the black middle class stood shoulder-to-shoulder in a determined assault on segregation throughout the 1940s and 1950s. The majority of middle-class blacks were not activists like Jones, Green, and Jackson. As John Dittmer reminds us in his analysis of the civil rights movement in the *Brown v. Board of Education* era, "scores of teachers and administrators," as well as journalists, clergy, and professionals, "through fear or indifference, refused to discuss racial problems in their classes and schools and avoided association with civil rights organizations."[38] The greater the fear of white retaliation, the more reluctant African Americans were to challenge the system. Luther Jackson understood this, as did M. Boyd Jones and Amzie Moore, but it was precisely this insight, along with the realization that racial amelioration required the support of influential black institutions, that motivated them to regenerate black political consciousness. They wanted to transform the black middle-class tradition of moral example into political leadership, to convince their counterparts that they should claim the political equality implied by their social accomplishments and extend it to all African Americans. This long tradition of middle-class leadership, along with the constellation of values that sustained it, framed the perspective of Johnella Frazer as much as Luther Jackson and the countless advocates of racial equality who moved like shadows on the dimly lit stage of civil rights in the years before Birmingham.

What we know, then, is that Frazer was no raging elitist, but her thoughts on music suggest a paradox at the core of prewar black middle-class culture. While she could not imagine the performance at the state legislature as anything but an expression of racial independence, she often strained her music and literature through the filter of cultural uplift. Able to escape cultural elitism in her own performances, she imposed it on her students, gravitating between the poles of white middle-class convention and African American cultural autonomy. Even if she hoped to transcend white paternalism, she often functioned on the assumption that young blacks would only advance when they absorbed the dominant values. Compulsory exposure to the European classics would have an ennobling, perhaps uplifting effect on impressionable young African Americans. For Frazer and the faculty at Virginia State, music, literature, and education intersected in a program of racial advancement. Many middle-class blacks were unwilling, however, to examine the assumptions about race and culture implicit in this program.

Personal Politics

Searching for common intellectual ground, Frazer and Jackson shared their thoughts on current events, politics, and letters. History was the most comprehensive of subjects, Frazer declared. "Your saying that you knew about the African Slave Trade before this summer," she mused, "led me to begin thinking of the many subjects that one would have to 'die and leave'—after studying an entire life-time."[39] Frazer was engaged in her own studies at the Virginia Normal and Industrial Institute. A weekly faculty club meeting provided a forum for teachers to examine pedagogical and intellectual issues. According to Frazer, the faculty frequently discussed the "New Thought" in education, which included the study of black history and literature. It also included the examination of pedagogical theories such as John Dewey's *Democracy and Education*. Searching out new material for the discussion group, Frazer solicited information from Jackson about intelligence quotient testing, which the United States Army had adopted during the First World War.[40]

Jackson reciprocated the interest in current affairs. In Virginia during the 1920s, the crusade for racial purity captured the headlines and exacerbated racial tensions. An extension of the drive for white domination that in 1902 had produced a state constitution featuring disfranchisement, the cause of racial "integrity" gained additional steam from the advent of scientific racism. Walter Ashby Plecker, Earnest Sevier Cox, and John Powell advanced the racial purity line in Virginia, fusing anthropology and eugenics into an argument for racial engineering built on the alleged dangers of black and white intimacy. They sported a form of scientific racism that fed on the racial antipathies prevalent in the 1920s. These views gained legitimacy at the national level through laws restricting immigration. In 1922, Powell, Cox, and their supporters established the Anglo-Saxon Clubs of America to mobilize support for state legislation to preserve racial integrity. Although the organization never achieved widespread support, it won legislative victories by pressuring sympathetic representatives in the General Assembly. The Racial Integrity Act of 1924 was one of these. It proscribed interracial marriage for whites and classified race by strict physiological standards. When a judicial ruling brought the law into question, club members revamped it by stringently defining a white person as someone "having no known, demonstrable or ascertainable admixture of the blood of another race," which the General Assembly approved in 1930. Among other goals, racial integrity advocates sought a law requiring racial segregation in theaters and at public events.[41]

The demand for legal enforcement of racial segregation at public events focused on the Hampton Institute, which, according to newspaper editor Walter Scott Copeland, promoted "social equality between the white and negro races." Copeland was the editor of the *Newport News Daily Press,* and his accusation stemmed from his attendance of a performance at Ogden Hall in February 1925. As Jackson explained in a letter to Frazer, the editor was perturbed that Hampton officials had "refused to give him a special seat according to the old custom of giving southern white people special seats and segregating our people." Led by Powell and Plecker, the movement enjoyed the support of "Trinkle and all his crowd," although, according to historian Richard Sherman, Trinkle had little use for the Anglo-Saxon Clubs and their attack on the Hampton Institute. Copeland disparaged Hampton principal James Gregg for allegedly adopting policies that encouraged racial contact and for failing to denounce the horror of "social equality." While Copeland appealed to Virginia's tradition, Jackson called it what it was, a demand by "the leading white people of Virginia" that "Jim Crowism" extend onto the campus of a historically black college and that "white faculty stop mixing with Negroes in a social way and that sort of thing." Jackson claimed that the situation was "really serious," and it was; the Public Assemblage Act of 1926 required racial separation in movie theaters, in public entertainment facilities, and at public assemblies, reinforced by fines for offending patrons and owners. Jackson's incredulity at white demands for "Jim Crowism" at the Hampton Institute echoed that of W.E.B. DuBois, who pointed out that whites were not required to enter into the "colored world" of Hampton Institute. For them to insist on racial segregation behind the racial veil was simply "monstrous."[42]

Religion was central to their lives, influencing both their relationship and their worldview. As much as Johnella Frazer attended to social issues, she leavened her intellectual concerns with religious convictions. Discussing intellectual history with Jackson, she observed that it seemed to be something of a "fad" for commentators to excoriate the Bible. She believed that critics should at least credit the Christian churches for their contribution to higher education. Their criticism of the Old Testament was unwarranted, since it was more a document of "Jewish history than anything else." She found it particularly difficult to accept the Old Testament image of God—a stern, exacting, and often-merciless deity. The Christian God was a "God of Love"; any amount of Old Testament iconoclasm could not shake her conviction that "so long as we cling to the Spirit of the *New*" and believe that "there is this All-knowing, All powerful Mind, that has supreme power—today and yesterday—all is well!" Frazer's evangelical sensibilities were manifested in the music she performed and in the life of the church she attended.

Jackson also sustained an active religious life. Having described a Palm Sunday service he had attended, she responded by encouraging his religious devotion: "It is really uplifting to *know* that a good service—singing and sermon all that you could wish—awaits you *every* Sunday." Although there was nothing explicitly religious about their joint decision to swear off alcohol, their teetotaling echoed the Protestant evangelical dictum that liquor was the slickening agent on the slope to perdition. Jackson once scolded his eldest son, Luther, when he came home one evening fragrant with booze. Luther Jr.'s only salvation was that he had been drinking beer rather than whiskey. Political interests and scholarship eventually crowded out Jackson's religious concerns, but he never lost sight of the church as an agent of black cultural cohesion and social consciousness.[43]

While he embraced his religious heritage, he also had an ecumenical streak that drew him to Catholicism. Meeting Woodson and others in Washington, he had the occasion to visit a Franciscan abbey that replicated the architecture of a monastery in Israel. He described the "special exercises," probably a high Tridentine mass, featuring "angelic music." Priests and deacons celebrated the mass with "great pomp, splendor, and ceremony—all kinds and colors of gowns and robes." Sitting at the front of the church, Jackson was fascinated by the moment of transubstantiation, "the converting of the wine and bread into the blood and body of Christ." Transfixed, he admitted, "It made a lasting impression on me." He had little enthusiasm for the institutional church and its hierarchy, but the experience deepened his appreciation of the religious ethos of the medieval period, one of the multiple subjects he covered in the tiny history department at Virginia State. His friend, Elmora, made him feel slightly uneasy as she followed the rubrics of the mass, repeatedly kneeling, responding in Latin, and making the sign of the cross. But Jackson was moved by the experience: "Say what you please the Catholics are certainly devout and sincere in their worship. We Protestants," he added, "certainly have a long way to go in this respect."[44]

No figure loomed larger in their early relationship than Carter Woodson, founder of the Association for the Study of Negro Life and History and editor of the *Journal of Negro History*. On Jackson's recommendation, Frazer read Woodson's *The Education of the Negro Prior to 1861*. She marveled, as did most that had learned little about blacks in traditional histories, that "so much was done during 'slavery times.'" Frazer planned to discuss slavery as well as a number of other issues the book raised the next time they met.[45] As much as she admired Woodson, she also encouraged Jackson's competitive instincts by pitting him against the master. Suggesting that she had found an area in which Jackson's research could improve on Woodson's, she added, "Haven't I *nerve*, now?" A reflection of intellectual confidence, her remarks also sounded a chord that would resonate throughout their years together. Woodson became a standard of measure for Jackson, a role model he consistently sought to emulate and impress. At the same time, both were scholars pioneering in the field of African American history appealing to the same audience. The competitiveness was natural, but when the two began to diverge on issues of race leadership, the sparks flew.[46]

Distance did little to deter their desire to exchange ideas as well as affection. Studying in New York, Jackson often sent Frazer copies of black newspapers such as the *New York Age.* Later they would exchange editions of the NAACP's *Crisis,* edited by W.E.B. DuBois. After reading one edition of the *Age* that Jackson had sent her in 1921, Frazer asked if he had read its coverage of the "lily black" Republican convention in Virginia. Denied admission to the caucus, the black delegates met separately to discuss strategy. Having discussed the issue with one of the delegates, Frazer added her own report on the events. Convinced of the impossibility of electing black state officers, the delegates, she claimed, were determined to mobilize as many voters as possible "just to show our strength in this state." Just for good measure, they vowed to run a slate of black candidates including John Mitchell, editor of the *Richmond Planet* and firebrand for the antilynching movement, for governor. "I wonder what DuBois will say to that," she mused.[47]

Like Woodson, DuBois became a yardstick on racial issues, the model of the engaged intellectual, an antagonist, and a goad to greater audacity in the assault on racial injustice. The architect of the Niagara Movement and the guiding voice behind the NAACP, DuBois had catapulted himself to fame with *The Souls of Black Folk,* a mystical, probing examination of life behind the "veil" of racial discrimination. A pioneering sociologist, a groundbreaking historian of Reconstruction, and a penetrating social psychologist who exposed the abscesses underlying the surface civilities of Jim Crow, DuBois was also an intellectual pugilist who suffered neither fools nor opponents gladly.

He took a circuitous route to his position as defender of black higher education and political equality. In the waning years of the nineteenth century, DuBois championed racial self-help, economic advancement, and middle-class values—the central tenets of Booker T. Washington's program for racial accommodation.[48] But subscribing to Washington's middle-class morality did not mean endorsing his political program. DuBois repudiated his tacit acceptance of disfranchisement and support for industrial education. He lashed out at Washington's tendency to blame African Americans for their own subordination. Civic equality and the franchise, not single-minded concern for property accumulation and good behavior, would restore black freedom. Despite the repeated accusation that DuBois was an apologist for the "talented tenth"—the black middle class that understood little about working-class blacks—his polemics held a mirror up to those who claimed to have reconciled moderation and racial integrity. He was the idealist for a generation weighted down by the realization that an entire country had tacitly embraced white supremacy. An uncompromising stand distanced DuBois from the majority of African Americans, particularly those such as Johnella Frazer who drew their livelihoods from institutions that imbibed a more accommodating message.[49]

On one occasion, Fraser vented her impatience with W.E.B. DuBois and his ideological inflexibility. "Do you know, Lute, there are times when I get heartily sick of DuBois [sic] continual ranting against everything and everybody except the N.A.A.C.P and DuBois. Of course, I know 'the Race' needs him, could hardly get along without him and his type, but I get tired of him nevertheless." According to her, DuBois had become the car-window sociologist he claimed to despise, pontificating on racial matters from the safe distance of New York. His address at Virginia Normal and Industrial Institute that fall, she claimed, "was very mild," a mildness she suspected was typical of all of his southern addresses. "When you are living and working with the southern whites as Moton and Fisher are, you can't take the radical stand that the editor of the *Crisis* takes." DuBois was free to generate as much "righteous indignation" as he could, but he should avoid "slinging mud at individuals who are doing constructive work in their particular fields," areas in which, according to Frazer, he was categorically unsuited. Apologizing for "ranting," she appealed for Jackson's opinion on the matter. His response is lost to us, but judging by his evolving social philosophy, it is difficult to imagine that he disagreed with her on any substantive points.[50]

Despite her impatience, Frazer remained a DuBois devotee throughout her life. In 1921, she purchased a copy of his *Darkwater,* a collection of poems and essays, from an itinerant book peddler who was earning money to study law at Howard University. Jackson had recommended the book to her, and Frazer had tried unsuccessfully to borrow a copy from the college library.[51] And while DuBois's militancy unsettled middle-class liberals, disciples of Washington also began to irritate the increasingly self-confident talented tenth. Jackson apparently met Moton at a social function and had few kind words to say about his racial outlook. Frazer concurred, describing him as "an uncertain quantity." She recalled a "black and white talk" he had given at a Virginia Normal and Industrial Institute commencement that they considered reprehensible. She added:

"DuBois and a few others are capable of holding their own with the speakers you mentioned. Not many!" According to Luther P. Jackson Jr., Johnella Frazer "was a red hot DuBois person," while Jackson was "somewhat inclined to Booker T. Washington." At least in the early years of their marriage, Frazer was "more radical than he was." Jackson's later association with the NAACP and his escalating political activism would strengthen his affinity for DuBois.[52]

Like most middle-class blacks of the period, however, Jackson was the product of two intellectual fathers, DuBois and Washington. Perhaps more accurately, his ideas suggest how elusive categorization can be, since neat dogmatisms accompanied neither of these leaders nor the lives of average African Americans. Jackson, like most middle-class blacks, absorbed the doctrines of racial self-help, economic independence, practical education, and property accumulation that Washington and the National Negro Business League espoused. For a considerable part of his career, DuBois embraced and espoused them as well. These broad notions of racial advancement and survival pervaded the cultural atmosphere that African Americans inhabited, finding expression in countless black weekly newspapers, church sermons, and school lessons. As August Meier once argued, racial ideologies of the early twentieth century can only be understood against the backdrop of disfranchisement, segregation, and extralegal violence. These were the realities that conditioned the programs and strategies of black activists in the twentieth century.[53]

Despite the appeal of assertive racial protest and black nationalism, most ambitious African Americans subscribed to the conventional morality of their white counterparts. Even those who embraced the militant nationalism of Marcus Garvey—and literally thousands of largely working-class African Americans did—imbibed along with his message of racial independence a heaping dose of admiration for middle-class American values, including practical education, self-reliance, and the American success myth.[54] Middle-class blacks persisted in a world molded by the experiences of racial resilience and bigoted hostility. But the ethic of market competition and self-control venerated by the dominant middle class also organized their worldview. Middle-class blacks did not march lock-step to the social and political program championed by Washington and his minions. Yet, as race relations deteriorated, the majority found it easy to subscribe to the basic ideas that gave Washington's creed such broad appeal. Economic improvement, racial self-help, and black unity made sense to southern blacks confronted with persistent lynchings, the hardening of Jim Crow, and the antiblack fury fueled by migration to the North.

Not surprisingly, Jackson endorsed Thomas Jesse Jones's accommodationist

Negro Education, published in 1917. Detailing the abysmal state of black education in the South, Jones advocated more money for vocational instruction and less money to the liberal arts colleges that DuBois had celebrated in *The Souls of Black Folk.* Jones used the study for a paper he was preparing on the "Negro in Education." According to him, *Negro Education* was a "monumental work" that would provide most of the data that he would need for his own paper. He also recommended the book to Frazer, suggesting that she would find Jones's observations on education in Virginia and in particular on Virginia Normal and Industrial Institute of interest.[55]

Jackson had known Jones since Fisk, and both had ended up at the Voorhees Institute in South Carolina. Jones went on to become field secretary of the National Urban League in Atlanta, where he managed the organization's work throughout the South. After World War I, the Urban League emerged as the leading welfare organization for African Americans, easing migrants into city life by operating as a housing and employment agency. Sustained by white philanthropy and managed by moderate whites and blacks, the League became an advisor on New Deal programs and orbited in Washington's sphere of influence. Jones's appointment probably had some connection to George Edmund Haynes, sociologist and author of his own widely acclaimed study on the social conditions of blacks in New York City. Fisk University invited Haynes to organize a sociology department and a program for training social workers. At the same time, a joint committee of two black social organizations studying a proposal for a national agency of social welfare turned to Haynes for expert advice. The committee eventually established the National Urban League.[56]

Jackson positively glowed in his assessment of Jones. He considered him "the very first of my friends," a person of sterling integrity. His work for the National Urban League was "splendid," the evidence of someone "destined to be a foremost leader of this race of ours in a short time."[57] Not everyone shared Jackson's opinion. Carter Woodson came out strongly against Jones. DuBois also took Jones to task for his educational philosophy. Both denounced a trip he took to Africa as part of the Phelps-Stokes African Educational Commission. Investigating missionary boards and educational facilities, Jones announced that technical education in the style of the Tuskegee Institute was in the best interests of Africans as well.[58]

For his part, Jackson was still pushing for industrial education in 1938. A member of the Petersburg Civic Association, he joined in a campaign to persuade the clergy of Petersburg to support a "Training for Vocations" drive.

Frank Greene, professor on the trade school faculty at Virginia State College, first brought the issue to the attention of the ministers. The committee then followed up on the initiative to direct young men into the skilled trades. It appealed to the ministers to offer sermons extolling the virtues of the trades. As the committee leaflet reminded the clergy, "the Bible fairly bristles with material dealing with the dignity of manual labor." In conjunction with the blitz on the churches, the committee planned an industrial exhibit to coincide with their father and son banquet.[59]

The campaign grew out of the concern that too many young men, enchanted by the promise of financial reward, had relinquished the skilled trades. "It is prompted by the fact," the committee maintained, "that nearly all boys today pass up bricklaying, carpentry, auto mechanics, etc. as life's vocations in favor of teaching or one of the professions." Claiming that they wanted to improve the wage earning potential of Petersburg's black working class, 90 percent of which was unskilled, the committee prescribed strategies of economic advancement that did not challenge racial submission. As the members unabashedly asserted, "Our drive is really pointed to getting our race back to the high position they once held as skilled workers." Instead of advocating the skilled trades as an alternative to the professions and to unskilled drudgery, the committee tried to discourage young blacks from following a career path that many favored. Even while Jackson championed political activism, he cooperated in efforts that countered the ambition for professional distinction and upward mobility.[60]

Although Jackson saw a place for technical education, he identified with the effort to link higher education to professional advancement. It was this program that would produce the leaders demanded by DuBois's racial blueprint. Both he and Frazer maintained connections to a group of Fisk graduates who pursued a range of careers. Students of Haynes's sociology courses at Fisk, many found opportunities in the burgeoning field of social work. His friends, both men and women, found work ranging from the Department of Labor to social workers and educators. James Robinson, graduate of Fisk in 1911, completed a master's degree at Yale and began a Ph.D. there in 1920. A native of Lexington, Kentucky, Robinson had started a dissertation on "The Negro in Cincinnati," a topic that immediately intrigued his hometown friend. Others in his circle of friends included "Fat" Harris, who had earned a master's degree from Harvard, and Robert Elgy, National Urban League administrator in Brooklyn, New York. As Jackson pursued his own teaching career, his network of academic and professional associations grew. The Association for the Study of Negro Life and

History alone introduced him to a world of like-minded professionals motivated by personal ambition and the hunger for racial justice.[61]

But as his Fisk associates found, educational ambitions competed with the demand for a steady income. In the middle of his first year at Columbia, the Summer High School in St. Louis offered Jackson a teaching position. Interested in the offer, he notified the superintendent that he would consider the position for an annual salary of $2,100. The money was enticing, but Jackson was also under pressure from his family to consider the position seriously. The chance to teach at a distinguished school was exciting; Frazer thought that it would be a "signal honor" that would give Jackson "prestige." But he was also reluctant to leave behind his education and the vibrancy of the big city. One consequence of the offer was the decision to move their wedding date up to September 1922. If he took the job, he planned to spend the following summer in Chicago with Frazer and her parents, who had moved there from Kentucky in 1921. He also hoped to enroll in the Ph.D. program at the University of Chicago.[62]

The plan to attend Chicago materialized, but the St. Louis job did not. Perhaps his salary demands were too high. Perhaps he simply decided that the Columbia degree promised a longer-term reward than a high school teaching position. What we know is that Frazer played no small part in bringing Jackson to the Virginia State Normal and Industrial Institute. Shortly after their decision to get married, Frazer started hinting at a possible move to Chicago. No doubt with some satisfaction, she wrote to Jackson that "President Gandy and Miss Lindsay [music school director] seem to be getting worried over the prospect of losing 'po'lil me.' Lindsay wanted to find some way of keeping the talented Frazer at the school. The president, on the other hand, seemed to like the idea of bringing Jackson to Virginia Normal and Industrial Institute. A Fisk graduate and a teacher with scholarly ambitions, Jackson fit into Gandy's plans to return the school to its collegiate status.[63] Gandy was so eager to bring Jackson onboard that he waived the school custom of employing no more than one married couple on the faculty.[64]

Jackson was not ready to jump at the offer. Teaching a patchwork of courses for an annual salary of $1,650, a full $450 less than he was willing to take at the Summer High School, hardly seemed worthwhile. Frazer tried to put the best gloss on the president's offer, emphasizing the opportunity to earn additional money from extension courses and save money by living on campus. Jackson was unmoved, even sending Frazer a pamphlet on Columbia Teachers College, which she then passed on to Gandy in an effort to emphasize his credentials and increase his bargaining strength. Frazer quickly became the mediator; after receiving Jackson's counteroffer, Gandy cornered her and told her that Jackson was demanding more money than they could offer.[65]

Frazer then shifted from mediator to counselor, urging him to hold out for at least $1,800. She based her advice at least in part on insider information: the school had recently hired a candidate of similar qualifications at that salary. She was also certain that Jackson had the stronger position: "But, Lute, let me tell you honey, if President really wants you, and I know he does, he can give you 1509–so you stick out for it. . . . Hold your ground, my Boy."[66] Although she promised not to try to persuade him, Frazer applied subtle pressure and plied him with information to prevent him from abandoning the offer. She wanted to get married, but she was not about to relinquish her own career without trying to reconcile the two. Established at Virginia Normal and Industrial Institute with a circle of friends that enjoyed a vibrant social life, she was reluctant to jettison the independence that teaching in Petersburg afforded. Jackson probably received the offer he wanted, though the correspondence does not confirm it. Although he accepted the position, he also started the marriage on Frazer's terms, a small victory before child rearing forced her to resign from her job. Without Johnella's mediation, Jackson may not have ended up at Virginia State, the college that would provide a haven for his activism and scholarship for another twenty-eight years. The college provided the framework, but it was Frazer's quiet determination and selfless support that would allow him to pursue his dreams of education and community action throughout their years together.

Maternal duties increasingly absorbed Johnella Frazer's time and energy after 1922. Joining her mother in Chicago on a maternity leave, Frazer gave birth to Laura Frances, followed soon after by Luther P. Jr. The letters provide no indication that Johnella was discomfited by her new role, but it is difficult to imagine that she embraced domesticity without some anguish, sacrificing her independence, her career, and the network of friends she enjoyed in Petersburg for life under her mother's roof in an unfamiliar city. Added to her difficulties was the strain of managing a young family without a husband and father present.

A demanding teaching load and the myriad professional activities that he accepted forced Jackson into long separations from his family. In August 1922, with Laura Frances on the way, Johnella wrote hopefully of Luther's return—

in November. Even that visit was uncertain, and Johnella—adopting the posture of the understanding wife—assured Luther that "we will just let the Spirit guide you in November." In April 1926, with Luther Jr. in tow, Johnella wrote: "September seems a long time to wait to see you again Luther. I knew you were to have a short vacation this time but didn't realize't would be only a few days." The letter offers only a glimpse of Frazer's frustration at Jackson's absence, but it is a glimpse nonetheless. While Jackson consolidated his career at the college where Frazer had pursued so many of her own professional goals, and while he took up the musical activities that she abandoned for motherhood, Frazer now held together the expanding family, alone. Separated from the world of day trips, tennis, like-minded friends, and teaching, one wonders if the slate gray of Chicago's winters seemed particularly bleak to Johnella Frazer that year.[67]

Circumstances, including one child's mysterious illness, shaped the couple's decisions, but so too did other factors, not the least of which were conventional notions of a woman's "place." After an account of his band's performance at another governor's day visit along with news about an invitation to address a principals' conference, Jackson wrote that his growing family made him feel "just so complete." The juxtaposition is intriguing—home and hearth fused to professional accomplishment, binary terms in a middle-class equation for domestic harmony. After sending one paycheck home, Jackson exulted: "My! But I feel so good in supporting my family even though to a limited extent. It makes me feel like a real man."[68] He connected manliness not only to career advancement but also to dependency. The image of a wife and children relying on a respected breadwinner to provide for their needs in a challenging profession harmonized with Jackson's plans. He also expected Johnella to play her part, by advancing his career and displaying suitable wifely submission. Praising Frazer for insinuating herself into Chicago's "music circles," Jackson emphasized the benefits that would accrue to him: "You are really paving the way so nicely for me. In this respect as well as all others you are playing the role of a real wife."[69] We can only infer that subsuming her career in his, relinquishing her financial independence, and almost single-handedly managing the responsibility of childcare fit comfortably into Jackson's definition of "the role of the real wife." For Jackson and a good many other African American men, women's independence compromised their maternal obligation, a responsibility that held implications for racial advancement: "It is unfortunate for the race that women of the standing of Myra and Edna do not marry and have children." Women of "standing"—presumably educated and well-bred women—could best promote racial uplift by bringing along the next generation; race leadership was something best left to men. Women could make their most valuable contribution to racial progress by following their biological imperatives, not their career ambitions.[70]

Despite the long separations and financial stringency, Luther and Johnella's relationship remained remarkably strong. They wrote to each other frequently, exchanging stories of family visits and meetings with friends, asking and offering advice, commenting on and searching for information about college football games, and detailing the minutiae of everyday life that provides the mortar of enduring companionship. Johnella missed Luther, but it went the other way as well. "I am just reving to see you sweetheart," Jackson wrote to his wife in March 1926. "I think of you and the children every hour in the day." Approaching a planned reunion, Jackson wrote effusively of his desire for his family: "How I long to see that child and in fact all of you!! Sometimes I even just have a craze to see you."[71] If Jackson found fulfillment in his academic pursuits, he found joy in his wife and children, deriving "inspiration" from the birth of his son Luther, showing off his photograph to coworkers at Virginia State, and regularly inquiring after Laura Frances's troubled health.[72]

Their correspondence hints at the tensions that Jackson's career and Frazer's sacrifices generated. Anticipating Jackson's return from an extended period of study for his Ph.D. in Chicago, Frazer confessed that she had grown "lonesome." With characteristic restraint, she added: "I'm not going to say much, but this isn't my easiest year by any means. I am just praying that it will hurry up and roll around real fast—that before we can realize it you will be back, happy, well, and thrilled to death with Juanita." Pregnant with "Juanita," Frazer endured the strain of managing a young family, which her husband's absences only aggravated. Jackson's educational pursuits promised to improve his earnings and their financial security, but they often came at the expense of his growing family. Proclamations of devotion aside, Jackson privileged his career and the social causes he championed over his family. As Luther P. Jackson Jr. recalled, "Daddy"—as he was affectionately referred to—"was busy all the time." While Edward, Luther, and John Tevis played basketball or romped in the woods, their father worked until 11:00 at his office, channeling his energies into his career and the movement: "He didn't want to be bothered. He wanted to do something that he thought would be more productive. Our mother played games. We did a lot of interesting things with her." According to Luther P. Jackson Jr., family activities were nonexistent.[73]

Despite his single-minded focus, he looked to his wife and children for companionship and counsel throughout his life. He in turn provided an anchor of stability and an example of self-directed achievement that each of his children sought to emulate. While social activities absorbed most of his time on the weekends, the family shared regular meals during the week, moments during which Jackson would hold forth on political issues, tell stories "punctuated with laughter" about the day's events, revel in his victories, and catch up on his children's activities. His laugh was "something else," his son Luther recalled, high-pitched and loud, the spontaneous expression of a man who took his work seriously and himself lightly. If Jackson spent little time in leisure activities with his children, he brought them into his world of politics and education. Luther Jr. once took a history class with him, receiving what he thought was a fair and inconspicuous final grade of B. Edward remembered accompanying his father to Washington on one of his many field trips to the Senate, the Library of Congress and, most important, the Supreme Court. Laura Frances became Jackson's most reliable typist and secretary, a task that gave her skills she would parlay into a federal government job in New York City. John Tevis, the youngest son, spent hours applying stamps to the steady stream of mailings that flew off of Jackson's desk, while Luther Jr. and Edward were put to work delivering newspapers and circular material. And though trips were unusual, the family did pile into the 1929 Dodge for a trip to Hopkinsville, Kentucky, and Nashville, Tennessee. The trip was not without misfortune. Jackson went off the road in Bristol, Tennessee, an accident that left a shard of glass in Luther Jr.'s leg and the elder Jackson with a permanent fear of driving. While it might be easy to cast Jackson in the role of self-absorbed careerist, he remained dedicated to his family and interested in their welfare despite painful absences.[74]

In a world that few whites cared to encounter, blacks lived lives that reflected the predilections and preoccupations of the wider society. And yet, through family traditions, religion, social commentary, community rituals, music, and literature, they molded identities out of the rich but tragic African American experience. They participated in an expanding consumer culture and shared the adversities of the Great Depression. Through satire and social criticism, they poked fun at the pretensions of southern whites and sharpened their opinions on a range of issues. And yet, as porous as racial boundaries were and as vibrant as the internal lives of middle-class African Americans could be, segregation distorted their experience. It reminded them that the accoutrements of middle-class distinction—the appreciation of fine music, the attention to public appearance, the classical education, the exhibition of Protestant virtues—

did not translate into social equality with whites. Class and race intersected powerfully in the region, even in genteel Virginia, where whites prided themselves on civility and presumed to understand African Americans better than their boorish counterparts to the South. For Jackson, the realization that class status did not equal equality propelled him into action.

Despite the social and academic commitments that pulled Jackson away from his wife and home, their mutual affection seemed to weather the years. Music, friends, and family bound them together during extended absences. Middle-class and educated, Jackson and Frazer avoided many of the deprivations visited upon rural and working-class southern blacks during the Depression. Yet, like other African Americans, they had to balance personal independence and self-determination against the code of racial etiquette. Life was neither an incessant struggle for racial advancement nor a charade of subservience toward whites. Frazer and Jackson found fulfillment by turning to traditional African American institutions—the family, the church, social clubs, musical groups, and the immediate community—as well as the professions of their choice. At the same time, they derived a larger sense of purpose from the movement for black equality. Frequently, through their work, family, and daily routines, they escaped the racial enmity that absorbed so much of the region's energy. Yet they did not entirely escape. In the racial dialectic of southern life, personal advancement behind the veil of segregation fueled the desire to eliminate the barriers standing in the way of full citizenship. In the 1930s, Jackson and Frazer would test their faith in the ability of hard work and self-reliance to breach the defenses of racial exclusion.

Chapter 3

Jackson, the Association, and the Meaning of Black History

Instructing children in the possibilities of change required teachers to look to the past, and no one understood this better than Luther Jackson. History offered the chronicle of glaring injustices and virtuous alternatives, but it also contained the keys to a cultural identity obscured by racial mythologies. What teachers, parents, and most African Americans understood, Jackson and his counterparts articulated. For most "vindicationist" historians, the study of the African American past was inextricably linked to the pursuit of racial equality in the present. His scholarship sought to recover African Americans from obscurity and remove the intellectual foundations that supported racial stereotypes. But scholarship was only one—and increasingly a secondary—method for achieving these goals. Through the Association for the Study of Negro Life and History (ASNLH), Jackson alerted African Americans to their history. It was a task that carried the implicit political message that blacks *had* molded the past, had asserted their identity in time, had thwarted racist imagery through their accomplishments, and could do so again. In this task, he shared the vision of the "father of black history," Carter G. Woodson.

But by insisting that activism take precedence over scholasticism, Jackson broke from Woodson, and the break was acrimonious. Jackson never proclaimed as much: if anything, he was a stalwart defender of the primacy of research, often complaining that his teaching load prevented him from pursuing his true love, research. Yet in this case, actions spoke louder than words. The Virginia State professor continued to pursue scholarship, but it was often subordinated to the myriad activities that absorbed his attention in the late 1930s and 1940s. Woodson, on the other hand, was no cloistered pedant. His studies and the association itself reflected his conviction that historical research should underwrite the ideological transformation that would carry the movement forward. Yet Woodson never allowed his convictions to compromise his notion of scientific research. For Woodson, the unmediated sources would speak louder than any propaganda, however well-intentioned. Jackson was no propagandist, but he did believe that historical research had to address the immediate needs of African Americans in their struggle for equality. Burdened by a heavy teaching load, family responsibilities, and multiple social commitments, Jackson had little choice but to let his research slip after his masterful book on black property-holders in Virginia. Contingencies alone do not account for their differences, though. He believed that the work of promoting the association, of increasing black voter strength, of politicizing and professionalizing black teachers, of supporting local business initiatives, and even performing in local choirs took precedence over brick-and-mortar research. While Woodson championed scholarship as the route to overturning racial oppression, Jackson favored community building and political engagement as the means for widening the cracks in the walls of Jim Crow. The two men crafted distinctive and often competing notions of black historical inquiry.

Woodson's association emerged out of the tumult of the early years of the First World War. Internal migration, imperial expansionism and the tottering of empires, anticolonial movements in the Caribbean and Africa, and racial clashes throughout the western hemisphere produced a group of African American intellectuals deeply attuned to the transnational problem of race. Like Arthur Schomburg and Tuskegee sociologist Monroe Work, Woodson adopted a macrohistorical approach to the black experience, examining the slave trade in Africa and throughout the Atlantic, patterns of slaveholding in Latin America, as well as education and religion in the African American experience. Besides producing his voluminous writings, Woodson joined Benjamin Brawley and W.E.B. Du Bois in challenging the dominant racism of the period, which denied African people any creative role in world history. In repudiating the image of African savagery, Woodson and others of his generation highlighted the African contributions to antiquity and to the Western tradition. In doing so, they established the intellectual foundations for challenging racial discrimination in the United States.[1]

Unlike most other historians, though, Woodson created an organization for collecting and disseminating black history. He graduated with a Ph.D. from

Harvard in 1912 and taught high school in Washington, D.C., until 1917. By 1915, however, he was dreaming of an organization that would illuminate African American historical accomplishments. Boarding at a YMCA in Chicago in order to attend the Exposition of Negro Progress, Woodson came into contact with NAACP, YMCA, and National Urban League activists who encouraged him to popularize African American history. That experience galvanized his commitment: he established the Association for the Study of Negro Life and History in September 1915 and four months later published the first edition of the *Journal of Negro History*. Assisted by historian John Franklin Jameson, editor of the *American Historical Review* and director of historical research at the Carnegie Institution in Washington, Woodson secured a $25,000 grant that reduced the association's debt while allowing him to relinquish his teaching responsibilities and devote himself to the ASNLH. Despite the largesse, the association continued to struggle on the financial front throughout his life. Luther Jackson would play a critical role in easing the association's financial burdens.[2]

Jackson had met Woodson earlier than 1925, but it was a meeting that year that crystallized his admiration for the ASNLH founder. The meeting, most likely the association's annual convention, proved "inspirational" for the young historian, who promptly resolved to establish a historical society in Petersburg that would include local citizens as well as the Virginia Normal and Industrial Institute community. In November of that year, the "great Woodson" participated in Jackson's historical society, an exciting development that provoked pangs of regret that he was not devoting more time to his own research. The September meeting also gave him the idea of taking his students on a tour of Washington. In addition to the Library of Congress, the White House, and the tomb of the Unknown Soldier, the professor and his students visited the headquarters of the ASNLH. Though Jackson was already committed to the teaching profession, his association with Woodson encouraged his scholarly proclivities and his desire for additional training. By March of the following year, he was "digging up old newspapers, books, etc" and "bringing out local history." His research methods followed Woodson's example of using census data and local materials to piece together a historical record from the ground up. Jackson also seemed to follow Woodson's research interests. His digging into local sources was part of a project on "The Education of the Negro in Virginia in the Reconstruction period," which sounded like an extension of Woodson's own *The Education of the Negro Prior to 1861*.[3]

By 1928, Jackson was enrolled in the Ph.D. program at the University of

Chicago under the direction of the venerable Avery O. Craven. He remained for the year and returned for another in 1932 to complete the course requirements for the doctorate. There he gravitated between the world of ideas and the world of servile labor that marked the experience of working-class blacks. When he was not studying at the Reynolds clubhouse or attending class, he was mopping floors and serving meals at a fraternity. If the menial work bothered him, he did not let on. Describing his schedule to Johnella, Jackson noted that he arrived at the fraternity house at 7:50, in time for breakfast and "just a little work." If he expected Chicago to be more progressive on race relations, though, he was disappointed. The white students were "very cordial and civil," but social interactions with them "go no further." He expected that Columbia by contrast might be more advanced "racially." Whether imposed from without or dictated from within, Jackson observed the southern taboo against social proximity between black men and white women. He had been invited to a dinner sponsored by the history graduate students but declined the invitation, concerned that "too many women folks" were involved. Patterns of economic discrimination against blacks were also replicated in Chicago and intensified by a faltering economy. Writing to Frazer, he noted that sixty-eight waiters at the Edgewater Beach Restaurant had been fired and replaced with white waiters: "It seems that more and more colored people are losing good jobs, which is of course true to some extent of the whole country." Chicago offered professional opportunities and a loosening of racial restrictions, but it consistently reminded him that he was still in America, a country where race mattered.[4]

For the most part, though, the Chicago experience was a positive one. With a neophyte's enthusiasm, he relished browsing through the library stacks for a half-hour each day, combing through books that were marginal to his courses but important for the dissertation he was planning to write on his return to Petersburg. Jackson was single-minded about his objectives. The research and the studies, he wrote to Johnella, were part of a program that would occupy him for "the rest of my days" and gain him a reputation "for you and the children." But like any student away from home and in a big city, Jackson enjoyed the nightlife. For a ten-cent admission fee, he absorbed the jazz and the electric atmosphere of the Savoy Ball Room. Even on campus he was able to breathe the cosmopolitan air that was in short supply in Petersburg. Studying at the Reynolds Club, a student hangout, he imbibed music ranging from "opera and church choir down to the lowest type of jazz—orchestras, bands, piano solos, vocal solos and everything imaginable." While Johnella struggled at home with two children and a third on the way, Luther satisfied his intellectual curiosity and his thirst for the myriad stimuli of Chicago in the 1920s. He realized it was not a fair exchange: "I think the husband gets off so light in the rearing of a family. I shall always be obligated to you."[5]

Some of the leading historical lights of the prewar period illuminated his intellectual journey. To Craven—historian of the allegedly avoidable Civil War and of southern nationalism—Jackson owed his interest in antebellum Virginia. In addition to Craven, he took courses with William E. Dodd (about whom Frazer asked if he was "prejudiced," considering his reputation for unreconstructed thinking), an Old South specialist, as well as William T. Hutchinson and colonialist Marcus Jernegan. It was Jernegan who impressed him the most, not only because of his encyclopedic knowledge of the period but also for his slant on the origins of the Revolution. Jernegan's progressive sensibilities found expression in his assertion that educated, college-trained leaders had guided the Revolution and towered over any of the political leaders that the 1920s could offer. His celebration of Adams, Jefferson, and Otis probably stimulated Jackson's yearning to play a leadership role in social affairs. The professor's emphasis on the classical sources of the Revolution may also have strengthened his conviction that the democratic claims of the present found their authority in the American past. Patrick Henry, the firebrand of the Revolution, may very well have become something of a model for Jackson, at least insofar as the Virginia activist provided the example of an uncompromising proponent of liberty. What is certain is that Jackson's courses stoked the flames of his own ambition to interpret the past. "As a result of my study this year," he wrote to Frazer, "I have determined to become an author of a book of some kind in the not very distant future."[6]

The book came later, but Jackson was already publishing the results of his research on free blacks of antebellum Petersburg. In 1927, "Free Negroes of Petersburg, Virginia" found its way into Woodson's *Journal of Negro History*; in 1930, he followed it with the "Religious Development of the Negro in Virginia from 1760 to 1860," a study inspired by a course he enrolled in on the "Negro Church in the U.S." The same meticulous research went into the production of his dissertation, "Free Negro Labor and Property Holding in Virginia, 1830–1860." Using county property records, federal census data, as well as the deeds, wills, and registers of free blacks often consigned to the dusty attics of the clerks' offices he visited, Jackson pieced together a picture of increasing free black ownership and independence after 1830. Far from declining into dependency once manumitted, Jackson's study argued, African Americans steadily acquired property and the middle-class virtues usually attributed to whites. In some cases, they themselves became slave owners. In addition to correcting the image of the dissolute free black—an image fostered by white historians concomitantly interested in underlining the merits of slavery—Jackson uncovered sources that advanced the study of local black history.

But Jackson's study was something more than a paean to black self-reliance. It warrants our attention here, at the crescent of Jackson's struggle for professional credentials. Skip ahead five years to the publication of *Free Negro Labor and Property Holding in Virginia, 1830–1860*, an event facilitated by the American Historical Association using funds from the American Council of Learned Societies. Perhaps better than anyone else, considering the exhaustive quantitative analysis that he poured into his study, Jackson dispelled the myth of the degenerate free black underlying the proslavery ideology. Proslavery advocates had argued that it offered a more humane system of production than the wage labor of the North, that it was necessary in order to prevent the degeneracy that invariably befell free blacks. As Jackson summarized the proslavery position, "Slavery, not freedom, was the normal condition for the Negro." Legislative proposals for colonization, the termination of free black schools, the prohibition of black preaching, and the end of jury trials for free blacks reflected the prevailing conviction that "slavery was the natural lot of the Negro and that in order to impress him with this fact a dreadful example must be made of the free Negro."

Demonstrating the steady accumulation of property by free blacks in antebellum Virginia, Jackson made the case that free African Americans could prosper despite persistent white antagonism. Here is how he described the study in a letter to Woodson:

> My general argument runs that although the 1830–1860 period was a dark era for the Free Negro insofar as the statutes and the frequent enforcement is concerned, yet from the economic angle this was the very period in which he made his greatest advancement. His labor was more valuable then [*sic*] ever, and consequently with the payment of wages he was able to buy property, real and personal, on a great scale. . . . Chapter VI tells the beautiful story of slaves securing their freedom chiefly through their own initiative, and then becoming owners of property and valuable citizens.[7]

By documenting the remarkable diversity of occupations in which free blacks engaged—wage-earning and independent farmers, blacksmiths, shoemakers, carpenters, boat operators, tavern keepers, factory operatives, butchers, and bakers—Jackson made the case that free African Americans had become "indispensable in the economic life of Virginia." His analysis carefully distinguished between rural and urban workers, independent proprietors and wage laborers, men and women, and skilled and unskilled workers, an effort that anticipated the methodologies of later social historians in search of a past that included the voiceless and the anonymous.[8]

His discussion also resonated with contemporary concerns. If slavery was not the "natural" condition for African Americans, and if free blacks in the antebellum period contributed to social progress and prosperity, then segregation was equally unnatural and an impediment to African American productivity in the present. His study reflected the sensibilities of middle-class uplifters, who privileged industriousness, thrift, and self-reliance in the struggle for black economic self-determination. It also resonated with the national mythology, which celebrated rugged individualism as the lever of social progress. What it did *not* do was suggest that property ownership was the precondition for political rights. Through historical analysis rather than polemic, he rejected the contention that black subservience was part of the natural order. The pathologies ascribed to free African Americans were the product of racial mythologies, not historical exigencies. The effort to contain blacks behind the barriers of segregation perpetuated the campaign to stigmatize free blacks in the antebellum period. What they had in common was the southern white fear of black competition and social equality.

The dissertation that became the book was his greatest source of pride. Writing to E. Franklin Frazier at Howard University, Jackson boasted that he had "examined and collected more than a thousand deeds of manumission" and "a dozen or more family papers." His collection of manuscript sources for free blacks in 1860 rivaled Woodson's collection for 1830. Not shy of challenging the "great Woodson," Jackson also reported that his conclusions on the status of black property holders "were at variance" with those of the editor of the *Journal of Negro History*. Jackson and Frazier connected on the issue of the black family during slavery. Frazier had just published his *Negro Family in the United States*, and Jackson's own research in the Register of Free Negroes and Mulattoes had invariably led him into the question of family stability, structure, and marriage legality. As Jackson informed the soon-to-be famous sociologist, the "Register of Free Negroes and Mulattoes"—which could be found in the city and county clerks' offices—was a "veritable gold mine, by far the most fertile field of information now in existence on the free Negro and also the slave." The professor volunteered to photostat materials from the "Register" as well as marriage records, birth registers, letters, and petitions and send them to Frazier, the Library of Congress, and Charles Johnson at Fisk University. The Howard scholar also expressed interest in the papers of prominent black families that Jackson had examined for his dissertation. At the same time, he provided sociologist Charles Johnson of Fisk University with data drawn from the "Register of Free Negroes and Mulattoes." Jackson offered to supply Woodson and "various institutions" with photostats of Virginia documents once "the war is over and normal times return."[9] Delineating the "unexplored fields" in black history in 1942, Jackson praised Frazier's pioneering study and advocated additional research on the black family, particularly on legal marriage among free blacks.[10] More than a pioneering scholar, the Virginia State historian became a conduit of research material for other black intellectuals and scholars, a role that mirrored the bibliographic efforts of Carter G. Woodson and Monroe Work, the Tuskegee sociologist and author of the *Bibliography of the Negro in Africa and America*. Through his scholarship and professional connections, Jackson challenged a historical profession that venerated Anglo-Saxon dominance.

Although his passion for recovering forgotten sources on African American Virginia continued, his focus shifted to broadcasting black history. On returning to Petersburg, he fused it to the program for political mobilization. Increasingly, his mind swam in the powerful currents of political activism, local business regeneration, and ASNLH promotion. Promoting Woodson's association came naturally, not only because of Jackson's own convictions but also because Woodson had published his articles and helped secure funding for his dissertation. Woodson had been appointed to the Social Science Research Council's (SSRC) subcommittee on interracial affairs. From that position, he was able to secure financial assistance for Franz Boas, E. Franklin Frazier, and Luther P. Jackson.[11] As timely as the financing was for the father of two, the grant represented a laying on of hands that raised Jackson's profile and prospects. "I should say he does have a high opinion of your work," Frazer exclaimed. "Think of the many people he might have offered it to and didn't. I am certainly proud of you Luther-boy." Despite the acrimony that lay in the future, Jackson never forgot the favor. His work for the ASNLH reflected this combination of ideological conviction and personal indebtedness, a debt to a scholar whom Jackson deeply respected.

Woodson expressed his confidence in Jackson by recruiting him to serve as state chairman for the association in Virginia. His appointment was part of Woodson's effort to generate revenues to compensate for the declining support from white-dominated foundations. Repeated applications for assistance from Rockefeller's General Education Board ended in frustrating rejections. As Charles Wesley, organizer of the association's "Nationwide One-Dollar Sustaining Membership Drive," argued, the turn toward popular support represented progress, since minor contributions were "of more real value to the Association than many times a thousand dollars from a foundation which desires to direct its publication and influence its thinking."[12] By the mid-1930s, African American supporters were already responsible for the bulk of the association's funding. Jackson responded enthusiastically, mapping out a plan to tap the intellectual and financial resources of the state's teachers. The strategy paralleled his voting initiative. Along with Maud Winston and Lutrelle Palmer, the Virginia State historian established a system for collecting annual contributions of fifteen cents from rural teachers, twenty-five cents from city teachers, and fifty cents to a dollar from college faculty. Donations would be sent to Virginia State, which became the association's central office in Virginia, and receipts would be fastidiously issued to the contributors.[13]

The association's program harmonized with Jackson's effort to connect the psychological and physical spaces that blacks used to foster cultural resilience. Since the college summer schools attracted teachers in the off-season, he would appeal to them—nearly two thousand, he estimated—at Hampton, Virginia State, Virginia Union, and St. Paul. Schoolteachers were critical to the larger program of expanding the association, but so too were college professors, tactically situated to influence their elementary and high school counterparts. The new chairman would solicit them through the college presidents while also plying the school principals and Jeanes supervisors for support. As Jackson built the Petersburg Voters League, he constructed a network of schoolteachers, principals, and citizens committed to disseminating black history. The two organizations would soon have overlapping functions.[14]

The indefatigable professor consistently moved beyond the campus in the drive for black history and the association. After reaching seventy-eight out of ninety-nine faculty and staff members at Virginia State, he reported that the local drive would "merge into the State wide effort in February." The organizational framework encompassing the states' teachers "is already perfected," he claimed. Jackson may have been exceedingly optimistic about the strength of the organization, but there was little question that he had laid the foundations for a vigorous ASNLH presence in Virginia. In advance of Negro History Week in February, the chairman launched two direct mail campaigns aimed at the Jeanes supervisors and principals of the city schools. The annual Virginia Teachers Association meeting provided an occasion for promoting the ASNLH as well as the cause of voting. He also planned to work through middle-class professionals and letter carriers to sell association memberships. In addition, he recruited traveling business people and the assistant supervisor of Negro education—a Virginia Normal and Industrial Institute graduate and former student—to drum up support for the association. He called for press publications covering the results of the drive and encouraged Woodson to accept President John Gandy's invitation to hold the annual convention at Virginia State in 1937. Earning a reputation for diligence and resourcefulness, Jackson was becoming a major figure in the ASNLH.[15]

He was also getting results. In January 1936, with more contributions still expected, Jackson reported that Virginia had contributed a total of $338.43 for the annual ASNLH drive. In 1937, Virginia submitted a total of $516.09, the second-highest contribution to the association, the District of Columbia (Woodson's territory) reporting the highest. By 1944, the Virginia chairman was reporting an income of $1,052 and confidently predicting that Virginia would produce $1,500 annually in the years to come.[16] Even as early as 1937, though, Jackson had reason to be pleased. In explaining the improvement, he credited the rising interest in black history rather than economic circumstances: "The outcome of this drive again proves that the people of Virginia are sold to the idea of supporting our association." He was determined to sustain the public support, not only through mail campaigns but also through the summer sessions "and the many odd times I meet them on various occasions."[17]

These "odd times" became critical opportunities to connect the issues of black history, voting, and civic education. The peripatetic Jackson became nothing less than a missionary for the cause, traveling throughout the state to promote the association and its principles. Meeting with Jeanes supervisors, school principals, social organizations, and teachers attending summer school at Virginia State, he doubled as booster for the association and exponent of African American self-determination. "I am going to sell the Association [to] the State Federation of Womens Clubs meeting at Franklin," he wrote to Woodson, observing that it would be an ideal opportunity to "capitalize" on the "race consciousness of many of our people," which, according to Jackson, had risen to an "amazing" pitch.[18] His archival searches merged with his drive to generate local support for political action and historical consciousness. "I have traveled for research and promotion," he wrote to Woodson in 1944, "and for circularizing the teachers, in a larger way this year than in any year of the history drive."[19] The association chairman used Negro History engagements at Shaw University, Virginia Union, Payne Divinity School, Jefferson High School in Charlottesville, and a night class of WPA workers to promote black history. Public meetings—such as the one that Jackson attended at the Astoria Beneficial Club of Richmond—became occasions for selling his popular history booklets and for holding forth on black history. Just as he linked the Virginia Teachers Association and the Virginia Voters League, anchoring both in Virginia State College, he worked to connect the Virginia Teachers Association and the ASNLH. "Membership in the Teachers Association," Jackson intoned, "must become identical with an annual fifteen or twenty-five cent contribution to the Association for the Study of Negro Life and History." While drawing upon the resources and constituency of the Virginia Teachers Association, Jackson promoted the larger objective of social commitment through education. Jackson credited the contacts he had made through the Virginia Teachers Association, the summer schools at Virginia State College, and the other colleges for generating historical awareness. But more than this, he noted to A. A. Taylor, the strong attendance of teachers at Virginia State had been critical in "the realm of developing a voting consciousness." Ultimately, Jackson, Woodson, Wesley, and others sought to build a movement for racial consciousness that began with history but ended with political activism.[20]

The association's growth reflected a new sense of black confidence in the early part of the twentieth century. The transformation of black consciousness in the twentieth century had its material roots in the Great Migration. Fueled by the demand of the First World War, northern and midwestern manufacturers increased production and hired African American workers to replace the European laborers who had supplied American industry before the conflict. Southern immigrants found work in steel mills, railroad yards, garment factories, and packinghouses at wages that would have been inconceivable at home. Nearly five hundred thousand blacks moved to the North between 1916 and 1919, drawn by unprecedented economic opportunities but also by the possibility of finding a foothold for equality analogous to what "forty acres and a mule" had once promised. Racial discrimination greeted the newcomers, but the absence of sharecropping, planter intrusiveness, and the climate of southern racial repression allowed blacks to build independent communities that sustained the hope of full-inclusion. Encouraged by a war that would convert the world to the gospel of American democracy, blacks began to despair as racial violence swept across the country in 1919. The violence reached an apex in Chicago. In July, roving gangs of whites attacked African Americans for transgressing the economic and social barriers dictated by race. After five days of bloody conflict, twenty-three blacks and fifteen whites had died, a conspicuous example of the violent energies coursing through the nation after the war. In all, more than seventy African Americans were lynched in 1919, several of whom were soldiers. Men who had worn the uniform embodied African American frustration over the denial of rights by a country dedicated to the enshrinement of those rights at the global level.[21]

Growing black militancy, particularly on the part of the NAACP, accompanied an intellectual reorientation that produced the Harlem Renaissance. More important to working-class blacks was the increasing strength of the labor movement exemplified by A. Philip Randolph's Brotherhood of Sleeping Car Porters. Yet white hostility and indifference closed off union membership to most blacks. Far more found a voice in Marcus Garvey's Universal Negro Improvement Association (UNIA), the vehicle for the Jamaican activist's message of racial regeneration through economic and cultural independence. With more than seven hundred branches and as many as five hundred thousand members, Garvey's UNIA offered "a political channel and a global perspective" for the ethos of racial pride that had been developing since the beginning of the Great Migration.[22] Fundamental changes were also evident in the wider intellectual atmosphere. Cultural anthropologists such as Franz Boas and Margaret Mead successfully challenged time-honored notions of genetic racial distinctions, the pseudoscientific basis of nineteenth-century racial classifications. Social scientists, artists, and media of the 1930s gradually abandoned the genteel racism that had supported assumptions about black regression and inferiority. Racial stereotypes did not disappear, but the intellectual respectability of racism faded beyond recognition.[23]

It was out of these developments that the determination to recover black history emerged. Founded in 1915, the ASNLH reflected the hopes and frustrations of the Great Migration era. Appropriately, Woodson inaugurated the association in Chicago, a major depot for southern migrants and—through the proliferation of jazz and blues clubs—a symbol of their cultural contributions to urban America. Through the *Journal of Negro History,* the association's main publication, Woodson sought to change white minds but also, according to historian Jacqueline Goggin, to "promote and encourage black achievement and a more positive self-image among blacks."[24] Yet this objective was part of a larger project of identity building premised on nationalist yearnings that produced Pan-Africanist movements across the western hemisphere and support for the UNIA at home.[25] Black historians including Woodson, Brawley, and Jackson wanted to create the intellectual superstructure of a cultural worldview that could challenge racist assumptions and support claims to full citizenship.

Despite the tactical and ideological differences, this theme of racial self-confidence united W.E.B. Du Bois, A. Philip Randolph, Marcus Garvey, and Luther P. Jackson. As Garvey wrote, "sloth, neglect, indifference, caused us to be slaves. . . . Confidence, conviction, action will cause us to be free men to- day." Justifying the all-black March on Washington, Randolph argued: "It develops a sense of self-reliance. . . . It helps break down the slave psychology and infe-riority complex in Negroes which comes . . . with Negroes relying on white people for direction and support." Echoing Garvey's themes of self-assertion and Randolph's notion of racial autonomy, Jackson asserted that cultivating "race pride" in young people was the only "sure method of making the Negro first think something of himself." In Jackson's view, the teachers' enthusiasm for the association's membership drive reflected their belief in "the cause" and their realization "that the inculcation of race pride and loyalty in the Negro youth serves as one of the main solutions of the so-called race problem." For each, it was a question of freeing African Americans from the weight of degrading racial stereotypes that reinforced the status quo. As Jackson put it, "It is an effort to have him shake off his racial inferiority complex." Even if middle-class elites downplayed the spiritual resilience of the people they sought to uplift while exalting themselves as saviors to the downtrodden, they expressed the convic-tion that progress required altered thinking and racial self-determination.[26]

For those who adopted a historical perspective on the black experience, the past was inescapably political. The association's objective had always been po-litical, a viewpoint considerably at odds with the historical profession's axioms about "scientific" history and objectivity. Dominated by whites enamored of myths of Anglo-Saxon nation building, the historical profession reconciled the ideals of objectivity and racial subordination, reducing blacks to inferior play-ers in the American saga. Teaching black history was the equivalent of teaching citizenship, since to graft African Americans onto the past in which Americans had forged their rights was to introduce blacks *into* the framework that in-cluded those rights. As Jackson explained to the people of Norfolk, "The observance of Negro History Week and the promotion of all other forms of historical activity constitute one phase of our rights and duties in a democracy." Once convinced that blacks had participated in crafting the nation's past, educators would fulfill their responsibility to instruct young people in their history. Teachers would then naturally insist that their students "pay taxes, that they vote, that they sue in court, and that they perform all the political duties common to all American citizens." Emphasizing black accomplishments over the chronicle of racial mistreatment and oppression, Jackson and others fashioned a past that was decidedly "usable." Minimizing black suffering, Jackson emphasized black heroism and virtue despite adversity. Regardless of the revisionist program, both he and his white counterparts would have agreed that the effort to reconstruct a past that included African Americans in the struggle for democracy had vital implications for a present in which black political powerlessness was the norm.[27]

In the same way that the association manifested themes of black nationalism and racial pride, it also reflected the shift toward larger social concerns among civil rights groups. Like the NAACP, it developed as a primarily middle-class organization, funded and administered by the black middle class. Under the strain of the Great Depression, it turned toward "the people," actively cultivating support and membership from African Americans of humble means. To be sure, Woodson's change of direction was dictated by expediency—Wesley admitted as much. Still, Woodson, Jackson, and others struggled to expand memberships in rural areas, enlist country schoolteachers, promote Negro History Week observances in small communities, introduce the *Negro History Bulletin* (a popular version of the *Journal* that appealed to teachers and laypeople), facilitate distribution through low subscription fees—in a word, make the association available to average blacks. And this initiative preceded the sustaining membership drive of the 1930s. It began in 1925 with the introduction of Negro History Week, celebrations that focused on black achievements and the accomplishments of prominent leaders. It grew throughout the 1930s and 1940s, expanding into rural schools, observed by social groups, fraternal organizations, libraries, churches, community centers, and adult education schools. Prior to the war, Negro History Week fared better in the Upper South and border states than in the Cotton Belt, where poorly trained, isolated teachers struggled against poverty and white hostility toward black education. Despite the regional variances, Negro History Week had become the vehicle for transmitting black history into the classrooms. By the 1940s, the ASNLH was no longer the exclusive possession of urban, middle-class professionals.[28]

Through Negro History Week, teachers and laypeople began to fashion a past that reflected their own needs. The association's campaign to raise historical awareness was mediated by people trying to negotiate issues of identity and power in a time seemingly ripe for change. Although leaders such as Jackson addressed countless Negro History Week gatherings, it was the teachers, students, and community residents who devised the "dramatizations" and "pageants" that brought African American history to life. Negro History Week became a temporal and psychological plane on which blacks staked their claim to the American liberal democratic tradition, celebrated their own great leaders, and established a connection to a past obscured by racial mythology and indifference. Woodson encouraged the ASNLH to adapt historical plays to suit the needs of children. The demand for Negro History Week materials and the limited capacity of the association to supply them also forced teachers to produce their own plays, the texts of which were reprinted and distributed.[29] Wellington Beal—an administrator at an orphanage for black children in New York—planned to hold Negro History Week exercises, give addresses, and invite guest speakers to participate. W. P. Bayless, the religious editor for the Pittsburg *Courier*, requested materials that would illustrate African American involvement in "racial progress and history." Echoing Jackson's uplift ideology, Bayless wanted to "inform, inspire, and rid our youth of inferiority complex" [*sic*]. Rather than celebrate racial distinctiveness, though, the editor hoped to encourage young people to see themselves as part of a common humanity, "human beings who are just as good, capable and responsible as individuals of any other racial group." World War II certainly created an atmosphere for egalitarian thinking, but most African Americans would be bitterly disappointed—though not surprised—to find that little changed. As blacks played an active part in shaping the nation's history—as soldiers, dockworkers, shipbuilders, women volunteers, and soldiers—they looked backward to the record of black achievement and forward to a time when those contributions would finally mean something.[30]

Jackson played the role of mentor and consultant for teachers planning Negro History Week exercises. Articles promoting black history and the association often sparked a response from teachers already absorbing Jackson's voting message. In conjunction with a social studies class examining "minority groups in America," S. Virginia Southerland of Fredericksburg requested information from Jackson that would help students "better understand the Negro and his problems." The crisis of the Depression and war focused the attention of many African Americans on social issues, a change registered by teachers planning Negro History Week exercises. Instead of great men and major events, Sutherland requested information on "the economic, social, and political problems of Negroes in America."[31] Others reflected the association's great leaders approach, which the *Negro History Bulletin* encouraged. Yet many *Journal* readers began to include Jackson in this list of great leaders, reflecting not only his impact on black social consciousness but also the teachers' determination to construct their own framework for black history. "My students read your column in the paper each week and I want them to know more about your life and work," wrote Ethel E. Love of Gloucester County. Love also sought information on A. P. Davis and Gordon Blaine Hancock, contemporaries of Jackson's and activists in their own right. The appeals for guidance also came from outside the schools. Claude Ruffin confessed that he knew "very little about the history of my race" and wanted to do something, "[b]oth for a vast majority of Negroes and myself who should know."[32] While some looked to integrate heroic black models into white-dominated narratives, others sought out historical perspectives on current economic and social problems.

Few, however, cared to separate the past from the present. In recovering leaders from historical obscurity, they also looked to prominent figures of the present, including Jackson, thus reinforcing patterns of middle-class dominance in the black freedom movement. At the same time, average people took *some* part in determining the outlines of the history they internalized. By selectively celebrating "great" leaders of the past—a list that rarely included Booker T. Washington or the "faithful" slaves of the Confederacy—African Americans of the World War II era said something about the leaders they would support in the present.

The role that women played in the association mirrored their contribution to the teachers' civic education initiative. The Jeanes supervisors—practitioners of home economics funded by the Anna T. Jeanes Fund—were almost uniformly women and stalwart supporters of the ASNLH. Poorly paid teachers at underfunded schools cobbled together exiguous contributions that testified to their commitment to the association and its ideas. One Jeanes supervisor requested a memento from Jackson in honor of the schools in her district, which had contributed $9.50 that year: "This is a sparsely populated country for Negroes, and this amount of money is double what they have ever given before."[33] Teachers often apologized to Jackson for submitting such small amounts. As Jackson reported to Woodson, Luru G. Fox and Ruby Vaughan of Faquier

County apologized for sending only $27.85, an amount they regretted was not larger "for such a most worthy cause." Maud Winston—the "faithful Mrs. Maud Winston," according to Jackson—apologized for submitting only $22.12. Like Winston, Hilda V. Grayson championed the association's cause, acting as a field agent in a manner reminiscent of Ella J. Baker and the countless women who built the NAACP from the ground up. According to Woodson, Grayson planned "to devote her whole life to the cause." The civil rights movement was developing, and women like Grayson employed organizations like the ASNLH to promote it along with as their own ambitions for public life and professional fulfillment.[34]

More than salespeople for the association, the teachers elucidated black history for their students. Laura Crawley of Dinwiddie wrote to Jackson requesting a graph of important events and dates in black history, as did Peggy Pender, Olivia Anderson, E. W. Lundy, and Mary Lancaster, only a few of the many teachers who wrote to the professor for classroom materials. While Jackson and others provided the charismatic leadership, teachers such as Winston and Vaughan became the voices of black history in the schoolrooms across Virginia and the South. Adopting the position of interpreters of the African American experience, they built on the tradition of teachers as respected leaders in African American communities. Woodson and Jackson may not have expected it—may not even have approved of it—but primary school teachers and Jeanes supervisors translated often inert historical material into social and political messages that resonated in the present. Part of that message was that women had a place in making sense of the past and in marshalling the energies of the young in the movement for change.[35]

Too much could be made of Negro History Week as a contested terrain over which laypeople and professional historians sought control. What we do know is that Jackson and Woodson thought of themselves as experts planning exercises for the unenlightened masses. In 1937, Woodson wondered whether the leadership should "restrict them to things abstract like the achievements of the Negroes in the political sphere, in education, in religion, in science, in art" or encourage teachers to "make their exercises chiefly biographical."[36] Educational and political elites played a critical role in sponsoring, even personifying, the association. The black intelligentsia found in the association a vehicle for their ideas and ambitions, and the association in turn increased their star power. According to Woodson, the public "clamored for orators," a claim supported by the dozens of requests for public appearances that flooded Jackson's office. Requests for appearances by Jackson at Negro History Week celebrations rivaled the dozens of requests he received for addresses on voting and citizenship. Of course, one cause flowed into another as Jackson combined voting, citizenship, and black history in a powerful appeal for black political revitalization.[37]

Other luminaries also evangelized for the association. In 1937, Charles Wesley disseminated the message throughout Texas and the Southwest, while Rayford Logan of Howard University addressed students at Lincoln University in Missouri. A. A. Taylor of Fisk University canvassed the Alabama State Teachers College, Lawrence Reddick covered Chicago, and bibliographer Arthur Schomburg advocated in the schools and churches in New York City. Nonhistorians such as Mary McLeod Bethune—an educator and Roosevelt-administration appointee—and Congressman Arthur Mitchell joined historian Benjamin Brawley and Howard University president Mordecai Johnson in delivering addresses in the Washington, D.C., area. Woodson pointed out that the supply of speakers was inadequate to meet the demand, since "history and oratory do not go far together." Transmitting historical information—the "facts" that would overturn racist folkways—was the responsibility of the trained professional. Despite the elitist assumptions, Woodson was careful to explain in his report to the readers of the *Journal of Negro History* that the addresses comprised "only one of the daily sessions of the week otherwise devoted to dramatics, art and the like." While Woodson, Jackson, Taylor, and others planned the kits that accompanied Negro History Week celebrations and monopolized most of the speaking engagements, they did so alongside teachers and students who adapted the programs, speeches, and publications to their own conceptions of black history and its place in the community.

Negro History Week did more than confirm group solidarity; it challenged racial stereotypes that pervaded school textbooks and curricula. The ASNLH vigorously opposed a curriculum that excluded, minimized, or distorted the role of African Americans in the American story. Yet black educators had been advocating African American history since before the turn of the century.[38] In the 1920s, several ethnic groups challenged schoolroom texts that overlooked their contribution to the American epic. Du Bois asserted that the NAACP should terminate its campaign to revise retrograde textbooks and instead write new ones that featured the black experience. As historian Jonathan Zimmerman points out, though, proponents of pluralistic textbooks had little interest in challenging the historical orthodoxies about the nation's great leaders and founding events. Ethnic pluralism did not automatically translate into a more critical perspective on the nation's past.[39]

Despite subscribing to nationalist myths, African American historians rejected school texts that romanticized slavery and lamented the alleged horrors of Reconstruction. After surveying textbooks in southern schools, historian Lawrence Reddick—a classmate and associate of Jackson's from Chicago—concluded that the image they presented was generally degrading: "As a slave, he was happy and docile. As a freedman he was shiftless, sometimes vicious, and easily led into corruption. As a freeman his activities have not been worthy of note." Since textbooks defined patriotism as the measure of American greatness, the exclusion of African Americans from the pantheon of national heroes meant black children had little reason to be proud of their heritage. In Woodson's opinion, Negro History Week celebrations exposed the unwitting complicity of teachers in the transmission of specious racial views. The demand for histories written by African Americans stemmed directly from the realization that "the public cannot depend on the oppressors of a race to give a true picture of those whom they despitefully use." Wellington Beal corroborated Reddick's and Woodson's observations. As far as "Negroes and Negro history are concerned," he wrote to Jackson, "the children know only the propaganda half truths which support 'the divine white right.'" Beal hoped that Jackson's advice would help him prepare a lecture series that would correct the students' misconception that "all Negroes in Africa are and were cannables" [sic]. The association struggled to extirpate representations of blacks rooted in a version of history that treated Africa's descendants as natural servants to the white masters of the twentieth century.[40]

Perhaps more than any other organization, the association reflected Jackson's commitment to the local community. Working closely with teachers through the Virginia Teachers Association and the ASNLH, he developed a personal investment in serving their needs and interests. As Woodson observed, "You are exceptional in that you love your people and you are trying to help them." If anything, the teachers became part of Jackson's extended classroom, admiring his erudition, charm, and social affection at least as devotedly as did his students at Virginia State College. His identity became closely entwined with his role as mentor, professional consultant, and intellectual authority for Virginia's African American teachers. This persona did not always harmonize with his role as research scholar in the tradition of Du Bois and Woodson. Pulled between his self-image as pioneering researcher and social activist, Jackson developed a dichotomous existence. Yet where others saw the roles of professor and social activist as distinct from one another, Jackson struggled to reconcile the two. A punishing course load, student demands, countless social commitments, and a family jealous of their time with him prevented Jackson from accomplishing many of the major research projects he imagined. As commitments grew and his own popularity increased in the 1940s, he tried to maintain a foot in the scholarly camp while fulfilling his sense of obligation to the teachers and to the movement. The combination was not always successful.[41]

Jackson was determined to reciprocate the teachers' support for the association. "For eight years the teachers of this state have given freely so that now I think it is time to extend them a token of some kind in recognition of their generosity." What he had in mind were two brief booklets, one highlighting the sacrifices of black Virginians in the Revolutionary War (eventually published as *Virginia Negro Soldiers and Seamen in the American Revolution*), and the other lauding the accomplishments of black officeholders during Reconstruction. His motives may have been more complex than simply reciprocating the teachers' affection. Considering the war and the push for black voting rights, he likely believed it an ideal time to link the heroism of black revolutionary soldiers to the contributions of black GIs in the European conflict. Booklets would also showcase Jackson's research in a popular format, perhaps encouraging recipients to purchase a copy of his recently published *Free Negro Labor and Property Holding in Virginia*. No less important, the booklets might encourage teachers to support Jackson's other ventures.[42]

He certainly imagined that they would benefit the association. In addition to "rewarding" the teachers, they would "serve as a big advertising scheme for the Association. It may result in the doubling of amount usually raised in our State." The altruism may have been diluted, but Jackson believed that the publication would promote the larger cause of disseminating black history among students, teachers, and the wider public. "I want to flood Virginia with the Association," he wrote enthusiastically to Woodson, "and the way to do that is to attempt to reach every individual in this commonwealth giving instruction to our youth." The format would also appeal to a broad public presumably interested in the accomplishments of self-sacrificing ancestors. "I would make this a popular description," Jackson confided, "giving the absolute facts but told and arranged in such a way that the simplest mind can appreciate." The patronizing tone aside, Professor Jackson believed the booklets would have more than entertainment value. Publishing lavishly illustrated encomiums on African American revolutionaries was one part of a larger strategy to make the association a vehicle for transforming black historical awareness.[43]

Woodson supported the venture, but he was less than enthusiastic. When Jackson asked for his opinion on a few stylistic matters, he responded indifferently: "The preface seems to be all right. I have no preference as to the title, either one is correct." Jackson pushed ahead nonetheless, publishing five thousand booklets at a cost of $692.47 to the association and distributing them to teachers, businesses, and public offices throughout the state. Once the booklets had been distributed, Jackson sought out his mentor's endorsement: "I judge you received my booklets on Negroes in the Revolution a week or two ago. From the standpoint of distribution this venture was an eminent success." Woodson may have been cool to the project initially, but the positive feedback on the booklet seemed to change his tune: "Everybody to whom I have given a copy . . . is favorably impressed with it." Woodson reported that he had given the booklet to a committee, composed largely of white teachers, that was studying the inclusion of "the Negro in literature" in the District of Columbia's schools. Although he "believed that it will do some good," he had nothing to say about the booklet's intellectual merit, an expanded version of which had appeared in the *Journal of Negro History* in 1942.[44]

If Woodson's reception of the first booklet was lukewarm, his response to the second was transparently contemptuous. The Virginia State professor had planned to document the political careers of several black city council, county, state, and congressional officeholders from Virginia. In this booklet, published in 1945, Jackson sought to highlight the accomplishments of black politicians and overturn the image of illiterate field hands exploiting Reconstruction for personal gain.[45] In the preface, Jackson was explicit about the book's purpose: it represented a "token of appreciation" for the teachers' contributions and for their "devotion to the cause of publishing and teaching the history of the Negro in the schools." That statement in itself signaled the book's character, but Jackson added that it was a "product of race, family and state pride," a premise that organized his other works but which had never been stated quite so explicitly, clearly marking *Negro Office-Holders* as a work of racial uplift.

Woodson may have been sympathetic to the objective, but he excoriated the final outcome as "the unfinished product of a race leader." He also took the opportunity to point out the shortcomings of the earlier project as well: "You compiled only some of the names of Negro soldiers in the American Revolution, and now you list only some of the Negro Office-Holders. Why jump from one task to another?" While acknowledging Jackson's desire to "give something back" to the teachers, he castigated him for compromising his professionalism.

"Although this book does not come up to the standard of the work of an historian," Woodson wrote condescendingly, "it has some value because the data, in spite of being inadequate, are valuable." Woodson was particularly miffed that his colleague had overlooked two of his uncles, lesser political appointees in Buckingham County. In his view, Jackson had overlooked the question of federal authority in Reconstruction as well as the political developments—namely, the independent Readjuster movement—that distinguished Virginia from other reactionary conservative regimes in the early New South. "Such a treatment," Woodson added condescendingly, "would be scientific whereas yours assumes the form of a compilation." For Jackson, the critique was devastating. The historian he most admired and most emulated had found his study wanting.[46]

More than the allegedly amateur quality of *Negro Office-Holders* may have irritated Woodson. Five thousand booklets would be distributed free-of-charge to Virginia's teachers and paid for out of the proceeds of contributions to the ASNLH, a plan that Jackson believed would pay for itself in future contributions. "The work is easily the most popular and saleable thing I have done," Jackson assured him. "Orders are coming in all the time and with them are coming a flood of congratulations extending from several of the nation's leading historians to the laymen on the streets." Since Woodson questioned Jackson on pricing, and since Jackson seemed at pains to justify the pricing scheme for additional booklets as well as the basic premise of the plan, it is reasonable to infer that the *Journal* editor was skeptical about the merits of his undertaking. He was probably also dubious about precisely who was to benefit from the booklets. Again, Jackson tried to assure him that "every step I make is in the name of the Association for the Study of Negro Life and History." Woodson was notoriously unwilling to concede control over the association to others, and Jackson's venture challenged the director's preference for unilateral authority.[47]

But there is probably another explanation. Jackson, the younger, still energetic historian and social activist was becoming *the* face of the association in Woodson's own backyard. He successfully combined scholarship and political activity, proving that academics had a place in promoting black civil rights. More than this, he was enormously popular; while black Virginians respected Woodson, they loved Jackson, and that realization must have disturbed a man who had dedicated his entire life to the cause of black history. As Lorenzo Greene, Woodson's research associate and fellow historian, suggested, the director was widely admired but deficient in close friends. As Jackson himself later confided to Dean A.A. Taylor of Fisk University, "Like everybody else I have had my 'run-ins' with him, but I have submerged instances of unpleasantness for the sake of the welfare of the organization." That may have been the case by 1949, but three years earlier, the wounds were fresh and the friendship in peril.[48]

After his restrained accounting of association debits and expenditures, Jackson finally confessed: "Your recent letter was a burning one. . . . You were so vicious in your attack on my methods and historical procedures that I would not think of showing this letter to my good wife or to President Foster." Jackson had already waited a full month to respond to Woodson's attack—a "cooling off period" that had done little to assuage Jackson's wounded pride. Whatever friendship the two had shared prior to the exchange had been irreparably damaged. Jackson continued to support Woodson, but he did so "for the good of the cause."[49]

Yet Jackson was not about to allow Woodson the last word, since his criticism had larger implications than the quality of the booklet. He could not have undertaken a more ambitious study since that would have required time that a professor teaching fifteen hours of classes for eleven months of the year simply did not have. Considering his involvement in the Virginia World War II History Commission and his multiple obligations to other social organizations, "you should wonder," he snorted, "how I get any Historical research done whatever." In addition to the travel involved in research—a function of the school's inadequate library and his commitment to uncovering archival material—he also wrote for the *Norfolk Journal and Guide* "in order to supplement a salary which is never large in a Negro institution." But he did more than excuse the limited research that went into the booklet. He also reminded Woodson of the book's objective, one that stood at the center of the ASNLH: to publicize black history to a broad audience.[50]

What Jackson was trying to do was define a place for the intellectual in the movement for civil rights, one that required a reconsideration of the meaning of historical inquiry. He was not interested in producing a thorough examination of Reconstruction; if anything, he clarified the limited scope of his analysis in the introduction. His booklet was not aimed at historians but "that great company of 4,200 teachers in the state and their pupils." Although he had no intention of impressing the scholarly crowd, it apparently paid him some compliments as praise rolled in from professors at Harvard, Duke, the University of North Carolina, Tennessee, Virginia, William and Mary, and "many of our leading Negro institutions." But more important than the formal praise from academics, Jackson received the warm endorsement of "people in general." He was becoming the popular historian who excites the imagination of average people and earns the opprobrium of specialists. He was trying to bridge the gap between "scientific" research and the public thirst for knowledge that sheds light on contemporary troubles. He was crafting a history that offered alternatives from a past filled with people not so unlike themselves. He was fashioning a history that would allow average people to mediate between the desire for immediate justice and the determination of whites to preserve a racially-stratified society.

Jackson met Woodson's implicit criticism head on—namely, that he was more the celebrity scholar than the serious researcher.

> You frequently cast aspersion upon my not staying in a cloister and mingling with the people instead. Yes I am affiliated with a large number of welfare organizations and I lead some of them. And out of my wide association with people I have learned more about the past and the people have learned [sic] me. Ultimately my success with my booklet stems back to my long association with people. They must think I have done something for them.

This was Jackson's manifesto, an impassioned declaration of his conviction that history was not reserved to those entrenched in the halls of academe. In essence, he violated the canons of his profession, which expected him to exercise authority over the past through exclusivist terminology, a scientific reverence for the "facts" unmediated by conviction, and a placid insistence that knowledge for its own sake was motive enough to undertake years of research. Jackson revitalized the idea that history was a conversation between the scholar, the reader, the sources, and the living memories of those who categorize and classify the past. On another occasion, when Woodson had indirectly attacked Jackson for belonging to the group of "Uncle Toms" that signed the Durham Manifesto, Jackson defended himself by insisting that his objectives ran beyond bringing the black experience out of historical obscurity: "Though essaying the role of the scholar in writing I have been motivated by the idea of trying to advance the Negro race."[51] He may have been content to play the role of "cloistered" academic before the war, but the political opportunities it opened shifted his perspective to the point where the past and the present merged almost imperceptibly. His *Negro Office-Holders* would produce "greater appreciation for Negro History by the thousands who are now reading and studying my small volume in the schools and in the homes of citizens generally." He might have added his unspoken assumption that the popular immersion in the accomplishments of the past would produce a vote-conscious people ready to claim the political inheritance won for them by the earnest black officeholders of the Reconstruction period. He would be "both the scholar and a worker among the people," he wrote to Woodson. In truth, he would be a race leader.[52]

Chapter 4

———•———

Voting for Freedom

Jackson and the Movement for Black Political Participation

Commenting on the political status of African Americans in the South at the end of the nineteenth century, H. C. Binford, a newspaper editor in Alabama, mused, "There is nothing in politics for us, it makes no difference which side wins none of them want the Negro." Binford later suggested that "we have gotten use[d] to being slighted and have ceased to kick. What's the use?"[1] The Alabama editor probably spoke for most black southerners in 1899. Hounded from political office by whites determined to restore racial control, blacks found themselves on the brink of political extinction by the end of the nineteenth century. Some blacks continued to vote in the twentieth century, but the deluge of disfranchising legislation after 1898 made exercising the franchise increasingly unlikely. Losing the right to vote was not the worst fate to befall southern blacks, but disfranchisement entrenched racial subordination in law and defined the political arena in racially exclusive terms. It was the final installment of a campaign aimed at erasing African Americans from civic life.[2]

Joining a growing number of middle-class activists, Luther P. Jackson struggled to revive African American political life in the interwar years. By publishing, organizing, and proselytizing on behalf of voting, he helped stimulate a political awakening among black Virginians. He simultaneously constructed a network of political institutions that sustained the later civil rights movement. Through voting registration drives, newspaper articles, and appeals to black teachers, he advanced a vision of civic participation that echoed the basic tenets of American liberal democracy.[3] His persistent optimism could not compensate for the weaknesses of a strategy predicated on voting registration. Yet by the war years, Jackson was advocating a strategy that included interest group pressure, civil litigation, and intense voter participation. He understood that the war had generated political opportunities that could be grasped only through voting. By exercising power at the ballot box, they could bend the political forces that operated on them at the local and national level. As black voting strength grew, political elites would begin to pay attention.

The South in Transition

No less than other African Americans, Jackson grew up in the shadow of racial discrimination. The South he inhabited bore the scars of racially motivated lynchings, debt peonage, inadequate schools, and black economic subordination. Beyond segregated public facilities, a battery of racial customs reinforced black submission. In Virginia, a tradition of racial paternalism that fostered the assumption that segregation was by "consent," as well as a disdain for unseemly violence, united white elites until at least the 1920s.[4] As much as southern whites wanted to solidify the color line, many African Americans opposed discriminatory treatment, particularly in public transportation, where racial boundaries eluded community control. Lawsuits and altercations accompanied efforts to regulate racial interaction on the region's streetcars and railroads. In countless challenges to the racial code, blacks put themselves in peril by challenging the rubric of inequality.[5]

Although whites were determined to maintain their monopoly on power, insurgent blacks increasingly challenged the racial status quo after World War I. Despite nationwide racism, the National Association for the Advancement of Colored People maintained a drumbeat of opposition to lynching and disfranchisement. The black nationalism of Marcus Garvey stirred the black working class with a vision of racial self-determination and solidarity. At the same time, the artistic blossoming of the Harlem Renaissance encouraged racial confidence and a new sense of black dignity among the urban, black middle class. So too did sophisticated historical investigations into the African American experience. Carter Woodson's Association for the Study of Negro Life and History supported research directed at restoring blacks to the American historical record. Woodson, along with Charles Wesley, Lorenzo Greene, and Luther P. Jackson, produced monographs that rescued African Americans, slave and free, from obscurity and the racial prejudice of white historians. While the NAACP challenged legal discrimination, A. Philip Randolph led an assault on racial inequalities in organized labor. Together with the Great Migration, these changes suggested a fracturing of the New South's racial order.

The Great Depression accelerated the forces corroding the southern racial order. In addition to encouraging agribusiness, New Deal agricultural policies drove one-third of southern sharecroppers out of the fields between 1933 and 1940. Rural-to-urban migration fundamentally altered social and race relations in the region, creating opportunities for collective action against the Jim Crow order.[6] Even before the Depression, Virginia's economic and demographic profile had become decidedly less rural, less agricultural, less prototypically southern. Never as dependent upon a single cash crop as some of its southern counterparts, Virginia became increasingly diversified in the twentieth century. By 1920, more than half of the Old Dominion's workers found nonagricultural employment. In the years before the Depression, Richmond became home to most of the state's tobacco processing operations, while Norfolk and Hampton Roads benefited from war-related federal investment. Petersburg hosted a number of industrial investors, Martinsville became the site for furniture manufacturing, Roanoke took on a mammoth rayon plant, and the city of Hopewell was transformed into a center for chemical processing and munitions manufacturing. African Americans joined the countrywide migration to the cities offering jobs, in the process increasing their numbers in urban areas by 32 percent between 1910 and 1920. In the period between 1920 and 1930, blacks left rural Virginia in droves, heading not for Richmond and Norfolk but out of the state and into places such as Baltimore and New York. An economically diversified, increasingly urbanized state featuring blacks and whites living in closer proximity and searching for similar economic opportunities was hardly the place for preserving the ethos of white paternalism. But white elites tried, and their efforts would meet the increasingly determined resistance of urban blacks and their middle-class leaders.[7]

While the New Deal transformed the world in which most blacks lived, it offered them at least some respite from the Depression. According to historian Ronald Heinemann, "black Virginians were provided a separate but almost equal share of the bounty."[8] Federal assistance through the Public Works Administration (PWA) and the Works Progress Administration (WPA) reduced African American unemployment, while support for collective bargaining increased union membership. In Richmond, Norfolk, and Petersburg, African Americans participated in demonstrations in support of the National Recovery Act, the New Deal measure that promised to regulate industrial production and guarantee workers the right to organize. The Civilian Conservation Corps

(CCC) hired more than two thousand African Americans in the state, although they followed the pattern of other CCC camps in the South by segregating black from white workers. The National Youth Administration provided scholarships to young blacks, the Resettlement Administration employed African Americans through its Homestead Project in Newport News, and the federal government built a school and a hospital in Norfolk. Blacks also received 36 percent of the relief money expended through the Federal Emergency Relief Administration (FERA). Although the fiscally intransigent Senator Byrd and Governor John Pollard became vigorous opponents of the New Deal, the Roosevelt administration channeled WPA, PWA, and FERA money into a state that desperately needed and benefited from it.[9]

The president's failure to endorse antilynching legislation, the persistence of racial discrimination in federal relief programs, and the exclusion of countless African American domestic workers from Social Security benefits exposed the limits of New Deal liberalism.[10] Yet, for many African Americans, the symbolism of the New Deal outweighed the results. Roosevelt's appointment of a "black cabinet" to advise him on African American issues and Eleanor Roosevelt's support of interracial groups enhanced the New Deal's image of racial liberalism.[11] The New Deal dislodged African Americans from their traditional allegiance to the Republican Party and led more and more of them into the Democratic camp. In regions where blacks could vote, they overwhelmingly turned out for the Democrats in 1934 and 1936. Government intervention in the lives of southerners—and the political fireworks it set off among conservatives and progressives alike—convinced blacks that political activity mattered. Joined by union organizers and the Southern Negro Youth Congress, the NAACP launched voter registration initiatives that produced minimal increases in rural areas but some impressive results in urban centers including Atlanta and Birmingham.[12] Jackson's voting initiatives of the 1930s stemmed from this regionwide political revitalization, which drew upon forces that only an instrument with the scope and power of the federal government could produce. If the Solid South had not exactly melted into air, the cracks in its edifice were showing.

Changes in the political landscape were abundantly evident in Jackson's Virginia. Lily-white Republicanism—which President William Howard Taft adopted and Herbert Hoover faithfully observed—antagonized many black voters. So too did Hoover's apparently tightfisted and distant management of the Depression.[13] A successful (1928) court challenge to the Democratic white primary in Virginia restored at least in theory a competitive electoral system and enhanced the appeal of the Democrats. Equally important, New Deal programs providing employment and improved public facilities for African Americans in Virginia clinched majority black support for the Democrats.[14] Despite these developments, a potent combination of voting restrictions and African American disenchantment inhibited political participation. Under the controlling hand of Senator Harry F. Byrd Jr., Virginia's political machine excluded most people from voting. As political scientist V. O. Key pointed out, a mere 11.5 percent of eligible voters participated in Virginia's Democratic primaries between 1925 and 1945. The restricted electorate meant that the Byrd gang had to win the votes of only approximately 5 to 7 percent of the state's adult population to nominate candidates for the governorship.[15] The organization had little tolerance for direct elections, vigilantly opposed the growth of public services that would benefit the poor of either race, and absorbed political challenges through patronage and coercion.[16] By exposing the contradictions of a country fighting for freedom abroad while denying it at home, the war effort stimulated African American hopes for genuine democracy.

These developments propelled the movement to advance black political prospects through local organization that Jackson had joined in the 1930s. As historian Steven Lawson points out, blacks capitalized on national wartime achievements to promote democracy in their own communities. Local groups held citizenship classes, promoted voter registration, sponsored poll-tax drives, and launched lawsuits against the Democratic Party for racial discrimination.[17] Rather than hew to a Washingtonian or Du Boisian line, Jackson launched a grassroots program of political activism that blended elements of both. Political influence was the objective, but the tactics operated within the boundaries of Jim Crow. As Jackson explained to Howard University historian Rayford Logan: "I believe there is a northern and southern method of attacking our problem and I am an ardent advocate of both. I don't think there should be any fight between them."[18] Jackson's thinking reflected the dominant ideas of most civil rights organizations in the 1930s. As Raymond Gavins argues, "the NAACP, Urban League, Negro advisors in New Deal agencies, and Northern Negro radicals, notwithstanding their bitter protests, followed the same pragmatic strategy." Segregation was not monolithic, but resistance had to be directed from positions of strength against points of weakness. For Jackson, the central weakness of segregation was the practice of political exclusion.[19]

It was his hope that pragmatism and political engagement would pave the way for African American self-determination. What we find is a pragmatic frame of mind in the service of democratic ideals that Jackson never lost sight of. Unlike many of his academic contemporaries, he spent little time defining his racial philosophy, analyzing the metaphysics of racial identity, or weighing the theoretical merits of black nationalism versus racial assimilation. Jackson privileged action over rumination, combining elements of black cultural nationalism and self-reliance in the search for political influence and legal equality. If we were to identify the ideological core in Jackson's thought, it would be the American liberal-democratic tradition crafted in the tumult of the 1790s, expanded in the Jacksonian period, tested in the crucible of the Civil War, reaffirmed by the Reconstruction experiment, and ignominiously abandoned by southern and northern elites for the better part of the Gilded Age. Jackson's scholarship and activism took for granted the indignity of racism, its conspicuous place in the American experience, and its corrosive legacy in his own time. Unlike W.E.B. Du Bois, Ralph Bunche, Charles Johnson, E. Franklin Frazier, and Rayford Logan—his intellectual contemporaries—Jackson did not struggle with the meaning of racial identity, at least not in his writings.[20] He could not ignore the nettlesome irony of racial inequality in a nation predicated on Enlightenment humanism. But he preferred to work these problems out through action, understanding racial discrimination as a historical reality susceptible to reform rather than as an abstract problem requiring theoretical insight. This may have been Jackson's weakness and Logan's and Bunche's strength. In any case, it suggests, paradoxically, Jackson's idealism, since his pragmatism had little to do with cynically pursuing power and everything to do with fashioning a democratic system that fulfilled the ideals enshrined in the nation's founding tradition. He placed a premium on voting, but he considered it more than a ticket to better services and schools. It provided a tool for achieving genuine equality, a society freed of racial discrimination, and the corridor through which black cultural pride could evolve into racial self-determination. His vision was simple, compelling, and characteristically American; neither he nor his supporters had much interest in making it anything else. Yet as much as Jackson threw his intellectual eggs into the basket of ballot box action, he recognized that it was not the only strategy available to dissidents. As the NAACP escalated its legal attack on segregation, he stressed the benefits of court action in overturning inequalities. Both techniques required political consciousness.

Organizing for the Vote

Already a politically conscious teacher and scholar at Virginia State College, Jackson's involvement in the Petersburg League of Negro Voters signaled his transition to political action. Formed in March 1935, the league united several black social clubs and civic groups in a political consciousness-raising campaign. It welded together college fraternities, a sorority, the Independent Voters League, and middle-class social clubs including the Civic Association, the Progressive Vigilantes, and the Elks. Headed by Jackson and D. A. Wilkerson, professor at Virginia State College, the executive committee featured the luminaries of Petersburg's black middle class, including attorney T. L. Taylor, Mary Jones, and Dr. W. F. Clarke. Jackson's credentials and magnetism vaulted him into the position of temporary chair and then president of the organization. From there, he cemented groups ranging from the National Ideal Benefit Society to the Daughters of David into a single vehicle for reform.

The voting leagues sought more than the full privileges of membership in the middle class. The Petersburg League of Negro Voters and its successor, the Virginia Voters League, provide a window into the lives of people who made black civil rights a standard feature of their workdays, their leisure hours, their social engagements, their everyday experience. By examining how these groups operated at the local level—the site of the black freedom struggle in the South— we move away from generalizations about the civil rights inertia of the generation before the *Brown* decision and into a fuller understanding of what racial equality meant in this era and what people like Jackson did to achieve it. In the New Deal era, voting rights activism was the leading edge of civil rights reform.

When Jackson and the Petersburg League of Negro Voters drafted a constitution, they anchored the group's activity in participatory democracy. The league planned to cultivate a sense of obligation "under a democratic form of government, for participation in the civic and political life." In the interest of negotiating the treacherous political waters of the Solid South, the league was strictly nonpartisan. In the broadest sense, it sought to generate political involvement, not mass support for a particular candidate. This was both the group's strength and its weakness. Instead of mobilizing voters behind the Democrats—the only viable party in the region—and articulating a program of political reform, the organization simply set out to maximize African American political action. Specific policies and issues were not its concern; exercising the vote was.[21]

The league aimed at increasing black voting through voter registration and poll-tax payment. The constitution also called for detailed research on African American voting in the state. Not unlike Du Bois and a host of academics molded by the progressive movement, Jackson believed that quantitative analysis would shed the light of reason on regressive folkways, encouraging social criticism and change. This assumption would guide his future work with the Virginia Voters League, as he meticulously amassed data on poll-tax payment and electoral behavior. By distributing literature for public edification, sponsoring campaigns for additional voters, and holding meetings to stimulate political consciousness, the league strove to make black political action visible again.

Not since the Union leagues had African Americans organized as extensively at the ground level. Eschewing behind-the-scene resistance, the league operated as a public vehicle of political action. Jackson hoped that voter registration would expand the political sphere and give African Americans the tools to make concrete improvements in a segregated world. "Many of the difficulties which beset us," he wrote in a mail-out to Petersburg residents, "may be attributed to our non poll tax paying and non-voting."[22] Attacking segregation would come later; for now, he and other middle-class reformers focused on gaining influence over the institutions that directly affected them. The organization hoped to legitimize black voting through meetings, mail-outs, and "personal contacts," a strategy that would expand the network of black "citizens."[23]

While the league tapped into the energy of local political groups, it also identified itself with the church, the institutional core of the black community, by holding its inaugural meeting at the Zion Baptist Church on Byrne Street. In addition to raising awareness, the organizers planned to register voters for the August primaries. In November, Jackson led the organization in a drive for the payment of the $1.50 poll tax. Contacting Petersburg's clergy, its 350 qualified voters, the faculty at Virginia State, and "hundreds" who had failed to pay the tax, his committee spearheaded a campaign to "awaken so many people from their lethargy." It distributed information concerning the final dates to pay the tax, the amount required, and the name of the county treasurer that collected the tax. In 1936, the league counted seventeen affiliated organizations. It also claimed that by April of that year it had increased the number of registered voters to 416.[24]

Jackson placed the development of "personal contacts" at the center of his voter registration initiative. He advised the league to produce several copies of the lists detailing those persons who had paid the 1934 poll tax. After assigning lists of twelve or more residents to teams of two investigators, the executive sent the students out to interview them. It was "urgent" that field-workers make "direct personal contact," a strategy that would allow the interviewer to apply direct pressure to the potential voter and present the tangible benefits of casting a ballot.[25]

Jackson appealed to Petersburg's elite, particularly its clergy, to support the movement. While field-workers canvassed poll-tax payers who had failed to register, the executive pressured the clergy. He reported to Wilkerson that they had the "full cooperation" of the five most influential ministers in the city. To convince the holdouts, Jackson applied tactical peer pressure: "Our duty now is to get out communications to all of them saying somewhat in these necessary words that several ministers of Petersburg in conference with the Executive Committee proposed that we undertake the united action for April 28th."[26] The mobilization of the black community's elite—a time-honored strategy among racial uplifters—figured prominently in Jackson's voting campaign. Targeting the clergy in 1942, he concluded that "ministers preach only a heavenly gospel. That the common man should participate in the affairs of government by voting is an idea quite foreign to the mass of these leaders." He chided the community's most respected institutions and asserted that "the so called democratic school and democratic church . . . are failing to promote the political democracy for which we are now fighting." He would continue to berate ministers who failed to vote and support the movement from their pulpits.[27]

Conceived as a middle-class enterprise, the Voters League sought to expand political participation and address working-class concerns. Proposing the question "Why Negro Should Vote in Petersburg and How They May" in a circular, Jackson gave his standard answer: citizenship required civic participation. But he added that only by voting could African Americans improve teachers' salaries and build better high schools, issues directly linked to economic opportunity and social advancement. Voting promised to rectify the injustices that African Americans routinely faced in the courts and at the hands of police. Only political involvement could put black persons on juries, pave the streets of black neighborhoods neglected by white lawmakers, and find blacks public employment. By emphasizing education and economic mobility, he tried to alert working-class blacks to the concrete rewards of political action. If he avoided attacking segregation directly, at least until the war years, he consistently mapped out the geography of racial equality and the political tools required to achieve it.[28] His work fostered the climate in which racial amelioration seemed possible.

Jackson also reached out to local workers through his favorite pastime: music. Just as he used the Elks lodge as a channel for disseminating the voting rights message, he deployed vocal ensembles to reach the "voteless." Jackson organized a choir among workers at the Brown and Williams tobacco plant in Petersburg, less than two miles from the college campus in Ettrick. The choir performed twice a year at the college, an event that became a social highlight on campus. While local residents found an audience for their talents, Jackson found another forum for inculcating political awareness among workers. The community choir provided Jackson an outlet for his musical energies, but he utilized it as a vehicle for reaching African American workers, mobilizing the local community, and subverting segregation.[29]

Despite the success in local organization, the immediate impact of the Petersburg Voters League on voter registration was limited. Although the change in allegiance of most black voters from the Republicans to the Democrats convinced both parties to court their votes in 1936, voter registration remained dismally low. For example, in Virginia in 1940, approximately 30,967 blacks had fulfilled all requirements to vote, but a mere 15,000 or so actually voted. Stubborn discrimination in Virginia's New Deal programs also suggested that blacks exercised only a nominal influence on the Roosevelt administration.[30]

Election officials in Virginia played no small part in enforcing racial inequality. In the transparent effort to deny registration, registrars asked applicants arcane questions, all under the guise of the "understanding and educational" clause, a measure that had been annulled in 1904. In one case, a registrar asked Charles Butts of Portsmouth how many patriots had signed the Declaration of Independence. If the understanding clause proved insufficient, registrars could subject applicants to a battery of technicalities, including the failure to sign a registration form the required number of times. Both methods effectively circumscribed black voting.

Even this barrier was beginning to crumble, though. In 1931, the State Supreme Court of Appeals ruled on a case in which a white registrar asked a black applicant a series of questions concerning the poll tax and residency requirements. The Court decided that the registrar had unfairly applied the now defunct "temporary understanding" clause in the registration process. Although registrars continued to use variations of the understanding clause into the 1940s, the decision forced them to be cautious. Registrars subsequently restricted their questions to matters relating to voting qualifications. When they did not, the NAACP and the Virginia Voters League (successor to Jackson's Petersburg organization) stood ready to intervene.[31]

Diagnosing the Voteless

If court decisions had removed the major legal obstacles to black voting, most notably the Democratic white primary, then Jackson wanted to know what explained continued black political apathy. In 1939, he supervised sixty students of Virginia State University in a house-to-house survey of black attitudes toward voting. The campaign covered some two thousand homes in the city. Part sociology, part salesmanship, the campaign grew out of Jackson's program to stimulate citizenship through "personal contacts." He wanted to examine the constellation of assumptions that conditioned African American thinking about the political system. The voting survey offers a snapshot of political attitudes beyond the ranks of the articulate middle class. It gives us a chance to listen in on conversations that went directly to the question of race and power in the South. The study was indispensable to Jackson's program for citizenship training, and it is essential for us in understanding the obstacles that Jackson faced.

Once they were assigned a street or a block to investigate, students approached residents with open-ended questions about the franchise. They then summarized their responses and submitted them to Professor Jackson, who synthesized them in a report titled "What the People Think about Voting in Petersburg, Virginia." What is most striking is the range of responses to questions about voting behavior. Rather than a disenchanted mass, African Americans in Petersburg chose not to vote for a number of reasons. One student editorialized about the "pathetic" illiteracy of his respondents between the ages of twenty-four and thirty-five. He also reported the widespread conviction that voting is for whites only: "Why boy, don't you know that votin' is fo' the white folks? We ain't got nothin' to do with that.... all we got to do is stay to ourselves, work hard and pray to the Lord. That's what we's supposed to do!" The use of dialect and the exasperation at illiteracy suggest as much about the class differences separating the interviewer and the respondent as they do about political consciousness among Petersburg's blacks. Still, the response represented at least one powerful strain of black thought about voting: political power was the prerogative of white people.[32]

Survey responses suggested that economic as much as political realities governed the decision to vote. According to one investigator, financial considerations were paramount in determining poll-tax payment. Inadequate wages and the cost of living made paying the poll tax a low priority: "Boy, I ain't worked in two years, and I ain't had hardly enough to eat in so long, I can't even remembah. I just ain't got no money to be payin' poll taxes." Virginia's $1.50 poll taxes were cumulative up to three years, a deterrent at the best of times and a burden during the Great Depression. In addition to the cost, the tax had to be paid six months in advance of an election, further complicating the qualification process. Clearly, the economic impediment built into the poll tax kept black and white undesirables from voting. Its effectiveness in reducing democratic participation was conspicuously evident in the 1936 presidential election. In the eight southern states that collected the poll tax, only one in four qualified voters went to the polls, compared to almost three in four elsewhere in the United States.[33]

While financial hardship curbed some poll-tax payments, competing financial obligations discouraged others. Some respondents simply privileged the church over political questions, vesting more meaning in religious faith and its institutions than in the vagaries of politics. Again, the inquisitor shed light on his assumptions by insisting that those who chose the church over the ballot "would not listen." Middle-class college professors, businesspeople, professionals, and students staffed the voting leagues; having glimpsed racial dignity in the public arena, they sought to expand it. For them, voting often assumed a mystical importance far removed from the concerns of working-class blacks. For many, of course, the issue was not an either-or choice between the church and the franchise, but the nagging doubt that voting made any difference at all. Several respondents echoed the disenchantment that stemmed from the southern white program to maintain racial hierarchy: "This is white man's wor' and he ain't gonna help us but so much. Jes a waste of time!" As part of the fabric of a "culture" of segregation, as historian Grace Elizabeth Hale argues, disfranchisement reinforced the assertion of black inferiority. Since black degradation was not a given, it had to be proven and demonstrated. Power substituted for reason in the tautology of segregation. African Americans never uniformly accepted the powerlessness that the Jim Crow system implied. Still, most African Americans in the 1930s would have grudgingly agreed with one respondent who believed that voting was futile, since "Negroes had no weight with lawmakers in Washington."[34]

Gender lines also made their mark on voting behavior in the 1930s. One student investigator found that the number of male voters and "prospective" voters far outweighed women voters. According to the interviewer, women took no discernible interest in local or national affairs, an observation difficult to reconcile with the political activism of women such as Mary Bethune and Ella Baker.[35] If the student interviewer found women unwilling to vote, he overlooked the less visible but powerful presence of women in social reform campaigns that sought political influence through alternative channels. As historian Glenda Elizabeth Gilmore has noted, disfranchisement fundamentally changed the nature of black political activism. As whites drove black men from public space, women occupied the void through social and religious organizations that expanded social services for the black community. They acted as mediators between white political authority and an increasingly separate black society.[36] Groups such as these—including the Ladies Auxiliary and Imperial Friendly Lyceum and the Daughters of David—belonged to none other than the League of Negro Voters. When it came to decisions about paying the poll tax, it was the husband who usually ended up casting the vote, further diminishing women's participation in the electoral process.[37] Bearing the burden of family and work outside the home, often in egregiously underpaid domestic service, and subordinate to their husband's prerogatives, many women must have viewed voting as a luxury at best.

Jackson and J. P. Spencer recognized the gender disparities in voting and sought to include women in the movement. Women were active on the executive, but the voters' leagues had made little progress in mobilizing the voiceless women identified in the Petersburg survey of 1939. Both Spencer and Jackson called for new "drives" to get women registered. Members also wanted to ensure that the commissioners of revenue included women on tax assessment lists. Although these were minor overtures to gender equality, the league understood the need for wide-scale opposition against a shifting front of racial barriers.[38]

While some student participants registered political indifference, others found black residents eager for full citizenship. Some Petersburg blacks welcomed the opportunity to vote but confessed little understanding of the poll-tax system. Others agreed in principle but seemed uncertain of the concrete benefits of registering to vote. In these cases, the failure to pay the tax and register to vote reflected a lack of training in political matters, not the absence of conviction; it was this deficiency that Jackson and his colleagues sought to remedy. Another worker found that interest in voting was strongest among the youth of Petersburg, a development he attributed to political education. He too recommended that "classes be held to enlighten the rest of the population as to the benefits of voting."[39] Whether tailored to what Jackson wanted to hear or the opinions of people newly awakened to political possibilities, the student canvassers were reading from the same page as their professor. More important, they were taking up the kind of democratic engagement that Jackson had been fostering at Virginia State since 1922.

The student surveyors were often greeted by suspicion. According to one participant, "most" of the people were "distrustful" and unwilling to divulge information. Furthermore, they became "indignant" when the interviewer probed them for their names: "nother white man's nigger, trying to get us into somethin.' We's bad off enough as it is . . . ' was the reply I received from one person, and even a few doors were slammed in my face." In the context of a southern legal system that discriminated against blacks, a political system premised on racial exclusion, and elites of both races who claimed to represent African American interests while defending racial inequities, this response is not surprising.[40]

Suspicious residents expressed a deeper current of opinion than Jackson and his contemporaries cared to explore. Instead of the cautious optimism characteristic of many middle-class blacks, some considered the world they inhabited hopelessly infected with the virus of racial enmity. For many, the poll tax and voting itself looked like another fragment in a mosaic of racial domination. Instead of cooperating in civic rituals that seemed to promise little in the way of change, many opted out completely. Others held out for a meaningful re-weaving of America's social and political fabric. Luther Jackson imagined a moral transformation of American society through democratic activism, but at least in the 1930s, he expended minimal energy to abolish the poll tax altogether or to address the economic foundations of black political inactivity.

Jackson ultimately concluded that indifference rather than legal obstacles explained the failure of blacks to vote. Writing in 1945, he echoed the findings of the Petersburg survey: "The poll tax is still in operation in Virginia, but the white primary and most prejudiced registrars have long since passed....All told, the failure of the Negro in these two states [Virginia and North Carolina] is not now the fault of the white man but the lethargy of the Negroes themselves."[41] Acknowledging Jackson's stress on voter training, he still sounded remarkably like Booker T. Washington in his conviction that blacks bore the responsibility for their exclusion. Jackson marveled that blacks were reluctant to pursue litigation when denied the right to register to vote. Confident of his rights, he seemed to lose sight of the social conditioning that prevented many from voting. Anxiety over reprisals from voting or indignities at the hands of capricious white registrars conditioned African American thinking about politics. For others, paying a tax six months in advance to vote in an election that seemed to have little impact on the structure of racial inequality was an exercise in abstraction.

The voting survey exposed the depth of political disenchantment and the need for a wide-ranging political initiative that reached the working class. Any meaningful voting rights campaign would also have to extend beyond local affairs. National developments sparked the voting leagues, but most tended to focus on local concerns in isolation from larger political issues. By 1940, Jackson was reaching out to voter education groups across the state. He maintained connections with the NAACP, civic organizations, and several voting leagues scattered throughout Virginia. Jackson proved particularly helpful to organizations in search of information about Virginia's black citizens, its voting laws, and statistics on registration. He also offered advice about establishing voting leagues. Contact with like-minded groups throughout the state raised his profile as a social leader and created the framework for a more ambitious initiative that bridged the gap between local powerlessness and larger political realities.[42]

The opportunity for wider coordination in the drive for voting rights came on May 3, 1941, at an education conference held at Virginia State. The teachers divided into groups to examine a number of school-related issues. When Jackson solicited suggestions for additional topics, one person, according to his account, "arose and declared that he would serve as chairman of a group to discuss the problem of voting among Negroes." Despite the dramatic moment, it is difficult to imagine that Jackson did not have something to do with the declaration. He almost certainly took part in the subcommittee that assembled to draft a constitution for a state voters' organization. His political expectations for the meeting are also clear. Representatives of Petersburg's League of Negro Voters had invited the chairpersons of voters' leagues throughout the state to the meeting. Finishing the constitution was a task that fell into the hands of none other than Luther Jackson and two associates, Raymond Valentine and Robert Cooley, both lawyers in Petersburg. They also became the ranking officers in the Virginia Voters League.[43]

Like the Petersburg League, the Virginia Voters League (VVL) functioned as a federation of voter organizations. Centered in Petersburg, it represented voting clubs in eighty counties and twenty-four cities in the state. Jackson eventually extended it into the remaining twenty counties of Virginia. Appointed chairpersons administered the local leagues and reported to the central office, while the executive encouraged the locals with diligent correspondence and periodic lectures. Yet the Virginia Voters League was no dictatorship. Jackson, Cooley, and Valentine used it to gather information and coordinate the efforts of local groups. The executive also placed voter education at the center of the league's agenda.[44]

For Luther P. Jackson, the Virginia Voters League provided the medium for propagating the message of social change through political participation. He relished the opportunity, quickly initiating a vast correspondence with league chairpersons and activists. He called on county chairpersons to organize their territories and to secure lists from the county treasurer of those blacks who had paid their poll taxes in the past three years. The president also asked for lists of voters in the years 1938 to 1940. In addition, he urged the county representatives to find out who the registrars were, to identify registered voters from the list of poll-tax payers, and to "Persuade Fellow Citizens to Vote in August." Like a sales manager with an eye on targets, Jackson appealed to the chairpersons' competitive instinct. He pitted them against one another in mobilizing the more than five thousand blacks who had paid poll taxes but failed to register. He also conducted "citizenship surveys" to determine the number of voters in a particular family, whether or not women had voted, and the status of poll-tax payments. Always eager to share his findings, he kept a steady stream of literature flowing to county representatives and "civic-minded citizens."[45]

But Jackson wanted to be more than a cheerleader for black voting. He proposed regional conferences to generate unity among county representatives. He encouraged local activists to leave the shadows and build the connections that would strengthen the voting rights initiative against inevitable resistance. He and his field-workers eventually held six regional conferences throughout the state. The summer school at Virginia State afforded Jackson the opportunity to fuse politics and education by encouraging young voters, most of whom were teachers, by recruiting organizers, and by promoting the work of the Virginia Voters League. At the same time, he and Robert Cooley investigated recalcitrant registrars in order to compel black voter enrolment.[46]

Convinced that empirical data could stimulate political change, Jackson started publishing the booklet *The Voting Status of Negroes in Virginia* annually. The booklet consisted of data on poll-tax payments that detailed yearly gains and losses. A second section explained the rubric and requirements of voting. Jackson thus fulfilled his dual impulse to publish the concrete data of racial discrimination and to educate his readers in the ways of democratic citizenship. Since the state did not collect registration and poll-tax information, he undertook the monumental task of accumulating data from county and city records. He meticulously assembled poll-tax and registration statistics into a five-page bar graph that broke down voting performances by county. The league distributed ten to twelve thousand copies of the booklet each year to affiliated groups as well as to libraries, Virginia's daily newspapers, and select state and federal officials.[47]

Jackson was eager to circulate the explicitly didactic booklet among Virginia's teachers. School principals and supervisors of the Anna T. Jeanes Fund, a philanthropic organization that provided assistance to black elementary schools in the South, distributed the booklets to their teachers. According to Jackson, 95 percent of the more than four thousand black teachers in Virginia received a copy of the booklet in 1944. In the hands of committed teachers, the booklets became tools for democratic instruction. Posters, folders, and circulars featuring information on teacher voting activity and notices of poll-tax deadlines also descended on school principals. Voting activists throughout the state turned to his booklet for concrete evidence of voting behavior. Fraternal lodges, civic organizations, and the NAACP also solicited Jackson's prodigiously researched booklet for stark illustrations of black political inertia.[48]

The significance of the voting surveys extended beyond Virginia. According to R. G. Higgins of the Agricultural and Technical College of North Carolina, Jackson's voting research was indispensable in attacking the "lethargy" that afflicted average voters and in eliminating the "insidious devices" used to prevent blacks from voting. Jackson's work had a profoundly personal impact on Higgins: "May I say with all sincerity, you are truly a pioneer, a trail-blazer, a credit to the profession. Your work has been most stimulating in stirring within me a greater desire to uncover and destroy the cantankerous growths that impede the progress toward democracy."[49] Political scientist V. O. Key, author of the seminal study on contemporary southern politics, relied extensively on Jackson's work and acknowledged its importance in fostering a critical analysis of the region: "I think you have been doing an extremely useful service in pulling together the facts about a subject in the discussion of which facts are usually ignored." None other than W.E.B. Du Bois turned to Jackson's voting surveys as a source for his research. The yearly study was arguably Jackson's most important contribution to voting rights activism in the South.[50]

Despite its growth, the Virginia Voters League never became the dominant player in the field of voter mobilization. Established in Virginia in 1915, the NAACP had grown to twenty chapters by 1935, a figure that would triple by 1950. As litigation at the national level increased during the New Deal era, the NAACP in Virginia launched a major voting registration drive that lasted from 1936 until 1940. Relations with the Virginia Voters League were harmonious since Jackson himself was a vigorous NAACP supporter. As groups affiliated with the Virginia Voters League withered during the war, NAACP chapters and Negro Organization Society locals replaced them. Enjoying greater financial stability than the Virginia Voters League, state NAACP chapters provided it assistance throughout the war. In 1942, Jackson went so far as to encourage city chairmen to align themselves with the NAACP if their cities could not sustain independent voting leagues. The Petersburg chapter routinely contributed to the Virginia Voters League. In 1943, Jackson requested funds from chapter co-ordinator Reverend C. L. Evans, reminding him of "the close connection be-tween the Voters League and the NAACP."[51] Before the era of sit-ins and free-dom rides, the NAACP and the Virginia Voters League forged a network of social organizations that shared the common objective of democratic inclu-sion. Under the leadership of activists such as Jackson, the voters' leagues pushed the issue of democratic participation to center stage in southern race relations, challenging assumptions about black political indifference and the racial status quo.[52]

The Four Freedoms, for Some

Although the Second World War accelerated the demand for change, the ra-cial order stayed depressingly the same. Yet the economic status of southern blacks improved as the region found itself caught up in a whirlwind of federal military spending and martial enthusiasm. Still in the grip of the Depression, all southerners greeted federal investment in war-related industries as manna from heaven.[53]

African Americans shared in the spoils of wartime spending, but employers followed the cadence of Jim Crow. Blacks enlisted in droves alongside white southerners but suffered segregation in the army and routine confinement to noncombat units. Racial violence also stalked military bases in Georgia, Missis-sippi, Texas, and Louisiana. In civilian life, government agencies and defense contractors hired whites over blacks. Out of one hundred thousand workers in the aircraft industry in 1940, only three hundred were African American. Glar-ing inequities only sharpened black discontent.[54]

Political and economic gains benefited blacks, but the rhetoric that accom-panied the war highlighted the American contradiction on a grand scale. Axis propagandists seized on the disparity between American ideals and racial reali-ties. Black newspapers and social leaders sounded the call for the "double V," a joint crusade against fascism abroad and segregation at home. While a growing number of black citizens challenged job discrimination, the NAACP broadened its activities against employment and housing inequities. Despite vocal reac-tion against wartime discrimination and the widespread mistreatment of black soldiers, the majority of African Americans did not protest. Historian Harvard

Sitkoff argues that the militancy of the March on Washington days declined dramatically once the United States entered the war. Rather than vigilant opposition to segregation, most blacks closed ranks in support of the war effort. As Sitkoff bluntly put it, "Despite the many transformations and upheavals triggered by the war, there would be no mass militancy in the World War II South."[55]

In Virginia, defense sector employment and the war overseas crowded out concerns about black voting. Voter registration increased only marginally during the war. In 1941, 30,748 blacks had registered to vote. By 1944, this number had crawled up to 32,889. Only in 1945, and largely because of returning veterans, did the number of registered voters increase substantially to 38,000.[56]

While Jackson followed the majority that supported the war effort, he adopted the more aggressive spirit that overtook the NAACP during the war. He also endorsed litigation as a strategy for countering racial injustices. At a meeting of the league in August that year, Jackson shared his observation that white attitudes toward blacks had improved considerably. Despite the climate shift, he strongly recommended that blacks report any effort to obstruct their right to register to a circuit judge, electoral board, or a sympathetic lawyer. Court action, not delay, was the proper response. Again, Jackson tied litigation to the overarching effort to include schools, churches, and other organizations in the movement to get people "vote minded." He had often called on African Americans to seek redress from voting injustices in the courts, so the turn to litigation reflected more of a change in emphasis than in strategy. For Jackson and his counterparts in the NAACP, litigation complemented the vote in the struggle for change.[57]

The Teachers and the Voting Question

As the war distracted attention from electoral politics, Jackson turned to the state's teachers to keep the movement afloat. Since the inception of the league, educators at Virginia State, Virginia Union, and elsewhere had supported the voting movement. Now Jackson worked to solidify that relationship and expand it to public school teachers. Six days before the Japanese attack on Pearl Harbor, he urged the Virginia State staff to pay their poll taxes and join the voting league initiative: "[W]e are now making a special appeal not only to the faculties in all our colleges, but to the four thousand public school teachers as well. If teachers vote then we may expect our graduates from high school and college to vote."[58] Integrating teachers into the voting effort made perfect sense for a movement premised on education for citizenship. In 1935, Jackson called for a direct appeal to the faculty of Peabody High School and volunteered himself for the task. Similar to his efforts with the NAACP, though, Jackson forged organizational links between teachers and field-workers that provided a continuous channel of information and influence for the Virginia Voters League.[59]

Mirroring the experience of middle-class blacks throughout the South, the Virginia Teachers Association grew increasingly militant in the years preceding the war. In 1937, it joined the NAACP in the movement to eradicate wage differentials between black and white teachers. Represented by NAACP lawyer Thurgood Marshall, Melvin O. Alston—a Norfolk teacher who had been encouraged to sue the state for salary discrimination—won a U.S. Court of Appeals decision. The court held that salary differentials for black teachers were discriminatory, a decision upheld by the U.S. Supreme Court later that year.[60]

It was probably with the salary equalization case in mind that Jackson encouraged the state teachers' association to endorse the Virginia Voters League. He had already forged close relations with them through the Virginia State summer school and the Association for the Study of Negro Life and History, of which Jackson was the state chairperson.[61] On his recommendation, the teachers assembled at the 1941 convention in Richmond approved the program of the Virginia Voters League. The convention nominated Jackson secretary of civic education and appropriated two hundred dollars for a program to train teachers and students in political participation. Professor Jackson stressed the connection between the teachers' association and the Virginia Voters League. In a letter to the chairpersons of the league, he urged them to support their teachers and to "give them no quarter."[62]

The decision to link the two organizations was more than a formality. As Adam Fairclough has pointed out, "Organization . . . provided the vital transmission shaft transmuting individual feelings into the *only* kind of resistance—purposive and collective—that could force change."[63] It was one thing for individual teachers to endorse civic education; it was quite another for their association to endorse black political participation and the social claims that voting implied. By endorsing the league program, the teachers' association signaled its transition from a professional alliance to a civil rights organization. But by instructing students in a history that whites had all but written out of public memory, black teachers had already engaged the crucial connection between social authority and education at the center of southern life.

Jackson's effort to combine the two groups challenged the misconception that blacks could separate education from civic equality. It also belied the notion that social progress did not require political engagement. Moving away from the individualism and status-consciousness that characterized black middle-class thinking on race, he envisioned a collective movement for gradual but fundamental change, one that mobilized the political potential of elites and average people alike. Under the pressure of wartime gains and postwar opportunities, the gradualism would diminish, the demands for change would increase, but the conviction that equality depended upon black ballots persisted.[64]

The civic education program was a departure for the Virginia Teachers Association, but it was not the first of its kind. Howard University historian Rayford Logan had launched an "Education for Citizenship" campaign as director of education for the influential Alpha Phi Alpha, a black college fraternity that included among its members W.E.B. Du Bois, Thurgood Marshall, Charles Hamilton Houston, Charles Wesley, and Paul Robeson. Like Jackson, Logan advocated enfranchisement as the key to black influence in local communities. Logan derived his inspiration for the citizenship school from his work with the Atlanta chapter of the NAACP, which initiated a voter education project under the leadership of Lugenia Burns Hope, the wife of Morehouse College president John Hope. In 1935, the year that Jackson and the others established the Petersburg Negro Voters League, the Alpha Phi Alpha chapter of Virginia State College's extension branch in Norfolk assembled a picket line to insist on the right to vote. Voting rights activism, citizenship training, and political instruction had already materialized by the time that the Virginia Teachers Association adopted the civic education position.[65]

As secretary of civic education, Jackson cultivated and documented the growth of political sensibilities. His work in this position is examined in chapter 4, but it is important to address it here briefly, since political participation and education were binary terms in Jackson's lexicon. He studied ninety-four schools, comparing the number of teachers who voted in the 1944 and 1948 presidential elections. He completed the study in 1948 and sent the results to the participating schools. Not surprisingly, he found a greater rate of political participation among urban than rural teachers. In addition, more than half of the 4,500 public school teachers were registered to vote. Most important, he reported an increase of between 15 and 20 percent in the rate of teachers voting in the presidential elections, a development he attributed to his work in the civic education department. Through a steady flow of literature and persistent pressure, the Virginia Teachers Association developed a "sense of civic responsibility among its members" that silenced those who claimed to see "no value in exercising the American right of franchise."[66] Although teacher anxiety about the repercussions of political activity continued, the association was building a sense of collective purpose that progressively dampened those fears.

For his part, Jackson turned his classes at Virginia State into a forum for political education. Connecting current events to a tradition of racial self-reliance, he used the data collected from his voting surveys to "hammer on my government classes" the status of black voting and the urgency of political action. He brought newspapers into the classroom and used them to spark discussions of contemporary issues. He took his students on field trips to Richmond and Washington to expose them to government and reduce the sense of alienation that perpetuated black political inaction. When they turned twenty-one, he insisted that his students register and pay the poll tax. Routinely dressed in a fedora and one of many second-hand suits he purchased from a pawn shop in downtown Petersburg, frequently humming John Philip Sousa numbers to accompany his marchlike stride across the campus, sporting an infectious laugh and easy smile that ingratiated him with students and teachers alike, Jackson cut a curious figure at Virginia State. But it was this radiant and endearing personality that opened doors for a message that many might have otherwise resisted.[67]

Jackson was a dynamic teacher and gifted storyteller whose enthusiasm for history and politics infected his students. On field trips to Washington, he would stand in the aisle of the bus and point out sights of interest, offering insight and anecdotes that made the excursions more than just a day away from the classroom. As former student and research assistant Sam Madden recalls, Jackson made his classes "interesting and exciting. On exams, he would limit student to five lines in answering a given question," all in the effort to elicit concise analyses that demonstrated genuine learning. As former student Elva Howell remembered, Jackson made dust-covered textbook events come alive: "Even when he lectured he spoke as if he were on the scene of action," whether the event was a Civil War battle or the storming of the Bastille. Moving back and forth across the plane that linked historical and contemporary consciousness, he convinced his students that the past mattered—to them.[68]

He was a vigorous practitioner of classroom primary source analysis, a strategy that invested history with a sense of immediacy. He took his classes on tours of the Petersburg battlefield and through old town Petersburg. As Lutrelle Palmer observed in 1950, and as Elva Howell recalled in 1984, his movement beyond the comfortable security of the campus impressed teachers and students alike. He "worked to abridge the gap between the school and community,"

Howell explained. Traveling to the Tuskegee Institute in repressive Macon County, Alabama, he acquired "first hand knowledge on our fight for social and political justice." More than erudition and social relevance, Jackson offered his students respect and compassion. He was "interested in the personal welfare of each student. He treated them as people—not as objects," Elva Howell observed.[69] In his classroom activities, his Negro History Week addresses, his presentations to local voting leagues, and his meetings with teachers and local leaders, Jackson exhibited that elusive quality that usually distinguishes leaders from followers. It was that quality that is much maligned in our self-consciously ironic and cynical age, one that is by no means the monopoly of leaders in commendable causes but is usually applied to more prominent activists: charisma.

The civic education portfolio gave Jackson a unique opportunity to observe the unfolding of democratic education. Before the ferment of the late 1930s, black educators had banished citizenship and "direct participation in governmental affairs" from the classroom. By contrast, teachers now registered to vote and instructed students on the mechanics of voting, elections, and parties. They also translated civic consciousness into political involvement in their communities. Much as Du Bois had expected, the "talented tenth" had started to foster political awareness in their students, a development made abundantly evident by the decision to hold mock elections in November. As Jackson reported (and as is discussed in more depth in chapter 4), students campaigned and held mock presidential elections at several schools in the state. The elections became exercises in civic participation. In institutions where whites expected blacks to learn little more than vocational skills, students absorbed the idea that the electoral process belonged to them as well. Decades before the freedom schools of Mississippi and the voter registration campaigns of the Student Nonviolent Coordinating Committee, Virginia's black students learned that voting was not simply "white folks' business."[70]

And their parents learned it as well, as teachers encouraged students to transplant the message in their homes. As Jackson observed, Leola R. Vann, a teacher at Hayden High School in Franklin, Virginia, went beyond the "traditional method of learning facts from civics text books." Vann convinced her students to "carry the voting message home to their parents while she in turn has followed up" by visiting the parents at their homes. Vann and others like her made the vital connection between education and political self-determination that white legislators had hoped to sever through disfranchisement and racial oppression. What happened was not revolutionary, nor was it the principal catalyst for the black freedom struggle. It was, however, the moment when African Americans began to claim the explicitly political terrain that few had occupied since the end of Reconstruction. It represented the decisive break with a tradition that had minimized electoral participation and black political prospects. In the process of repudiating political indifference, teachers such as Vann became more than "mere teacher[s]—they became "civic leaders."[71]

Rising Expectations, Persistent Frustrations

Invigorated by the Virginia Teachers Association and the heady wartime atmosphere, Jackson found multiple outlets for his growing assertiveness. Acknowledging Jackson's growing prominence in the civil rights struggle, P. B. Young—the editor of the *Norfolk Journal and Guide,* one of the South's leading black newspapers—gave him a column to disseminate his voting message.[72] Launched in 1942, Jackson's column, "Rights and Duties in a Democracy," became a forum for the voting registration campaign, his appeal for teacher involvement in political affairs, his campaign for black history, and his commentaries on the status of the civil rights campaign. He used the space to appeal for white support in the anti-poll-tax campaign, a subject he had avoided during the 1930s. Spurred by the work of the National Committee to Abolish the Poll Tax (NCAPT)—a division of the Southern Conference for Human Welfare—and the Southern Electoral Reform League (SERL), liberal forces mobilized around the Geyer-Pepper Bill to eliminate the poll tax. The initiative proved to be an interminable source of frustration as southern congressmen filibustered it into oblivion. Yet the persistence of the anti-poll-tax supporters—among whom were included Virginia Foster Durr and Eleanor Roosevelt—suggested the liberal determination to realign southern politics despite the growing political conservatism of the war years. Liberal activist Moss Plunkett of the Virginia Electoral Reform League—the state branch of the Southern Electoral Reform League—looked to Jackson to spearhead the anti-poll-tax initiative in the African American community. Jackson threw his support to the initiative, offering up columns that called for the abolition of the poll tax, circulating anti-poll-tax petitions, and joining letter-writing campaigns targeting senators and congressmen. Jackson also joined the Southern Electoral Reform League, but he balanced his anti-poll-tax activism against his continuing appeal to pay the tax in order to get rid of it.[73]

He also joined what was for the period one of the boldest African American initiatives for racial amelioration in the South. In 1942, Gordon B. Hancock, a professor of economics and sociology at Virginia Union University in Richmond, wrote an article for the Associated Negro Press that called for interracial cooperation to avert the escalating violence on the home front. "Interracial Hypertension" sparked the interest of Jessie Daniel Ames, an antilynching crusader and field secretary for the Commission on Interracial Cooperation. Meeting in Richmond to discuss the article, Ames and Hancock decided to hold the Southern Conference on Race Relations. The idea was to bring together the black elite to formulate a plan of action to which a committee of leading whites would then respond. Hancock implored Jackson, who became the conference's treasurer, to do "some hard thinking about this conference" so that it might produce "something more than 'just another conference.'" Plans were made for a preliminary conference to be held in Virginia to determine the scope and the participants for the larger meeting.[74]

The trouble began when Jackson and the others had to decide who would attend. Jackson, Henry J. McGuinn of Virginia Union, and Wiley H. Hall of the Richmond League fervently agitated for a conference that would include African Americans from outside of the South. Hancock was afraid that if the conference included "northern radicals," it would give white southerners the ammunition to dismiss the group's statement as the product of "subversive elements etc." After rancorous debate, it was decided to send invitations only to southern blacks, many of whom had belonged to the now largely discredited Commission on Interracial Cooperation. Jackson had opposed the decision, but now he was on board with an organization committed to finding a southern solution to racial conflict, one that would win the support of white liberals.[75]

Meeting in Durham, North Carolina, in 1942, the group produced a manifesto that condemned segregation but conceded their willingness to "address ourselves to the current problems of racial discrimination and neglect." Despite censuring discrimination in wartime industry, racial inequalities in public education, persistent lynchings, and inadequate public health for blacks, the Durham Conference could not avoid being entangled in the contradiction of denouncing segregation but proposing a "sensible and timely" program to improve "race relations within the democratic framework."[76] Meeting to strike while the iron of war was hot, southern black intellectuals and academics temporized on the very question that made a meeting in Durham necessary.

Northern African American newspapers pounced on the manifesto, deriding it as a compromise of principle for a mess of interracial pottage. White liberals including Ralph McGill applauded the document for pursuing reform along "realistic lines." What critics and supporters seemed to miss was that for the first time, leading black southerners demanded racial reform rather than white patronage. Although influential whites were the target audience, and although white cooperation was the objective, the Durham Conference repudiated segregation as a matter of principle rather than expediency. Critics also seemed to ignore the crucial turning point at which southern blacks had arrived: the decision to pursue racial reform through politics. They finally put to rest the ghost of Washingtonian political submission that had haunted interracial initiatives throughout the early twentieth century. While Washington had insisted on segregated equality and the abandonment of political and civil justice, "the cornerstone of which is the exercise of the suffrage," the Durham conferees had "entered this field with all the vehemence of the other fields," clearly distinguishing themselves as a "new group."[77] Conference participants advocated the abolition of the poll tax and the white primary, condemning at the same time the prevention of black voting by fraud and intimidation. The Durham Manifesto resonated with Jackson's conviction that voting was the "safeguard of democracy." Any limitation on electoral participation represented an abridgement of freedom and "the integrity of the State." Two years before historian Rayford Logan assembled the team of leading African American scholars that published the landmark *What the Negro Wants,* Hancock, Jackson, and others had delineated the terms for future discussion. Southern blacks might be willing to concede the impenetrability of segregation for the present, but they put liberal whites on notice that racial separation and American democracy could no longer be reconciled. In dispelling the notion that blacks favored segregation, the Durham Manifesto also discredited the myth of white paternalism that had endured since slavery.[78]

Under the leadership of Jesse Daniel Ames of the Commission on Interracial Cooperation, a group of white liberals met in Atlanta to respond to the manifesto. When representatives of both groups met in Richmond in 1943, they decided to replace the ineffectual CIC with the Southern Regional Council. With its emphasis on education and research, the commission exuded the regionalism of Howard Odum, who—along with his protégé, Guy Johnson— initially headed the organization. Interested in racial moderation and economic growth, the commission resisted endorsing desegregation until 1949. Nonetheless, its support for studies of black voting behavior in the South kept Jackson active in the organization following the war.[79]

For Jackson and his colleagues, the greatest wartime breakthrough came with the 1944 Supreme Court decision eliminating the white primary, the principal weapon in the South's arsenal against black political participation. In *Smith v. Allwright*, the Court decided that the key electoral function played by the Democratic primary meant that any use of race to limit participation violated the Fifteenth Amendment. Jackson observed, "The Texas primary case was the beginning of a complete revolution in our thinking on the right of suffrage."[80] The decision propelled the NAACP and the Southern Conference for Human Welfare (SCHW)—an interracial organization established in 1938—into aggressive voter registration drives. Blacks also revived and expanded local voters' leagues that had fallen dormant during the war. By 1954, more than one million blacks had registered to vote, a number almost four times that of registered voters in 1944.[81]

Jackson's political ventures extended beyond the cautious Southern Regional Council and the Durham Manifesto. He also aligned with groups that sought to build a liberal-labor coalition in the South. Despite the fact that Jackson's ideological trajectory incresingly put him at odds with the group's moderate interracialism, it was the SRC that gave him his widest exposure and an opportunity to play a distinctive part in regional affairs. In 1947, the SRC commissioned him to undertake a wide-ranging study of black voting behavior in the South. His odyssey took him to cities throughout Alabama, Mississippi, Georgia, and Tennessee. In Montgomery, Jackson met with Aubrey Williams—former head of the New Deal's National Youth Administration—and "Big" Jim Folsom, governor of Alabama and, according to Jackson, "a semi liberal for a southern governor."[82]

The experience was professionally and personally satisfying. "This trip means everything to me," he wrote to his wife, Johnella. Whether a function of his connection to the SRC, his unmitigated optimism, or the impact of racial advancement since the war, Jackson suffered little of the brutality of segregation: "Have not had the slightest hold back in anything I have attempted to do. Today I have an appointment with the editor of the *Birmingham Age-Herald*." He also found it difficult to generalize about black voting behavior: "Localities in a state differ so much in racial attitudes toward voting that one has to visit a number of points in order to arrive at the whole truth." Whether Jackson ever found the "whole truth" about voting is uncertain, but Executive Director George Mitchell applauded his report, which was published as "Race and Suffrage in the South since 1940" in *New South*. One wonders, though, whether Jackson's interviews with courteous southern liberals went much beyond the surface niceties of most interracial meetings.[83]

He may have engaged in some wishful thinking, but his study documented the political developments that were transforming the South in the 1940s. The story of the South's political "awakening," as Jackson described it, belongs to chapter 7, but the importance of his article should be highlighted here. While liberal activists celebrated the apparent increase in political activity across the South, Jackson documented it, placing it in the context of national and regional developments favoring black voting. His study convincingly underlined the cumulative gains in black voting between 1940 and 1947. The elimination of poll-tax requirements, critical Supreme Court decisions, African American litigation against unfair registration practices, political organization in states such as South Carolina, as well as voter registration campaigns accounted for substantial gains in a number of states. In Georgia, for example, the number of registered African American voters climbed from 20,000 in 1940 to 125,000 in 1947. There, in 1946, black voters cast ballots for the first time since Reconstruction after litigation compelled Georgia and several other southern states to eliminate the white primary. In Virginia, the number of black registered voters tripled from 15,000 in 1940 to 48,000 in 1947. Taken as a whole, the twelve southern states that he investigated reported a 26–percent increase in the number of qualified African American voters. Still, Jackson was realistic: despite the dramatic changes, only 12 percent of blacks had registered to vote. Yet the numbers did not tell the entire story. Jackson was able to report that "politics seems now to be everybody's business." More profound in the Upper and Border South states than in the Deep South—with the notable exceptions of South Carolina, Georgia, and Florida—the political new day seemed to be dawning, and Jackson was a key witness.[84]

But Jackson also stressed the concrete benefits that flowed from political activity. Voting had produced better parks, playgrounds, swimming pools, community centers, and better policing, including the hiring of black officers. Political activity had improved relations between whites and blacks, insofar as the former had "become more civil in their dealing with Negroes." African American politicians had also won seats on city councils, city commissions, and school boards. In Richmond, Jackson exulted, a biracial coalition elected attorney Oliver W. Hill to the city council in 1948. But he did more than applaud these important but minimal changes. He also exhibited greater empathy toward the majority who remained disfranchised. Blacks often failed to register, he observed, because the registration "involves a social relationship which Negroes have always been taught never to infringe." Since registration in rural areas was often conducted in private homes, African Americans shied away from violating "the unwritten laws of racial etiquette" that dictated that they only visit the home of a white person "as a servant or on business." The tradition of nonvoting extended back to early-twentieth-century whites and "race leaders, from Booker T. Washington at the top to the thousands below" who advised African Americans to relinquish political participation. By 1948, then, Jackson had grown closer to average African Americans and had cut himself adrift from his earlier Washingtonian moorings. Although he reminded white readers that the growth of the black electorate had not reached the point of threatening "white supremacy," he confidently concluded that the movement toward political equality was probably inexorable. The *New South* article documented not only the South's political progress but also his own.[85]

The article also resonated well beyond the boundaries of Virginia. Letters of support and congratulations, queries about his methodology, and protests against his findings poured in from across the South and from outside of the region. His report struck a nerve in the electric atmosphere generated by the increase of black voting rights agitation throughout the South in the run up to the presidential contest of 1948. As Mabel Smythe—a former student of Jackson's who was then working as a research assistant for Du Bois—noted, Jackson's article had produced "a lot of publicity." Considering that it was an election year, "with Negroes fighting for rights in the courts, the NAACP getting a lot of attention through that case in South Carolina [against the white primary], and Moon's book on Balance of Power: The Negro Vote, well it is understandable the hulla-baloo that is being raised." As Jackson exulted in a letter to a friend from Lexington, the pamphlet had brought him "nationwide publicity" through articles and editorials on it in major newspapers throughout the country. Jackson, the Virginia professor and civil rights activist, had become a public intellectual of national stature.[86]

While working through regional organizations like the SRC, he continued to advance on Virginia's political fronts. He eagerly cooperated with the NAACP in promoting poll-tax payment and voter registration, using the pages of the *Norfolk Journal and Guide* to extol its virtues and promote popular support for its programs.[87] He employed the *Journal* and the *Teachers Bulletin* to educate African Americans and pressure them into voting, all the while intervening on behalf of those trying to register to vote. He fused the Virginia Voters League and the Virginia Teachers Association together in the conviction that municipal reforms, educational improvements, and economic mobility required political influence. When the voting initiative declined during the war, Jackson bolstered the Virginia Teachers Association and stressed litigation as the means of dismantling racial barriers.

If Jackson's strategy allowed for racial conciliation, his vision of racial progress included equality before the law and political self-determination. Both were goals that deviated from the Washingtonian script. While endorsing the Durham Conference's pragmatic call for the improvement of segregated facilities, he reminded readers of the *Norfolk Journal and Guide* that "the sixty or more Southern Negroes who comprise this body detest segregation." He subscribed to the doctrine of racial self-reliance, but he argued that "Most Negroes oppose segregation and maintain that if the walls were battered down the present inequality would no longer exist."[88] Repudiating accommodation, he adopted the racial strategy of the NAACP, pursuing relief simultaneously through the courts and voter mobilization. By combining a variety of religious, social, and fraternal organizations that the NAACP could not reach, voters' leagues like Jackson's played a crucial role in the early black freedom struggle. Building on local connections, they expanded the range of political organization and awareness. But Jackson was not content to build citizens' groups from the ground up. During the war—and long before his cross-country trip for the Southern Regional Council—he decided to work through existing professional organizations, particularly those that could influence the largest number of young African Americans. He would focus his energies on awakening the teachers from political somnolence.[89]

Fig. 1. Luther P. Jackson on his graduation from Fisk University.

Fig. 2. Johnella Frazer.

Fig. 3. Luther and Johnella on their wedding day in 1922.

Fig. 4. Mattie Jackson, Johnella, and "Mama Laura."

Fig. 5. Jackson and the Virginia State chapter of Omega Psi Phi. Fraternities, like the Elks Lodges and the local business associations, provided important vehicles for generating political action and unifying African Americans behind civil rights.

Much Property Held by Negroes In Richmond in Days of Slavery

Many of Race Distinguished Themselves for Development.

This article in two sections, printed today and tomorrow, is an outgrowth of the author's doctoral dissertation at the University of Chicago, 1937, called "Free Negro Labor and Property Holding in Virginia," 1830-1860. Like the original dissertation, it is based on State and local archives as found in the State Library and the City Hall. The tax books in the State archives, Land and Personal Property, and the deeds and wills in the chancery records at the City Hall constitute the basis of the findings represented here. Among printed materials, Mordecai's "Richmond in By Gone Days," certain works of travel and the Richmond newspapers of the period were helpful.

By LUTHER PORTER JACKSON.

LUTHER P. JACKSON.

D. Jackson is Professor of His-

Activity Among Freed People Often Expression of Filial Devotion.

liam Marshall, John Logan, Richard C. Hobson, Michael Brooks, John Norman and Henry Matthews bought their wives or wives and children, and set them free; Maria James, her husband; Hope Butler. John Logan and William Marshall, their daughters; Samuel Anderson and Caiberry Burton, their sons; Charlotte Smith, John Elson and John Hopes, their grandchildren; while James Johnson, in 1856, set free his mother whom he had purchased from Thomas Roberts.

Filial Devotion Shown.

This activity among free Negroes was frequently an expression of filial devotion. The case of John Logan was like that of many others. Said he in 1841: "Now, therefore, in consideration of the natural love and affection that I bear them I do hereby emancipate and forever set free (my wife and children) Maria Logan, Mary Ann Logan, and Sarah Frances Logan." That love and af-

Fig. 6. Luther P. Jackson, circa 1942. By this time, Jackson was an established historian and a prominent civil rights activist.

Fig. 7. Jackson and the ever-present suit, hat, and smile.

Fig. 8. The faculty at Virginia State University, ca. 1946.
Jackson is at the end of the second row from the back, on the left.

Fig. 9. Watercolor of Jackson, completed shortly after his death.

Chapter 5

———•———

Teachers Struggle for a Voice

From Professionalism to Political Action

Few African Americans commanded as much respect as teachers, and few understood this better than Luther Jackson. If young people were going to become politically active, their teachers would have to lead them. The clergy cast a wide net but carefully avoided the role of political visionaries. Teachers, on the other hand, presided over institutions that promised social mobility and the intellectual tools for challenging the status quo. Average blacks looked at education as the road to improvement and their teachers as exemplars of self-reliance.[1] They were in a unique position to craft political consciousness, but first they needed to exercise it themselves. Getting them to act was Jackson's principal task in the Virginia Teachers Association (VTA).

Jackson promoted the twin objectives of professionalization and political action, yet he was a latecomer to the upper echelon of the Virginia Teachers Association. To understand his role as secretary of civic education, which he undertook in 1941, we have to examine the development of the association from teachers' salon to advocate of professional and political rights. Jackson's 1937 chronicle of the VTA is central to this reconstruction. Because of southern realities, the effort to professionalize necessarily involved black teachers in the struggle to achieve racial equality, since the character of the social order, its historical origins, and its susceptibility to change was implicit in almost every classroom lesson. Jackson understood that political action to improve the position of black teachers could lead to something more than higher salaries; it could become the leading edge of the movement against the caste system.

Black Teachers and the South

Racial inequality was anything but an abstraction for black teachers; it had immediate implications for their livelihoods and careers. As racial discrimination widened the gulf between black and white public education in the New South, it created salary disparities between black and white educators that lasted until the 1950s. As late as 1940, for example, the average annual salary of female African American teachers in Virginia was $553, compared with the $805 paid to white females in the same profession.[2] Poorly financed, neglected by white administrators, and feared as a potential source of black social advancement, African American schools occupied a precarious position in the modern South.

The generally poor quality of training for black teachers only exacerbated the problem. In 1933, Ambrose Caliver, an African American researcher working on behalf of the U.S. Office of Education, published a revealing study of academic training among black teachers in the District of Columbia and sixteen southern states. Caliver found that, in 1930–31, 35.8 percent of black teachers in the rural South—as compared to 4.5 percent of white teachers—had achieved no more than a high school education before they started teaching.[3] When southern state governments started using exams to certify schoolteachers, African American prospects in the teaching profession declined further. In the rural areas, where the majority of African Americans continued to live until the 1950s, discrepancies between black and white schools and teachers' salaries were extreme. Additional training and education among white teachers made them eligible for higher certification levels, which translated into better salaries. White administrators could then justify lower salaries by claiming that black teachers failed to meet the certification requirements achieved by their white counterparts. State administrators tried to solidify caste distinctions by advocating separate exams and certification procedures for blacks. Leading black educators, including sociologist Charles Johnson, vigorously opposed separate standards for teacher qualification or for the classification of black high schools and colleges. Against the backdrop of these pedagogical and political challenges, black teachers' associations throughout the United States sought to strengthen their position. Efforts to elevate classroom instruction, improve the quality of black schools, achieve certification, and secure equitable pay converged in the drive to organize African American teachers. Professionalization enhanced the status of black teachers and broadened their political perspectives, just as whites had long feared.[4]

By the time that Jackson penned his chronicle of the association in 1937, the VTA had become an important presence in Virginia. Like other associations in the South, its origins were fairly humble. Established in 1887 as a "reading circle" for the enrichment of teachers, the association spent most of the early twentieth century trying to counteract the effects of inequitable state funding on black schools. It worked to upgrade the physical facilities of black schools, lengthen the school terms, and raise the salaries of black teachers. The school improvement drive mirrored the education crusade that swept over the South at the beginning of the twentieth century. White reformers in Virginia inaugurated the movement in 1905, offering African American educators little more than platitudes. Administrators struggled under the threat that state politicians might reduce public funding to match the taxes paid by African American citizens. The threat—based on the widespread assumption that black schools were financed at white expense—was absurd, since by 1910 public funding for black schools already approximated the percentage of taxes paid by black citizens. Southern state governments allocated taxes paid by blacks to support white schools and realigned school districts to disqualify black schools from local tax support. In Virginia, state authorities attracted campaign contributions by maintaining a low tax policy at the expense of public education. Political hostility in these years of "crisis" forced school personnel to deepen their dependence on local community resources and support.[5]

The crisis that Jackson described in his history of the VTA also strengthened the organization as a vehicle of African American activism. In its early days, the association offered teachers little more than an annual meeting featuring uplifting lectures on "The Teacher as a Factor in Social Progress" and "Education in the Home." Controlled by college faculty and administrators, it left many of its members cold. Its meetings provided a distraction for teachers enrolled at the Virginia Normal and Industrial Institute's summer school, but the self-help exhortations produced limited enthusiasm among teachers worried more about dismal salaries and certification requirements than moral improvement. Despite the negligible membership fees, the association failed to take root at the community level. In 1903, it counted fewer than 150 members out of approximately 2,000 black teachers in the state.[6]

The School Improvement League widened the scope of the association's activity and diminished some of its elitism. Founded at Virginia State in 1907 by English professor James Phillips, the league directed school improvement throughout the state. Educational improvement dated back to Reconstruction, but white hostility toward black education in the early years of the twentieth century fueled the drive to upgrade rural schools. Since the league and the state teachers' association operated under the auspices of Virginia State, the decision to fuse the two in 1909 made sense. Even so, it changed the character of the teachers' organization. The association joined the effort to promote school reform at the ground level. Moreover, the league constructed an organizational network that later supported Jackson's voting and citizenship campaign.[7]

The School Improvement League gained the popular support that had eluded the association. The Hampton Institute provided most of the leadership for this progressive campaign to advance farming techniques, domestic science, cleaner homes, and better schools, all in the spirit of Washington's crusade for black uplift. Whatever its pedagogical thrust, it spawned local affiliates and linked with existing school improvement clubs. Instead of esoteric exercises, the association engaged in a campaign for community support and parental involvement. Moving in this direction, the Virginia undertaking paralleled efforts throughout the South to enhance school facilities and local support for education.[8]

Teacher involvement was critical to local school improvement. It solidified the connection between extended school terms, upgraded schoolhouses, increased teachers' salaries, and professionalization. According to Jackson, the First World War accelerated the growth of the association as members learned "the effectiveness of group action." Now virtually indistinguishable from the School Improvement League and its Hampton ally, the Negro Organization Society, the association boasted six hundred local leagues. Mass meetings and a steady correspondence from the headquarters at Virginia State carried the educational message into communities throughout the state.[9]

The College and Its Professional Teachers

In the 1920s, Jackson and a stream of talented educators arrived at Virginia State, bolstering the college and the Virginia Teachers Association. Founded in 1882, the Virginia Normal and Collegiate Institute was the brainchild of Alfred W. Harris, an African American lawyer who served in the House of Delegates from 1881 to 1888. Harris belonged to William Mahone's Readjuster Party, that curious, progressive anomaly that briefly offered an alternative to conservative dominance. The Readjusters promoted, among other things, public education, a position that included support for African American higher education. Against stiff opposition from the conservative Funder Party, which recoiled at the prospect of spending tax dollars on liberal arts education for blacks, Virginia Normal and Industrial Institute opened in 1883. The college was perched atop Fleets Hill in Ettrick, a mill village contiguous to Petersburg and populated largely by poor whites. Featuring academic, normal, and college programs, Virginia Normal offered an educational haven for Virginia's African Americans despite persistent political intrigue in the post-Reconstruction period. The respite did not last long. The wave of disfranchisement and segregation that spilled out of Mississippi in the 1890s eventually washed over Virginia in 1902. That year, the state adopted a new constitution that disfranchised African Americans. With the electoral purge of African Americans, and with the growing enthusiasm among whites for the Booker T. Washington style of industrial education practiced at Virginia's own Hampton Institute, the political foundations for liberal arts training at Virginia Normal crumbled. A new charter eliminated the college program and converted it into a high school and industrial institute. Despite an increase in students from 131 in 1883 to 481 in 1906, the Democratic legislature reduced the institute's appropriation from $20,000 to $15,000 annually. In the face of considerable hostility, Virginia Normal continued to fill the ranks of a gradually expanding African American middle class.[10]

The school operated as an industrial institute until 1923, when President John M. Gandy succeeded in restoring its collegiate program. The fact that the school had been designated the recipient of land grant funds through the Morrill Act and the Smith-Hughes Act helped, since both measures were intended to support practical education at the collegiate level. So too did the movement toward high school accreditation, which required teachers to have college degrees instead of the traditional normal school certificate. Once the institute became Virginia State College for Negroes, Gandy set about recruiting high-caliber faculty, an initiative that netted Luther P. Jackson, Doxey Wilkerson, Edna M. Colson, Wilhelmina Hamlin, and others from "the best institutions of the land."[11] With advanced degrees from distinguished northern and southern colleges, the Virginia State faculty compared favorably with many of its counterparts in the region. In a 1933 article on black normal schools in the South, Colson claimed that Virginia State was one of only two in which every education and psychology instructor held a master's degree. Jackson corroborated the trend, writing to Johnella that "[a]ll of our college teachers are rapidly acquiring the master's degree."[12] By 1937, the year that Virginia State added graduate studies, it included among its faculty ranks four Ph.D.s, including historians James Hugo Johnston and Jackson. Paid abysmally low salaries, teaching a collegiate program that had grown to 1,524 by 1934, and carrying a heavy teaching load that meant for some more than twenty-five hours in the classroom and responsibility for more than 150 students, Virginia State's professors struggled on the margins of the academic profession.[13]

Yet it was academic notables such as Eva C. Mitchell and William Cooper of Hampton who took up leadership positions in the Virginia Teachers Association, adding an aura of expertise and professionalism to the organization. Men monopolized most of the key leadership roles, but women played an indispensable part in the association. Women such as Hamlin and Colson exercised racial leadership not only as administrators but also as public speakers at the annual conferences. They functioned as academic experts in scholarly journals and the association's bulletin. Amelia Felton controlled access to the organization's funds as its longstanding treasurer. Kate Colson, a high school teacher in Richmond, and Eva C. Mitchell, director of elementary education at Hampton, both wielded clout in the organization. But it was Rose Butler Browne who broke the male hold on the presidency. Starting out as a "mere class room teacher," in Jackson's status-conscious expression, she gained the confidence of the rank-and-file membership through her peripatetic work as director of the college's extension department and through numerous convention appearances. After Gandy's departure, Browne was elevated to the presidency in 1932 and remained there for two years.[14]

Others followed the divisions of labor set by dominant gender conventions. Mary E. Branch and Tossie Whiting, both Virginia State faculty members, undertook the daunting correspondence that held its local chapters together. While Gandy, Lutrelle Palmer, and Jackson took the limelight at the conventions, Branch and Whiting diligently maintained the records of the association's departments and reported them in the college gazette. Despite the persistence of time-honored gender practices in the VTA, women created opportunities for leadership that reflected their considerable presence in the profession. By setting the context in which African Americans could question reigning assumptions about racial inequalities, the VTA created an environment in which women could dissolve invidious gender distinctions.[15]

As the status of the college improved, the VTA became increasingly professional and bureaucratic. It added a president, district vice presidents, an executive secretary, a secretary of educational research—responsible for investigating the condition of rural education—and a treasurer. Spurred by President Gandy, the association supported educational reform and built on the achievements of the School Improvement League. By 1927, local affiliates of the national and, presumably, more stable Parent Teacher Association (PTA) had replaced the league chapters.

For all of its democratic trappings, the association was a thoroughly hierarchical organization. College teachers dominated the conventions and subject groups, "point[ing] the way for their high school colleagues by showing them the weak points in their instruction." Jackson confidently reported that the college elite "operated as the main cog in the machine of all the lower bodies." Among the VTA's major players, status ambitions often coexisted alongside sentiments of racial advancement. In practice, however, hierarchical stratification reflected the growth of decisive leadership and a functional division of labor that accommodated its multiple educational ventures.[16]

The executive committee strengthened the lines of communications connecting the association and the local chapters. Under the editorship of Lutrelle Palmer, the VTA began publishing the *Virginia Teachers Bulletin,* which disseminated the latest educational theories, information on salary litigation, thoughts on teaching African American history, reports of the conditions facing black students and educators in Virginia, and political developments relevant to the membership.[17] After the *Norfolk Journal and Guide,* the *Bulletin* served as Jackson's central platform for the voting campaign.

The association also reached out to teachers and the public through the Speakers Bureau. The bureau sponsored lectures by experts, educators, and activists such as Jackson, who used it to spread the voting message throughout Virginia. The Speakers Bureau gave Jackson a vehicle for ranging far beyond pedagogy and schoolyard beautification. In 1943, the Lynchburg NAACP invited him to address them on a proposed voting project, noting that his services "can probably be secured through the State Teachers Speakers Bureau."[18] The Teachers Association of Leesburg also turned to the Speakers Bureau for Jackson's expertise in a public meeting dedicated to "The Negro and Civic Participation." Reflecting the political cross-fertilization between African American institutions, teachers in Heathsville secured Jackson for an "educational day" address at the Sharon Baptist Church. The Jeanes supervisor who invited him must have expected more than pedagogical platitudes from the popular orator, since the application indicated "No special topic" for his address. Exemplifying the growing synergy between church and politics, one that would become increasingly common after the Montgomery bus boycott of 1955, the Cumberland Training School invited Jackson to address the local teachers association at the Tearwallet Baptist Church. The president of the local association, S. D. Womack, urged Jackson to think broadly about the "advancement of the Negro, not only in Virginia but through out the nation." The quasi-evangelical meeting included singing, an "invocation," and Jackson's address. Although the spiritual undercurrents were strong, Womack made it clear that "the question of voting should be stressed."[19]

Under the auspices of the Speakers Bureau, Jackson delivered Negro History Week addresses at training schools, teachers' associations, and high schools throughout the state.[20] While the Speakers Bureau drew the local church and voters' leagues into the VTA's orbit, it also forged connections between black historical and political consciousness. In December 1941, E. N. Talioferro, president of the local teachers' association, invited Jackson to deliver an address at a "mass meeting in the interest of a fuller civic participation by Negroes in the life of the Community." The meeting would also launch Negro History Week, giving Jackson the chance to address issues that were "near and dear" to him. Organizers were determined to "develop a civic consciousness among our citizens," which they planned to achieve through the PTA. Civic consciousness was becoming inseparable from historical awareness, from a sense that the past shaped the present and offered it alternatives.[21]

Negro History Week invitations gave Jackson the opportunity to advocate political participation and the legal defense of black civil rights, but they also allowed him the rare chance to conduct research. As he explained to C. W. Seay, secretary of educational activities for the VTA, "My reason in accepting as many as I do is that these trips afford me an opportunity to do other things: see the chairmen in the counties in my Virginia Voters League, see people about history and conduct research in the clerk's offices in the counties."[22] He reinforced the bureau's political function by encouraging lawyers to enlist for speaking engagements. "I do this," he explained to Seay, "to supply the needs of such groups of teachers who wish information about voting requirements, particularly the problem of combating a few die-hard registrars in the state."[23] The number of invitations alone suggests Jackson's popularity as a civil rights orator, but some used them as an opportunity to express their admiration for him. In one invitation, the principal of A. T. Wright High School in White Stone confessed that he felt "elated to think of you turning your thoughts again toward Lancaster County," reassuring Jackson that, "I know of no other man more diplomatic and capable of delivering that needed punch."[24] Education, historical consciousness, and political involvement merged through the Speakers Bureau and in countless other public meetings that brought middle-class African Americans together in this pivotal period.

The Speakers Bureau and the *Bulletin* reflected the association's effort to move beyond the innocuous formalities of the annual meeting. The VTA now tried to sustain communications with rural teachers, expose them to current issues, and upgrade their training throughout the year. The bureau linked professionalization and educational reform, challenging a racial status quo built upon limited opportunities for black children and discrimination against black teachers. By initiating an employment bureau, a teacher recruitment week, a fund for impoverished schools in rural counties, and a teachers' institute staffed by college faculty, the association transformed itself from educational booster to professional advocacy group. At the same time, it expanded its political capabilities and created the communications network required for civil rights activism.[25]

Under Phillips and Gandy, the VTA joined a collection of organizations involved in racial advancement. Self-interest and social reform converged as the association engaged a cluster of issues centered on racial equality. As Jackson explained, "It actually became a clearing house for many other interests and movements of vital importance to the Negro race." While supporting local conferences that addressed the problems of rural schools and teachers, it also cooperated with YMCA chapters, parent-teacher groups, and its own National Association of Teachers in Colored Schools in examining the nexus of education and racial equality. In the 1940s, the PTA became one of several organizations fostering political awareness and support for the Virginia Voters League. As Lessie Evans Hogart explained to Jackson, members of the East Suffolk PTA had "discussed voting from many angles" and had decided to form a local voters' league: "I have been teaching here a number of years and their interest in voting is higher than I have ever known it." Hogart also asked her former professor for information on voting and assistance in launching the voting league.[26]

In the 1930s, this network embraced the NAACP and the Association for the Study of Negro Life and History. In one sense, the fusion of the teachers' association and the School Improvement League followed the long tradition of African American self-reliance in educational matters.[27] The critical difference was that the association tied Virginia's teachers to other reform groups, creating a network for exchanging information, resources, and personnel. It also created the framework for defining a common agenda. Association leaders and teachers increasingly cast professional issues in terms of African American advancement.

Even so, some teachers were skeptical about the association. As Jackson adroitly observed, "The lowly teacher, on a low salary, in one of the backward counties, might well claim that the Association has meant nothing to him." The "lowly" teacher had good reason to be skeptical, considering that in 1928–29, the average African American educator earned a monthly salary of $69.72, while her white colleague took home $111.36 for the same period. The problem was not that Gandy and others had failed to understand the concerns of average teachers. What they lacked was the political influence and social consensus needed to correct even the most glaring injustices. Organization building created the potential for change, but even optimist John Gandy admitted in 1920 that, "at present there is no hope for Negro people to share directly in determining the educational policies of this country."[28] Deficient in political leverage, the VTA focused on improving chronically unstable schools.[29]

Informal alliances did not transform the racial order or produce a coherent ideology of social change. Until the salary equalization drive of the late 1930s, the VTA continued as a largely annual affair of addresses and sessions dominated by college elites. Yet by developing a stable organization aligned with other groups willing to raise troubling questions and consider solutions, the association expanded the range of political possibilities. The VTA did not crusade for civil rights, at least in the 1920s, but it did provide a laboratory for ideas about racial amelioration, even equality. Through the teachers associations, the local leagues, and activist colleges such as Virginia State, African Americans developed the argument that education was at the center of the struggle for racial equality and self-determination. Part of the equation was the improvement of teachers' salaries and certification. At least until 1930, however, educators subordinated these professional concerns in the effort to counteract discriminatory school policies. This was the context in which Jackson's political activity and the association's drive for salary equalization unfolded.

Racial Pride beyond Harlem

The intellectual sparks that set Harlem aflame in the years of the literary and cultural renaissance also triggered brushfires in the VTA. If the "New Negro" meant anything to Virginia's teachers, it meant a curriculum freed from hidebound notions of black inferiority and historical insignificance. Jackson certainly imbibed the mood of African American confidence radiating from Harlem. For most black teachers, including Jackson, history provided the touchstone for a renewed sense of African American pride. Du Bois and in particular Woodson—whose ASNLH promoted school observance of Negro History Week—fashioned a historiography that resuscitated African American cultural accomplishments and challenged the visceral racism poisoning the study of the nation's past. In an address at an ASNLH meeting that Jackson organized at Virginia State, Grace Hays Johnson, a Bennett College instructor, proposed a Western civilization course that focused greater attention on African "ethnology" and the anthropology of slavery. History, Johnson believed, should instruct and inspire: "Any member of any race has the right to the self respect engendered by legitimate pride in racial achievement. . . . . All through school the Negro is taught the history of Western Caucasian civilization and almost nothing is included which relates to the ethnic background of his own race."[30] According to Jackson, the cultural relativism of the new history would lift the burden of racial degradation that weighed on black teachers and students alike: "A close study of the history of mankind has revealed to Negro educators that such social conditions as heathenism, slavery, and serfdom is the common heritage of all races today and not alone to persons of African descent."[31] Beyond the campuses, the NAACP and others called on school boards to offer courses in black history and use textbooks that incorporated the African American experience. Although Woodson and the ASNLH institutionalized the study of black history, teachers had been promoting it since the late nineteenth century. In the 1930s, though, knowledge of African American history became the standard by which teachers would measure their claims to local leadership.[32]

The dissemination of black history, the ethos of the "New Negro," the growing strength of civil rights organizations, the demographic shifts in the African American population, and the political response to the Depression made the 1930s a fertile period for promoting black civil rights. According to J. Rupert Picott, these developments crystallized the association's commitment to "1, participation in the affairs of government and 2, the use of Negro life and history as subject matter in the schools." The change from moral exhortation to political action mirrored the tactical adjustments made by black teachers' associations throughout the South. In Kentucky, the Negro Education Association lobbied for the Anderson-Mayer Bill requiring states to finance African American graduate students. They also enlisted the support of the NAACP in the drive for equal salaries. The State Association of Negro Teachers in Missouri promoted legislation to enlist an African American in the job of state inspector of Negro schools. The most progressive of the state associations was in West Virginia, where teachers agitated for better salaries, a tenure system, a nine-month school term, and the equalization of salaries across racial lines for teachers with equivalent credentials and experience.[33] Expansion, astute leadership, and the professionalization of its membership placed the VTA in a position to follow suit.

But it was the economic collapse of the 1930s that galvanized the teachers' support for political action. For black teachers earning an average monthly salary of $69.72 in 1928–29, losing an average of $21.00 from their monthly salary between 1931 and 1937 was crippling.[34] As Jackson observed, teachers' associations had become channels of professional self-interest: "[T]hey no longer exist simply to 'advance the cause of education,' but, in European fashion, they have turned to the more material aspect of teachers trying to gain something for themselves." The association duplicated the growing activism of white teachers' professional organizations. They gravitated toward the "labor union idea," relinquishing the preoccupation with pedagogical techniques and emphasizing in its place teachers' salaries, federal involvement in education, the improvement of school budgets, and lobbying for favorable school legislation. It was certainly a hospitable time to entertain the "labor union idea," considering the federal government's support for collective bargaining, first through the National Industrial Recovery Act and then the landmark Wagner Act of 1935. The combination of communist agitation and the challenges of the Depression also forced the NAACP to focus greater attention on economic problems, including those of beleaguered southern teachers.[35] Jackson was on the margins of the early salary equalization initiative, but its progress is essential for understanding the relationship between Jackson's political activism and the VTA as well as the organization's activity in the 1940s.

A Hesitant Crusade

The Buckingham County Teachers Association first challenged salary inequalities in 1930. Led by Thomas Dabney and Charles Allen, and supported by P. B. Young's *Norfolk Journal and Guide*, it enlisted six hundred teachers at a meeting of the Hampton Institute in its crusade for minimum salary standards across racial lines.[36] Together with persistent friction between urban and rural teachers, Governor John Pollard's decision to combat the Depression by reducing the salaries of all government employees coupled with the dismissal of local association president Thomas Dabney terminated the fledgling movement. As in the post–World War II voter registration drive, the NAACP lit the flame for a renewed salary equalization campaign in Virginia in the 1930s. The salary initiative was part of a regionwide NAACP campaign to equalize black and white education. In challenging black proscription at graduate schools and by attacking school segregation by demanding school improvement and salary equalization, the NAACP aimed to make Jim Crow education financially untenable.[37] In 1936, the organization launched the drive for equal salaries in fifteen southern states.[38] A sustained NAACP effort to convince teachers of the benefits of litigation as well as the successful court action by African American teachers in Montgomery County, Maryland, persuaded Virginia's teachers to endorse a frontal assault on salary disparities.[39] Meeting at the Hampton Institute in November 1937, VTA members authorized a joint initiative with the NAACP to generate five thousand dollars for litigation against salary inequalities.

The 1938 case of *Missouri ex rel. Gaines v. Canada, Registrar of the University et al.* gave the teachers' initiative an unexpected boost. Lloyd Gaines had applied to and been rejected by the University of Missouri law school. Assisted by NAACP legal counsel, he took his case to the state courts and eventually to the Supreme Court. The federal court decided that the state was obligated to offer educational facilities for all citizens, regardless of race; out-of-state scholarships did not meet the "separate but equal" requirements of the law. The decision forced southern legislators to provide graduate and professional opportunities at existing colleges or—in subtle defiance of the ruling—supplement their out-of-state aid for African American students. According to Harry Roberts, head of the Department of Sociology at Virginia State, the Gaines case together with the support of the VTA persuaded at least a handful of teachers to undertake legal action against discriminatory salaries.[40]

Encouraged by the vulnerability of legal segregation, the NAACP—led by attorneys Thurgood Marshall, Leon Ransom, and Oliver Hill—moved ahead in Virginia. They filed a suit on behalf of Aline Black, a teacher at the Booker T. Washington School in Norfolk who had volunteered to serve as a plaintiff in the salary case. The circuit court dismissed the suit, citing Black's consent to the terms of the yearly contract, which fell under the jurisdiction of the city government. The NAACP lawyers agreed that the city had the authority to establish salaries but rejected the assertion that they could violate the Constitution with impunity. The NAACP lawyers filed an appeal, but the city of Norfolk struck first, notifying Black that her contract would not be extended the following year. Despite protests and newspaper indignation, the city adhered to its decision, forcing the VTA and the NAACP legal team to search for another volunteer.[41]

They looked no farther than Melvin O. Alston, the president of the Norfolk

Teachers Association. Alston and his lawyers filed suit in federal district court against the Norfolk school board, claiming that it paid equally qualified teachers different salaries based on racial considerations alone. Issuing his decision in February 1940, Judge Luther B. Way recapitulated the legal reasoning of the judge in the Aline Black case. He asserted that Alston had understood the terms of the contract when he signed it and thus had abdicated his constitutional right to challenge the school board's policy. Unwilling to tolerate the legal chicanery, Alston appealed to the U.S. Circuit Court of Appeals. The court returned the remarkable decision that the school board's salary differentials were unconstitutional. But it was not finished: contrary to Judge Way's opinion, Alston's petition qualified as a class-action suit, which rendered the decision in his case applicable to *all* African American teachers. The decision was a landmark, but the outcome in Norfolk disappointed those expecting to break the tradition of racial discrimination against black educators. In an effort to stall equalization, the school board proposed a three-year period for incremental equalization. While Marshall and the NAACP lawyers dismissed the proposal, fearing it would only weaken the impact of the decision and transfer leverage over equalization from black teachers to local white authorities, P. B. Young and Lutrelle Palmer, president of the VTA, objected. They convinced Norfolk's teachers to accept the proposal in return for a new elementary school and amicable race relations. Teachers voted for the compromise proposal 134 to 34.[42]

The deal might have reduced racial tensions, but it failed to achieve the uniform equalization that the court decision had promised. Bitterly, "Aline"— the letter is signed only Aline, but considering the content it is safe to infer that the author is Aline Black—wrote to Jackson in 1943 that, "the salaries have not been really equalized. The principals, heads of the departments and some who were 'appeasors' during the fight have been either brought up to scale or placed above them . . . on the scale. So they continue their appeasing roles." Black noted that Jimmy Archer, president of the Norfolk Teachers Association and holder of a bachelor's degree, received the "top salary" of $250, while she, "the only Master of Science in the city," earned $230 a year. Deflated by the minimal progress and the subterfuge of some highly placed teachers, Black believed "that all of my fighting was in vain and I am disgusted to say the least." Highly trained women encountered discrimination not only as black teachers but also as women. They might have enjoyed leadership roles in the VTA, but they suffered conspicuous sexism at the hands of male administrators in the educational hierarchy. Black's observations also shed light on the attenuated accomplishments of the early

civil rights movement. As a middle-class movement rooted as much in professional self-interest as in racial justice, the salary equalization cause afforded
individual teachers ample opportunities to satisfy their own interests with little
consideration for larger issues.

Considering the financial burdens weighing on black teachers, it is no sur-
prise that they endorsed a strategy promising the greatest material improvement for the least risk of retaliation. Aline Black's experience only confirmed
the dangers of challenging white authority. Given the opportunity, white administrators exploited the teachers' professional and legal vulnerabilities. The
compromise solution that Palmer and Young arranged also reflected the exigencies of civil rights initiatives prior to the Second World War. Teachers had
every reason to expect retribution from white authorities who resented court
interference in local matters. School administrators were more than willing to
delay full compliance as long as federal authorities failed to enforce judicial
rulings. This was particularly the case in the early stages of the movement, when
few school boards had to defend discriminatory practices in court. None were
more cognizant of these realities than local black leaders. Like Jackson, Young
and Palmer operated in "the world of civility and racial accord," one in which
confrontation threatened livelihoods and the prospect of additional gains.[43]

The NAACP lawyers were in no mood to tolerate backsliding. To Marshall
at least, the decision to accept the board's gradual approach represented "the
most disgraceful termination of any case involving Negroes in recent years."[44]
By focusing on the compromise settlement, though, it is easy to overlook the
larger significance of the Norfolk case. First, it opened the floodgates of litigation for equal salaries throughout Virginia, demonstrating that legal action
could achieve results while highlighting the uncomfortable contradictions of
the entire system of segregated education. Second, it exemplified the development of the teachers association as an instrument of racial advocacy. As Earl
Lewis notes, members of the local teachers association operated as channels of
information for city residents as the case unfolded. When Black was dismissed,
the organization launched street demonstrations by local schoolchildren featuring banners that read "Our School Board Has Vetoed the Bill of Rights" and
similarly spirited proclamations. At one point, twelve hundred students, parents, and citizens signed a petition calling for the school board to renew Black's
teaching contract.[45]

A politically aware and organized Virginia Teachers Association generated
public support and maintained internal cohesion throughout the court cases.[46]

Equally important, the VTA expanded the salary case into something more than a middle-class issue, something that resonated among Norfolk's working-class blacks. For a fleeting moment, it drew a community together on the common front of education and racial dignity. Drawing attention to salary inequalities for the community's elite invariably led working-class blacks to examine the economic injustices that marred their own lives. By addressing salary differentials, teachers drew attention to the full spectrum of injustice that followed from being African American. If the salary case fell short of forging racial solidarity, it suggested the possibility that blacks could overcome class differences in the pursuit of collective interests.[47] And while the final outcome failed to satisfy NAACP expectations, it graphically illustrated the self-determination of Norfolk's African American teachers—albeit a divided group subject to the persuasive powers of the legal elite and the racial uplifters with access to white authorities.[48]

Jackson and the Widening Movement

At the time of the salary case, Jackson was preoccupied with the voters' leagues, but he could not ignore the developments in Norfolk. If anything, they convinced him that salary equalization could become the leading edge of the civil rights movement. Jackson attributed the growing support for salary adjustment to the influence of the black history movement and to the consensus for political action. Voting dominated his field of vision, but the Norfolk incident expanded his definition of political activity. Now, litigation, public protest, and other forms of political pressure were legitimate strategies for challenging racial injustice. He applauded the association for inviting Charles Hamilton Houston, dean of the Howard Law School, to address teachers on the Fourteenth Amendment and the legal struggle for equalization. Like countless other civil rights activists over the course of these decisive years, Jackson broadened his understanding of equality and the tools that could achieve it. His thinking suggested that the ideas of freedom, equality, political action, and racial justice were not static notions transmitted from one generation to the next. Jackson did not hew tenaciously to a line of racial accommodation mapped out by the National Negro Business League and the Afro-American Council. His thinking, like that of his contemporaries, evolved dialectically along with the circumstances and people that molded them.[49]

In "Citizenship and Government Participation," published in both the *Bulletin* and the *Virginia State College Gazette,* Jackson elucidated his expanded conception of political activity. Government produced laws through its executive and legislative branches, but it also corrected injustices perpetrated "by one individual or group on another group." The courts could remedy transgressions against individuals, but they could also rectify historical injustices inflicted by public officials: "Governmental participation means, then, not only the act of influencing law making . . . it also means the ready use of the courts by the individual whenever he feels he is suffering a wrong contrary to the intent of the United States Constitution."[50] He was thinking about the legal impediments to black voting, but the courts could be used as effectively in eliminating racial barriers to a decent education as they could in neutralizing a recalcitrant white registrar. Increasingly, litigation and voting became binary strategies in the movement for racial change.[51]

His involvement in the salary initiative increased as chair of a citizens' committee that petitioned the school board of Chesterfield County to equalize the salaries of black teachers. The committee submitted the petition in December 1940; in February, Jackson prodded the superintendent to take action. Chesterfield officials adopted the delaying tactics deployed by school board officials in the Norfolk case, the same tactics that would become the mainstay of segregationists throughout the civil rights struggle. Despite a resolution to equalize salaries, school officials did nothing to correct the disparities.[52] The Chesterfield County Teachers Equalization Committee suffered no illusions that the board would respect the petition. In 1941, they began legal proceedings, assisted by Richmond attorneys Hill, Martin, and Robinson, the same firm that had represented the Norfolk plaintiffs. Despite a flurry of activity including the filling out of questionnaires and the signing of forms authorizing legal action, the case had made no progress by 1946.

Exasperated at the attorneys' apparent foot-dragging, Arthur Freeman— who replaced Jackson as chair of the committee—and James Spencer appealed to VTA executive secretary J. Rupert Picott to find new legal counsel. Whatever momentum the Alston case might have generated, the legal inertia eroded the morale of the teachers and citizens embroiled in the equalization campaign.[53] Picott immediately fired off a letter to Jackson, now a member of the NAACP Salary Equalization Committee, complaining that "people continue to write" for information on the case, but little had been accomplished in the way of "court action." Picott wanted to know precisely what the committee was doing on the matter and what Jackson thought about hiring a lawyer to work on the case full time. Picott likely turned to him as much for his prominence in the VTA and the larger movement as for his position on the Salary Equalization Committee. Jackson dismissed as "foolish" the suggestion to replace the attorneys, exposing perhaps his own stake in the NAACP's bureaucratic order but also his commitment to the organization as the only viable instrument of racial reform. The case had stalled, Jackson believed, because of the difficulty of finding a second plaintiff, which the lawyers mysteriously insisted on securing before proceeding. Considering the prospects of dismissal and sanctions against participating teachers, it is little wonder that the legal team struggled to find a second plaintiff. Despite the delay, Jackson still believed that "One good suit in Chesterfield . . . will wake up many other superintendents."[54]

Jackson also urged Picott to send a copy of Spencer and Freeman's letter to the lawyers. Their response vividly illustrates the challenges facing civil rights litigators in the 1940s. On behalf of the firm, Martin A. Martin admitted that it had been "delinquent" but not "derelict" in pursuing the equalization case. By taking the case, the firm and others similarly engaged by the NAACP were "charting a new field," which meant that accomplishments could not be measured by "the amount of money recovered by the school teachers involved or the additional school facilities secured in the individual county or city." Hill and his associates, like Jackson and his voting supporters, were committed to a program that included but went beyond paved streets, higher salaries, and better material conditions. Martin argued that attorneys in civil rights cases were trying to accumulate a series of rulings that would "secure additional, long range and permanent advantages, not only to the school teachers and to the school children, but to the race as a whole." The cases had to be tried in courts presided over by judges no less susceptible to racial prejudice than most white southerners. Considering that the decision could establish a "precedent and possibly a bar to filing further suits," attorneys had to minimize the chances of losing them. Instead of neglecting the case since 1941, Martin claimed that the lawyers had spent the summer of 1946 drumming up prospective plaintiffs, collecting additional data, and filing complaints against the school boards. Perhaps most tellingly, the legal team had to wait six months until the teachers responded to their request for three plaintiffs in the case. What Martin's letter does not address are the financial challenges facing a small law firm managing a slate of paying clients as well as financially risky civil rights litigation.[55]

His comments also suggest the clashing perspectives that frequently divided groups within the movement. For some teachers, opening the doors to racial equality across a wide social front was a desirable consequence of court victories, but improving their own living standards and professional status took precedence. A good many also considered economic improvement inseparable from the question of racial advancement. Any other definition of racial progress sounded quixotic and hollow. Certainly this was the conviction underlying the efforts of the VTA and the Negro Organization Society to upgrade dilapidated schools and improve the professional qualifications of rural teachers in the early twentieth century.[56] For civil rights attorneys and activists, however, material improvement was part of a larger campaign to dismantle racial inequalities and advance African American interests, even if those were filtered through a middle-class lens.

For black teachers in the South, justice meant something tangible. The frustration of litigating a principle that had already been established in Norfolk offered a painful reminder of the original injustice—being paid a fraction of what their white counterparts earned despite comparable qualifications. By challenging discriminatory practices that affected them directly, they unleashed energies that surged beyond the drive for improved salaries. As James Spencer, secretary of the salary equalization committee for Chesterfield, wrote to Jackson after the successful conclusion of their protracted court fight: "We must not stop upon winning the salary fight. We must fight on to break down other unfair practices prevailing in the county."[57]

The mobilization of teachers in the salary cases created the conditions under which African Americans could stretch the meaning of equality. While teachers focused on quantifiable change, they participated in a process of democratic revitalization that paralleled the experience of the voters' leagues. "The striving for equal salaries is a bid for economic democracy," Jackson claimed in 1943. "Going to court for the redress of judicial wrongs is like paying the poll tax and registering to go to the polls for redress of legislative wrongs." Each was part of a languishing democratic tradition that could only be restored through an active citizenry. And yet, while editorializing on the salary cases, Jackson recapitulated his Washingtonian conviction that teachers, like non-poll-tax payers, had only themselves to blame for failing to exercise these rights. The salary struggle, like the voting initiative, the interracial crusades of postwar years, and the segregation challenges of the late 1940s, tested and transformed racial assumptions that had seemed axiomatic in the 1930s. Jackson was a civil rights leader, but he was also a participant trying to reconcile familiar assumptions with new circumstances. Even if Jackson was circumspect about them in print, the struggle produced luminous insights into the sources of racial inequality, the potential for social change, and the identities that lurked behind

the racial veil of modern America. But those changes would not come over-
night.[58]

The Richmond firm did eventually prosecute the Chesterfield case, which
ended up in the U.S. Circuit Court of Appeals in November 1948. The court
decided in favor of the teachers' association, and Jackson exulted in the ruling;
writing to the obstructionist Superintendent Greene, he claimed it a "significant victory" for "those Americans who disbelieve that because an employee of
a governmental agency is a member of the Negro race, his pay should automatically be less than that offered white persons." Jackson hoped the "wicked notion" of black inferiority would be "banished forever in Chesterfield County in
Virginia, and indeed the whole Southland." In a tone of restrained contempt
that would have been unthinkable before the Second World War, Jackson re-
counted the committee's appeal for fairness and the school board's mendacity
in issuing an equalization order they never intended to honor: "The principle
was attained only after you were dragged through two federal courts at great
expense to the county and to the plaintiffs involved." Jackson probably spoke for
most teachers when he admonished the school boards to "see the handwriting
on the wall" and equalize not only salaries but the schools as well. In one of
his most confrontational episodes, Jackson challenged white authorities to acknowledge the duplicity at the core of a segregationist tradition cloaked in
paternalism. Jackson was doing nothing less than challenging the tradition of
black subservience that persisted in the modernizing South.[59]

Fellow committee member James Spencer recognized that his letter represented a repudiation of interracial conciliation. According to Spencer, it was
"the Magna Carta of your public relations as I have observed such in Virginia."
Suggesting the larger implications of the salary dispute, Spencer applauded
Jackson for unequivocally reviewing the facts of the Chesterfield case: "We need
more frankness in these vital cases and less beating around the bush when
important principles are at stake." According to Spencer, it was N.B Greene's
advice that convinced the board to ignore the request for equalization, a course
of action that made the superintendent sufficiently "ashamed" to withhold
Jackson's letter from the board. Spencer believed that Jackson's letter served as
a warning to school board officials that the public would not tolerate reprisals
against black educators involved in the federal court case. If racial cooperation
for school improvement had been the theme of earlier VTA efforts, militant
confrontation in the achievement of racial equality was the dominant motif in
its postwar activity.[60]

The Chesterfield case drew Jackson into the fray, but the Newport News case thrust him into the foreground of the equalization movement. The case followed the pattern established in Norfolk, Chesterfield, and, more recently, Richmond, where the VTA and the NAACP supported Antoinette Bowler's bid to compel the city to equalize teachers' salaries. In Newport News, the association sponsored Dorothy E. Roles in a case against salary discrimination. Now a weekly columnist for the *Norfolk Journal and Guide,* Jackson had a vehicle for addressing developments in the equalization movement and establishing its connection to the statewide voting crusade. Shortly after the United States District Court ordered the Newport News school board to equalize teachers' pay, Jackson celebrated it as a victory for democracy. In an effective rhetorical flourish, he asserted that "freedom from bondage"—the goal that had propelled chattel slaves—drew together the defense of the Scottsboro Boys, the decision in the Lloyd Gaines case, and the movement against inequitable salaries in Virginia in a historical vindication of the legal system. African American educators in other states benefited from the *Alston* decision of 1940. In 1941, teachers in Louisville eliminated a 15-percent salary discrepancy to achieve parity with white teachers; in North Carolina, where the NAACP did not launch a campaign, the legislature announced the equalization of salaries in 1943, a policy that would take effect in the 1944–45 school year.[61]

Yet African Americans in Virginia soon discovered the limitations of legal victories. In June, the school board fired Lutrelle Palmer, principal of Huntington High School in Newport News and leader of the local salary initiative, along with five other principals and teachers, including J. Rupert Picott. The unilateral decision, Jackson observed, was "so sudden and sensational that it affects the morale of school and college teachers everywhere." It struck at principals who were actively transmitting the message of social change through political action—principals "whose schools are veritable laboratories for the teaching of full fledged citizenship."[62] Retribution against teachers involved in equal pay cases was not confined to Virginia. In Palm Beach, Florida, Charles Stubbins found himself out of work after becoming the plaintiff in a local salary case. In Louisiana, white opponents of litigation for equal pay used violence and intimidation to drive members of the NAACP out of town, although the organization quickly rebounded, adding 150 members shortly after the episode. Threatened by reprisals throughout the South, teachers still turned to the NAACP as the best hope for equalization and racial progress.[63]

The Newport News story captured national attention and ignited local civil rights activism. In Jackson's account, the NAACP immediately met with Governor Darden while African Americans in Newport News held "an overflow mass meeting." In addition to plans for public demonstrations, the Parent Teacher Association and community churches joined what he described as a "nation wide agitation."[64] Teachers and their supporters formed a Committee of Action that solicited funds for the impending court appeals and petitioned the school board to reinstate the six teachers. Jackson called on the "thousands of backers" throughout the state to sign petitions and contribute to the committee defense fund. He poured his indignation into his columns, but he recognized that this was a crucial moment in the salary equalization drive. The victories in the Alston and Roles cases were too limited to guarantee success in a salary equalization drive. If the courts upheld the school board's dismissals, the prospects of salary equalization for Virginia's black teachers looked grim. Yet Jackson's optimism prevailed; the dismissals provided African Americans a chance to demonstrate that democracy worked and that transgressions could be remedied through the courts and the ballot box. Having adapted himself to an upbeat tone in what often seemed like the losing battle of black voting, Jackson found it reasonably easy to locate the silver lining in the teachers' struggle. And considering his long-term view of racial reform, there was no other course of action available.[65]

Throughout the protracted legal battle over the dismissals, Jackson tried to "keep the pot boiling."[66] Reviewing racial developments over the year, he declared the Newport News case "The Tragedy of 1943." The decision was a tragedy not only for the schoolteachers of Virginia and the VTA but also for "liberal white opinion in the South," abundantly manifested in the recently established Southern Regional Council.[67] If anything, his association with the biracial Southern Regional Council made him optimistic about the potential for white liberals to link arms with black progressives in a march toward equitable race relations. In Jackson's estimation, the force of reason and moral suasion would permit the alliance to overwhelm white reactionaries. Anticipating the trial in which school officials would be called upon to defend their actions in the Newport News incident, Jackson believed that it would "determine whether Negroes and minority groups the world over are to enjoy that freedom for which the present war is being fought."

Although he championed the principles involved, he carefully reminded his readers that the salary disputants were not revolutionaries. Instead, black teachers engaged in the salary cases sought to redress their grievances "in the best and most orderly fashion." They might have been critics of the segregated order, but the teachers still abided by the strictures of American due process of law. They wanted to secure existing rights, not to disrupt the liberal-democratic order, and they used the conventional instruments of court and ballot box to achieve them.

Jackson was trying to deflect the accusation of un-American radicalism increasingly hurled at African American civil rights activists in the post-Depression era. Despite the moderate tone, he insisted that the salary case was the product of a system of racial exclusion that extended beyond the boundaries of the South: "For as Negroes are discriminated against in the matter of teachers' salaries, so are they discriminated against in most phases of American life." The salary dispute was not simply an exercise in professional self-improvement but rather a flashpoint for a larger struggle for equality. While a victory in the salary disputes would improve black education, it would also "pave the way for equality in work and wages, equality in housing, equality in recreation facilities" and "every phase of the welfare of Negroes in our country." The ramifications of the teachers' dispute went well beyond Virginia's African Americans.[68]

The professor/journalist extolled the virtues of the dismissed teachers and heaped opprobrium on "a small group of local Negroes" for their complicity with school board officials in the firings. Perhaps it was his involvement in the Chesterfield case, or the growing strength of the Virginia Voters League, or the increasingly aroused audience for which he was writing, or perhaps simply the heady atmosphere of the war years that encouraged Jackson to abandon diplomacy and castigate the teachers who broke ranks. Fashioning itself an "advisory group," the junta of collaborators threatened to "pull down the State Teachers Association, the N.A.A.C.P., and even the race itself in order to kill these six citizens who may have incurred their wrath." Jackson thundered that the "voice of the people" in the Newport News case was the "voice of God."[69]

No one was more grateful for Jackson's support than Lutrelle Palmer. Thanking him for an encouraging letter, Palmer commended his *Journal and Guide* article as "a trenchant and searching indictment of entrenched injustices and the quislings among Negroes who contribute so much to the perpetuation of our social and economic slavery." Deference to white interests might have been a tactical necessity in the past, but the momentum of the salary equalization issue fueled anger at flagrant collusion with white power brokers.

Racial consciousness was undergoing a seismic change. Palmer the conciliator was now Palmer the militant, and Jackson was not far behind. "When I have the opportunity," Palmer wrote, "I will tell you the depth of infamy to which this school board and their Negro stooges have gone because I dared to challenge the system."[70] Palmer's comments may have stoked Jackson's indignation, perhaps even his sense that intrigue made good copy, because he returned to the conspirators again in December. "The greatest tragedy . . . is that a small group of Negroes cooperated secretly with the Board in their act." Jackson could not document the accusation, but Palmer's testimony and the "repeated statement that Negroes, playing the role of Benedict Arnold, committed treason upon their race" seemed evidence enough. Privately, Jackson was eager to expose the collaborators. He hoped that the hearings on the teachers' dismissals would force the school board to divulge "that Negro traitors were their allies." Although a year had passed since the episode, Jackson considered the outcome of the case a "matter of the welfare of school teachers throughout the South." Bitterly, he added, "the nasty affair" was "just as fresh with me today as it was the day after it happened."[71] Through his newspaper column, his work as secretary of civic education, and his support for the citizens' committee, Jackson drew attention and public support to the salary case and fused it to the southern movement for racial justice.[72]

Jackson did not settle for rooting out the Newport News offenders. Learning that Walter Ridley—a professor at Virginia State and secretary of educational activities for the VTA—endorsed the school board's decision, he lashed out, asserting that "this attitude eats into the vitals of our very harmonious State Teachers Association," and ominously suggested that "perhaps we need to do something about this gentleman."[73] In an episode that dramatically illustrated the politicization of the VTA, the executive convened a meeting at which Ridley was expected to "give an account of himself in the Newport News affair." Jackson requested a written affidavit from a teacher who had discussed Palmer's looming dismissal with Ridley and the prospect of an opening for a principal's position at Huntington High School. The professor also noted that he would serve as a "star witness against him." Jackson may have had a personal vendetta against Ridley—both taught at Virginia State and both vied for top positions in the VTA. What is more likely is that, following the *Alston* decision, the stakes had been raised in the Newport News affair. Palmer was a high-profile educator and the executive secretary of the Virginia Teachers Association. By dismissing him as well as Picott, another key figure in the VTA, white school authorities struck at the nerve-center of the teachers' association and its campaign for professionalization.

Salary equalization meant more than additional annual earnings; it implied recognition of professional status and social equality. It would confer a sense of dignity that African Americans had granted their teachers but that most whites jealously withheld. For Jackson, Palmer, and other leading figures, winning the salary dispute required more than class cohesion. It demanded that the teachers' association, a key organization in the early stages of the movement, exercise control over its membership and operate as a vehicle of political action. In this way, the VTA closely approximated "the labor idea" that had accelerated union organization in the New Deal era. School improvement was now an essential part of the drive for economic democracy.

While censuring offenders, Jackson encouraged the VTA to take a more active part in the Newport News affair. Writing to C. W. Seay, president of the VTA, he recommended that the association make an official statement to the press and a formal expression of support to the Citizens Committee of Action. Once again, Jackson emphasized the larger implications of the Newport News case, this time stressing its significance for "the entire teaching profession in the South." Despite the tension between the appeal to white beneficence and the call for change that riddled Jackson's public life, the demand for action prevailed: "I stand ready to do anything: attend meetings, make a financial contribution, draw up resolutions, or anything to support . . . L. F. Palmer." Jackson also wrote directly to the Committee of Action, encouraging them, volunteering his time, and offering financial support to assist the reinstatement initiative.[74]

By the time that Jackson called for action, C. W. Seay and others in the VTA were already mobilizing against the school board. In the days immediately following the dismissals, William Cooper and Eva C. Mitchell, both Hampton Institute professors and VTA officials, had been busy convincing Palmer that the association should make its presence felt in the Newport News dispute. Seay did not need Jackson's prompting to announce that the VTA "should assert every ounce of pressure on this case which we can manage to muster." He wrote to Governor Darden; Dabney S. Lancaster, the superintendent for the state board of education; and the chairperson of the Newport News school board; and he sent circular letter to principals, Jeanes supervisors, and presidents of the VTA local affiliates. Carefully pitched to each audience, marked by a tone of both diplomacy and urgency, the letters highlighted the ideological contradictions that entangled the United States during the war. To the governor, Seay pointed out the political conundrum of official racial discrimination at a time when "we are emphasizing Democracy and democratic procedures in settling the problems which confront us." Since the firings were carried out under a cloak of secrecy, Seay reminded the governor of due process of law, observing that "[e]ven the criminals in our State are given the opportunity to face their accusers and defend themselves in court." His appeals registered the change in African American consciousness. Teachers as well as "citizens in all walks of life," Seay observed, "expect justice and fair play from our public officials." Black southerners, even Virginians, had little reason to expect "fair play" from white officials in the New South; something had changed. And if it had, it was not simply a function of an economic reconfiguration that made a stable agricultural labor force disposable, or a newly activist federal government, or a mobile black working class, or a national party in search of a powerful minority's votes. It had as much to do with the schoolchildren protesting Aline Black's dismissal and Luther Jackson's impassioned editorials as it did with larger social forces. Restoring the teachers was not a matter of white paternalism; it was now a question of legal justice.[75]

Appealing to the superintendent of the state board of education for a public hearing on the dismissals, Seay clarified the political significance of the case. The Newport News firings were only a symptom of more profound white anxieties, since the board's decision was a retaliatory strike against black teachers promoting salary equalization. The school board was trying to interfere with an effort grounded in widespread convictions about social change: "Obviously such tactics will not stop the movement. They can only lead to increasing bitterness and suspicion which will surely reflect itself in the classrooms throughout this state."[76] Jackson corroborated Seay's observation: the salary initiative *had* developed the momentum of a social movement. Twenty years before the Newport News affair, Jackson argued, the board's "violent action" would have affected only the teachers immediately involved. Now, "such action reverberates through the nation." The removal of six teachers in Newport News was no isolated episode of racially motivated retribution—it reverberated among four thousand teachers throughout the state.[77]

Seay also targeted the Newport News school board by using the rhetorical swords that the war had forged out of the ideological ploughshares of American liberal democracy. Holding a public hearing would provide school officials "an unexcelled opportunity to practice here at home some of the Democracy which we say we are fighting for all over the world." While pressuring white authorities to reconsider the dismissals, Seay also directed his attention to the rank-and-file teachers in the VTA. Playing on legitimate fears that the firings "could have happened anywhere in the State," Seay implored teachers to fight the decision by using "every weapon at our disposal," including the courts, public opinion, political action, and "protest and petition." More dramatically than in his other correspondence, Seay outlined the political issues at stake: "If fascism wins in this instance it will be easier for any of the rest of us to be the next victims, because the pattern will have been set." In his estimation, the salary cases were part of a worldwide movement for racial liberation: "If Democracy is worth fighting for in Africa it is worth fighting for in Virginia." The teachers responded quickly. By early June, Seay reported to Jackson that the teachers in his hometown of Lynchburg had raised one hundred dollars for the defense fund.[78]

Groping Toward Collective Action

Like the Norfolk case, the Newport News incident engaged black Virginians in a political struggle that raised larger issues than equal pay for teachers. In the flush of the salary dispute, Palmer exulted at the growing popular support for the VTA. "Newport News is aroused as I have never known it to be," he proclaimed in a letter to Jackson. "With the exception of the few Negroes who are being used as stooges, the community is solidly behind the movement to have the Board give the dismissed teachers a hearing." At this stage, Palmer had every reason to applaud "the way in which the Negro people are standing together on this great public issue." Jackson certainly would have agreed that the case had struck a chord in the public conscience. School board officials faced not only an enlivened community but also an increasingly politicized teaching profession, an aggressive NAACP, and an emboldened black media that expected white political accountability.[79]

Despite mounting public support, the teachers' initiative suffered from internal instabilities and external pressures that prevented the development of a widespread social movement. The teachers enjoyed the support of African Americans who valued their profession and saw their own grievances reflected in the equalization cases. Even so, the drive to improve their wages never lost its middle-class moorings. The teachers' fight could not improve the wages of black workers, create employment opportunities, expand social services, eliminate police harassment, or by itself dismantle segregation. Since salary equalization required litigation at the municipal level, teachers not engaged in a case could sink into blissful indifference or—when authorities struck back against activist teachers—paralyzing fear at the prospect of retaliation from their own school boards should they take similar action. The latter seemed to be the case in Richmond. Following a meeting of the VTA, Palmer wrote disconsolately to Jackson that he was "astounded" by the conservatism of the city's teachers, including members of the VTA's own Executive Committee. In striking contrast to his earlier jubilance over the "unity and intelligence" of African Americans engaged in the dispute, the mood of the Richmond meeting convinced him that the Newport News affair had produced "a profound weakening effect upon the morale of Negro teaches in the State," particularly African American principals. Even more disconcerting was Palmer's realization that leading educators, "fearful of their security, will go any length to appease school superintendents and school boards."[80] As Mark Tushnet points out in his account of the Norfolk salary case, the dismissal of Aline Black polarized advocates of immediate action and conservatives who considered Black's departure a warning of the dangers of agitation.[81] Unlike later civil rights initiatives in which broad cross-sections of a community faced reprisals from white authorities, teachers conspicuously involved in the salary disputes exposed themselves to reprisals in a hazardous legal campaign that offered no guarantee of success.

Despite the ideological limitations of the teachers' cause, the salary initiative *did* fragment the edifice of segregated schooling. When the VTA challenged racial discrimination in teachers' wages, they exposed the duplicity of the separate but equal doctrine. They also highlighted the hypocrisy of the southern dogma that blacks received fair treatment from the better class of whites. By asserting that qualified African American teachers should receive salaries equal to those of their white counterparts, they dragged the assumptions about black inferiority that underlay Jim Crow out of the shadows of southern folkways and into the light of public scrutiny.

Yet school officials held most of the cards. By installing compliant principals and paying them to act as "informers," as Palmer described it, "reactionary school boards" tried to crush the "liberalism in Negro schools." School administrators also worked through cooperative black principals to collect the names of teachers that had contributed to the defense fund the previous year. Yet, as Palmer realized, white administrators were able to combine intimidation and obstruction with a ruthless strategy of divide and conquer in the effort to scramble salary equalization. School authorities had remarkable leverage in challenging the salary initiative. Since the state had no tenure law for teachers, the attorneys in the Newport News case decided after an unfavorable federal court ruling not to appeal the case to the Virginia Supreme Court.[82]

Like so many episodes in the early civil rights movement, the salary equal-ization campaign produced a mixed victory. Palmer was never reinstated, but the board—after it was found in contempt of court—finally honored the *Roles* decision mandating equalized salaries. By 1950, according to Henry Allan Bul-lock, salary differentials based on race had become the exception rather than the rule in the South.[83] The Virginia equalization campaign ultimately generated $50 million for augmenting black teachers' salaries, schools, and buses.[84] The salary cases proved that NAACP legal action could produce results and force change, even if those changes were incremental, delayed, and costly.

More than anything, the salary cases demonstrated the political capabilities of the Virginia Teachers Association. Once it established a network of commu-nications and professional support, the VTA could mobilize financial support for court action and apply political pressure, forcing public officials to account for racial inequities that had achieved axiomatic authority in the New South. Palmer thoroughly enjoyed watching Superintendent Joseph Saunders "per-jure himself over and over again." He was sure that Jackson would have been gratified to "listen to the ridiculous argument submitted by the Board's counsel in defense of the discrimination which the records abundantly disclose." Po-litical pressure was ultimately insufficient to restore Aline Black's or Lutrelle Palmer's job, but Palmer's observations are critical notwithstanding, because in the Newport News case, white officials *did* have to account for their behavior. They adopted a tenuous line of reasoning—that not all black teachers were paid less than white teachers, proving that discrimination is based on experience, not race—to defend decisions transparently rooted in the determination to main-tain the racial status quo. By pursuing court action, black teachers met white public officials on a level plane defined by the American traditions of due pro-cess and equality before the law. They started redeeming the courts as a public space for approximating justice rather than compelling black subservience. Salary equalization did not end segregation, but it fractured some of the ideo-logical and political girders that held the structure in place.[85]

As Palmer made clear, racially motivated reprisals demoralized black teach-ers who could only rely on the courts and their own voices for protection. Before the advent of mass demonstrations and sit-ins, the protest activities of organi-zations such as the VTA were chronically fragile, susceptible to white opposition and internal dissension. It is obvious but important to point out that internal dissension was not unique to the early stages of the civil rights movement; if anything, it intensified in the later struggle, bifurcating organizations such as

CORE and SNCC along lines of race, generation, and ideology. It is less obvious but equally important to emphasize that Jackson, Palmer, Picott, the VTA, along with the citizens of Norfolk, Newport News, and several other Virginia towns *did* engage in protest, albeit of a less confrontational brand than the one that characterized the later movement. Commenting on the equalization of salaries in North Carolina, where the NAACP did not launch a case, Jackson asserted that "advancement for one group of people is often made by peaceful means simply because another group of people previously sought to gain their ends by *militant* means" (emphasis added). In other words, since North Carolina and Virginia shared the area covered by the Fourth U.S. Circuit Court of Appeals, it also shared in the benefits of the *Alston* decision and the Newport News case. To Jackson, the lesson was clear: "Before there can be a settlement of differences there must be a fight." Jackson and the teachers did fight, but they did so in a manner that reflected prevailing assumptions about the proper paths to racial equality.[86]

They participated in a middle-class movement, but it was a movement nonetheless, one that briefly generated popular support while sparking widespread hope that the salary cases might breach the walls of segregation. It confirmed the importance of the courts as an avenue for advancing racial equality. In a moment of optimism preceding the contempt of court hearings over the school board's obstruction of the equalization order, Palmer wrote to Jackson, "I am more and more convinced that this technique bears within itself the seeds of success perhaps to a larger extent than any other now available to us."[87]

Jackson certainly supported litigation as one of several strategies available to civil rights activists, but he cautioned his readers that court decisions had to be supported by community action: "Local school boards may never carry out the mandate of the federal courts respecting equal salaries unless the local teachers and local citizens press them to act."[88] The NAACP had proven this principle in its own struggle, that "regardless of the edict of a higher federal court the legislators will never repeal old segregation laws or any form of discriminatory law unless they are forced to do so by the votes of the people."[89] In 1948, as the Virginia Civil Rights Organization (V-CRO) sponsored bills to desegregate common carriers and public accommodations, Jackson reminded expectant readers that legislation was only one line of "attack," one that had to be accompanied by political pressure and litigation.[90] Palmer never convinced him that litigation was the best method of social protest, but Jackson had no quarrel with the suggestion that legal action could eliminate stubborn barriers to racial improvement. Both realized that it challenged deeply ingrained social customs.

The critical lesson was that teachers could take political action and the public would support them. The VTA became more than a school improvement league, more than a self-conscious interest group. It developed into a professional organization dedicated to achieving social reform, however moderate that reform may seem in retrospect. The hesitant movement was a function of organization and the impact of the salary equalization campaign, but it was also a result of Jackson's Speakers Bureau, his ceaseless effort to raise awareness through the *Journal and Guide,* and his support and encouragement of key players throughout the course of the salary initiative.

But Jackson's involvement in the teachers' movement extended beyond his newspaper articles and letters of support. As secretary of civic education for the Virginia Teachers Association, he crystallized the emerging conviction that the interests of all black southerners were best promoted through political channels that included voting, lobbying, and litigation. More than this, his work as secretary of civic education helped raise the sights of a generation of teachers and students beyond received institutions. Encouraged by committed teachers, students surveyed the range of possibilities that political action and self-determination offered. For Jackson, education was inherently political. It reflected on the fundamental questions of one's place in society and the institutions and structures that determined that place. If teachers would lead, then they would have to set the political example. The place to start was in the schools.

Chapter 6

The Curriculum for Change

Jackson, the Teachers, and Civic Education

African Americans may have been willing to march on Washington for jobs, but most were still too afraid to vote. If a later generation considered the NAACP a study in moderation, Jackson and his contemporaries understood precisely what it represented: the only organized challenge to the racial status quo. Fellow activists in Halifax County testified to the anxiety that NAACP activity generated among conservative blacks. Even as teachers mobilized around the voting message, the majority worried about the consequences of casting a ballot. Asked to address a voting rights meeting by Vincent Estill—a civil rights leader and physician in South Boston, Virginia—Jackson was informed that the teachers would "not attend in mass" if it were advertised as a "Voters League" or "Voters Meeting etc." Estill told Jackson that "the teachers are afraid of the NAACP"; a public announcement of its involvement would simply "frighten" them away.

The intimidation of vulnerable teachers and the example of Aline Black had been enough to subdue the teachers of Halifax County. Even before the Norfolk case, the NAACP had recruited no more than twelve from approximately 150 African American teachers in the county. Instead, teachers joined politically neutral and white-dominated organizations such as the Red Cross. To soothe the teachers' anxiety, Estill removed Jackson's affiliation with the Virginia Voters League from the handbills as well as any references to the Virginia Voters League or the NAACP. Students weren't the only ones who had to be schooled in political freedom.

In the early years of the Second World War, any effort to stimulate political action threatened the racial status quo. In his struggle to generate support for voting, Jackson confronted deeply rooted fear about the consequences of casting a ballot in a society that denied the legitimacy of black political participation. Yet he recognized that teachers offered a point of entry to the hearts and minds of those in the best position to throw off the nonvoting tradition. The civic education program touched students and teachers, but it taught Jackson something as well: many teachers had already internalized the political message. By engaging these teachers, he could achieve a powerful synergy in the quest for political action.[1]

The Civic Education Program

Whether or not Jackson proposed the position of secretary of civic education for the Virginia Teachers Association (VTA), it seems clear that the organization tailored the position for him. Serving in this elective office from 1942 until his death in 1950, Jackson crafted it into another channel for political revitalization. It certainly suited his ideological propensities, since the overriding objective of the office—according to a notice Jackson sent to the state's Jeanes supervisors and high school principals—was to "produce a body of vote conscious young people who may face the future determined to participate in the affairs of government in contrast to the non-participation of our people during the past generation." Established at the association's 1941 convention, the office of civic education allowed Jackson to promote voter registration among one of the black middle class's most influential groups. Appealing first to the Jeanes supervisors and high school principals to register, Jackson planned to extend the campaign to all of Virginia's African American educators.

The program for the civic education office paralleled the strategy of the Virginia Voters League. Like the VVL, it would recruit the black leadership caste through a combination of positive propaganda on the merits of political activity and public humiliation of those who deliberately remained "voteless." Just as the VVL targeted the black middle-class elite, the secretary of civic education would operate hierarchically, appealing first to black school administrators, then to college educators, and finally "down to the four thousand public school teachers below." Typical of most civil rights initiatives before the 1950s, Jackson operated on the assumption that racial progress required the leadership of a talented tenth ready to champion African American interests in an orderly manner that respected political conventions and the formal protocol of Jim Crow. But he wanted to do more than inspire teachers to fulfill their civic duty.

He hoped that the VTA program would encourage them to set an example for their students and stimulate in them an appetite for government participation. More than any other group in the African American middle class, teachers offered the medium through which civil rights leaders could reach young African Americans and mold their political expectations. What Jackson and other voting rights activists grasped years before the sit-ins at Greensboro and the freedom rides was that racial change would have to begin with young African Americans, albeit under the direction of their responsible elders. As Jackson wrote to attorney Moss Plunkett, chairperson of the Virginia Electoral Reform League and perennial white liberal, "You recognize that in the final analysis our growth is dependent on the school room." Teaching political action in the classrooms was not simply a matter of generating support for equal educational facilities; it was a precursor of social activism.[2]

Jackson detailed the consciousness-raising tactics he would pursue. He explained that the office of civic education would collect data on teachers' registration and voting activity and publish the findings in handbooks that included instructions on voting procedures. Mirroring the tactics of Woodson's history association, it would also support a "Voting Week" in April featuring statewide instruction on electoral protocol for teachers and students. In addition, the office planned to coordinate with the Virginia Voters League in promoting voter registration.[3] As Jackson emphasized when he launched the VVL, the Office of Civic Education would operate publicly and would seek the cooperation of school authorities in registering black teachers to vote.

Jackson's civic education program reflected the changing prospects for black civil rights, but it did more than simply suit the times. It also launched changes that advanced the drive for racial equality. Together with the organizational accomplishments of the Virginia Teachers Association and the salary equalization cases, Jackson's civic education and voting project fit into a pattern of civil rights activism that sociologist Doug McAdam has described as the "political process model," which elucidates the rise of African American insurgency in the 1950s. The political process theory locates three critical factors in the growth of effective social protest: levels of organization among the oppressed group; consciousness about the potential for collective political action; and the configuration of political interests and groups in society. The "structure of political opportunities"—which until the New Deal had been dictated by one-party dominance and the pervasive cotton tenancy system in the South, along with federal disinterest in southern racial matters—began to shift in the early

1930s in favor of black civil rights. McAdam suggests that between 1931 and 1954, a combination of factors gradually transformed the political and economic order that had maintained black subordination. The decline of cotton tenancy in the region, the migration of African Americans into northern urban-industrial centers, the corresponding growth of black support for the Democratic Party, the ideological energies unleashed by the war, and increasing federal attentiveness to African American interests realigned the political landscape, creating the possibility that concerted black action could generate political results.[4] The rise of the VTA as a professional association geared to political action, as well as Jackson's own development as a voting rights activist, paralleled these broad social processes.

Jackson and key members of the VTA transformed political opportunities into a movement for social reform. Through the teachers association as well as the Virginia Voters League and the civic education office, he helped construct the organizational framework that stimulated social discontent. By forging group cohesion, Jackson established the basis for meaningful political activity. According to McAdam and other sociologists, organizational networks provide the fiber of collective action. Members are "recruited along established lines of interaction" rather than for psychological or personal idiosyncrasies. Through its annual conventions, extension lectures, and school improvement undertakings, the teachers' association recruited educators and citizens into a network linking education and civil rights. Jackson's voluminous correspondence strengthened those membership ties and made political action the standard of membership in the teaching profession. Social organizations also provide "communication networks" that "determine the pattern, speed, and extent of movement expansion." Although McAdam rightly emphasizes the critical role played by the NAACP in this process, the teachers' association in Virginia provided the communications system that supported the movement there. Jackson's Speakers Bureau lectures, his newspaper editorials, his convention seminars on civic education, his voting surveys and correspondence, as well as the association's *Bulletin*—which Jackson also used to spread his message—provided the channels of communication that bound teachers together in their struggle for racial equality. No less important to social movements are leaders who can "lend their prestige and organizing skills to the incipient movement." Jackson furnished this in spades. As much as average teachers supported the movement for racial justice in the profession—often having cultivated political sensibilities even before Jackson's civic education project started—he and others such as Palmer galvanized these into a reasonably unified campaign for salary equalization and school improvement.[5]

Yet the organizational structures and favorable political climate created the conditions, not the determination, to dismantle inequality. This is what Jackson's consciousness-raising efforts produced, and what McAdam describes as "cognitive liberation." The critical problem in the emergence of social protest movements is the translation of advantageous political developments into a widespread *perception* that those developments have in fact created opportunities for real change. Following the political process theory, an oppressed group must arrive at the point where it no longer accepts the legitimacy of the existing arrangement *and* believes that it can be reformed by collective protest. Modified perceptions about the possibilities for reform are not based upon individual assessments of objective information, much as Jackson had hoped they were. Instead, adjustments in thinking about the prospect for racial reform are a function of group cohesion. Lacking a collective dynamic fused together by personal bonds rather than abstract propositions, the sense of despair will continue *despite* the belief that change has become possible. Cognitive liberation, then—the "vote consciousness" that Jackson relentlessly drilled into the heads of teachers and students—developed in response to favorable political factors *and* Jackson's exhaustive efforts to create "interpersonal networks."[6]

This is the significance of his mountainous correspondence with principals and teachers, of the frequently emotional letters written by teachers recently "converted" to voting, and the testimonies of those eager to share their revitalized political convictions. More than the empirical data that he meticulously accumulated, his efforts—as well as those of teachers Eunice Bundy and James Spencer—to connect teachers to political groups outside the schools, to inject political instruction into the classroom, and to excite students about racial equality through politics created the social connections that fostered "cognitive liberation."

No less important, Jackson helped interpret those developments for activist teachers, filtering them through an idiom that resonated with African American traditions of self-reliance and racial pride. But that ideological filter also included the liberal democratic tenets embedded in the Constitution and its civil rights amendments. Quoting Murray Edelman, McAdam argues that the transformation of political consciousness does not depend on "observation" but rather on the signs generated by people who collectively construct the meaning they impose on contemporary events and on the future. Analyzing teachers' voting behavior, interpreting the salary equalization campaigns as an entering wedge for the larger movement for black equality, expounding the importance of civic education in the classroom, and encouraging teachers to set the example of civic responsibility through voting and public engagement, Jackson helped formulate the larger meaning of the war years. Voting was important, he argued, because the climate and the political alignments had made it possible to mold the future for African Americans. Changes in federal policy and the achievement of critical Supreme Court decisions produced "a cognitive revolution" among blacks concerning the possibilities for dismantling a segregated social order. In this electrified atmosphere, teachers could become the lightning rods of political reform.[7]

But in fostering this political reawakening, Jackson couldn't resist the Washingtonian habit of ascribing responsibility for political powerlessness to African Americans: "If then, the colored people fail to get justice in this country it is not the fault now of the law of the land or the learned justices who interpret it. In each instance the fault lies with the folks back home."[8] Mobilizing against racial exclusion, he often pointed the finger at those with the strongest reasons to be skeptical of the political system. Admitting that nonvoting teachers feared the loss of their jobs from voting, Jackson dismissed it by insisting that this "so called fear is nothing less than an excuse offered by teachers for their failure to exercise one of our greatest privileges." Jackson's program would feature all of the strengths as well as the limitations of the VVL's liberal strategy for racial equality.[9]

Building the Case against the "Voteless" Teachers

In an article that year for the *Virginia Teachers Bulletin*, Jackson expanded on the political implications of nonvoting educators. Detailing the generally dismal level of poll-tax paying in the state, he concluded in Du Boisean fashion that "many leaders have failed to encourage the people to vote." Political activity was highest among urban teachers, but rural teachers, who comprised 75 percent of all Virginia's black educators, fell woefully behind. Jackson later argued in the pages of the *Norfolk Journal and Guide* that nonvoting teachers were "nonreading teachers," unacquainted with current affairs and untrained in the rubrics of voting. But Jackson generally overlooked the economic and cultural forces militating against teacher involvement in politics. Even so, his limited empathy for the rural teachers did not obscure his grasp of the consequences of a politically disfranchised teaching profession. Jackson believed that politically disengaged teachers not only would produce adults with little understanding of government affairs but would also impoverish the students' capacity to succeed in a ruthless and atavistic society. Students of the politically indifferent teacher would find themselves poorly prepared "to face the problems of our ruthless, capitalistic society." Never having learned the benefits of "the organized labor movement," or the merits of consumer cooperatives, or the political dividends paid by pressuring office holders to legislate responsibly on matters affecting jobs and "social security," those students would fail to climb the economic ladder. Although Jackson returned to his familiar trope that teachers, like black citizens, had only themselves to blame for nonvoting since most of the formal mechanisms of disfranchisement had been swept away, his case for political instruction in the classroom demonstrated a strain of social consciousness missing from many of his earlier paeans to ballot casting. The social perspective imparted by the New Deal expanded his own political consciousness, heightening his awareness of the intersection between structures of class, race, and political exclusion.[10]

Jackson quickly followed through on his program to disseminate the voting message among educators. He dispatched over two hundred copies of his voting instruction handbooks to Jeanes supervisors, school superintendents, high school principals, college professors, and "influential white citizens." The booklets became a standard feature of Jackson's program, testifying to voting progress, statistically documenting the limits of black political activity, and providing a tool for political education in the classroom. He also wrote to administrators of historically black colleges appealing for them to encourage registration and voting among the faculty.[11] Distributing literature to school officials and writing to key administrators, Jackson also championed voting in the pages of the VTA *Bulletin* and the *Norfolk Journal and Guide*. In addition, he addressed local teachers associations and the faculty of Virginia State College, directly entreating them to register and set the example of political involvement for their students.[12] Jackson was convinced that quantitative data as well as persistent appeals to racial responsibility would be sufficient to overcome the inherited weight of traditional political torpor.

Teaching Political Engagement

Cajoling teachers to vote was only one part of Jackson's strategy; the other was inserting political instruction in the curricula of Virginia's schools. Shortly after the appeal to the Jeanes supervisors, Jackson called on school principals to adopt voting exercises in their history, civics, and social studies classes. His reasoning is important, because it underscores the psychological dimensions of racial exclusion and the physical strategies required to overcome it. He believed that "mere book instruction" on social questions would never be sufficient to galvanize support for political involvement. Just as activists in Montgomery and other communities would discover, political change required collective rituals of defiance, self-confidence, and democratic participation, actions that graphically countered the customary subservience expected of African Americans while at the same time pointing toward the inclusive practices that protest would presumably make possible. As Jackson explained, "In order to get action and instill a voting consciousness in our youth they should go through some form of *dramatization*" (emphasis added). What Jackson had in mind was a mock election for a primary in which students paid the poll tax, registered to vote, and then cast a ballot. Although a far more individualistic exercise than the sit-ins and boycotts of the later movement, the mock elections would give students the opportunity to imagine themselves in the role of active citizens. As Jackson explained to L. F. Palmer, the object was not simply to instruct students in the mechanics of voting but to introduce them to "the larger program of participation in the affairs of government."[13]

It would be easy to romanticize the mock elections and overlook one of the key flaws in the exercise—the paying of the poll tax—which reinforced the system of racial exclusion. Even so, Jackson and the teachers carried out political instruction at a time when schools conditioned black students to racial submission. By instructing students in the rubrics and importance of political participation, Virginia teachers anticipated the freedom schools of the Student Nonviolent Coordinating Committee's (SNCC) 1964 Mississippi campaign. By adopting Jackson's program for making political participation a visible and conceivable experience, Virginia teachers approximated the Mississippi Freedom Vote initiative of 1963, in which African Americans cast ballots in a mock election supervised by the SNCC and the Committee of Federated Organizations (COFO). Like SNCC activists in the Magnolia State, Jackson and those teachers who supported the civic education project created the conditions in which—in the words of one historian of the Freedom Schools—African American southerners could grasp "the intersection of education and political action" and contemplate even briefly "a life unmarked by racial oppression."[14]

Jackson's multipronged initiative generated an immediate if not overwhelming response from teachers and administrators, some of whom were already offering voting instruction in the classroom. The responses to Jackson's program as well as the continuing correspondence between him and the educators he targeted provide a barometer of political awareness among Virginia's African American educators. They also offer insight into the political expectations of African Americans in the wake of the salary cases, the Supreme Court rulings against the white primary, expanded opportunities for public employment, an emerging liberal-labor coalition hospitable to black voting, and a social climate favorable to racial issues.

For principal James Spencer of Richmond, Jackson's mail-out campaign was a "timely civic recommendation" to promote voting among students. Well in advance of Jackson's program, however, Spencer's school had been conducting classroom instruction, field trips to the General Assembly, and student visits to the polls to witness teachers casting a ballot. Moving beyond Jackson's recommendations, Spencer also planned to contact students who had graduated in the last seven years to determine their voting status and remind them of their civic obligations. His local voters' league and civic association appealed to area ministers to preach the benefits of poll-tax paying and voting, and the county teachers' association printed circulars and posters for distribution to black business establishments. For Spencer and the teachers of South Richmond, inculcating political consciousness in the classroom was part of a wider program of social and political activism.[15]

Spencer was uniquely willing to commit his convictions about teaching and politics to paper. Well before the office of civic education was established, Spencer admitted to Jackson that he had discerned "a close correlation between good teaching and voting. The teacher who is interested in getting close to the community needs and serves well in the community, votes." Like Jackson, Spencer believed that school officials would not punish the voting teacher: "One told me once to drop my garden hoe and go out and scare up some votes for good county officials who were up for election." One can only wonder what, according to the school administrator, constituted a "good" county official, and whether or not he would have encouraged African American voting in the event that candidates supportive of racial integration and equality ran for office. In any case, Spencer reported that out of forty-five teachers in the county, twenty-eight had voted, by no means a stellar level of participation but certainly an indication that the voting message had registered among teachers, particularly those in the urban centers.[16]

Spencer continued throughout the 1940s to organize and advocate for racial progress through education. He routinely replied to Jackson's queries, updating him on the status of teacher voting and the progress of civic education in his school. He encouraged Jackson and congratulated him on his work, while reporting on local political developments. In 1949, for example, Spencer discussed voting with his five teachers and determined the voting status of parents as well. He sponsored mock elections and civic programs in the school, and, as noted, drove students to the polls to witness electoral democracy in action. As a leading member of the Virginia Voters League and an NAACP stalwart, Spencer traveled throughout the state "spreading civic information" through speeches, addresses, and lectures.[17]

As much as Spencer supported Jackson's program, he was no lackey, and he took Jackson to task on racial practices at none other than Virginia State College. Having "declared war" on the American Legion for its support of segregation, he criticized Virginia State for permitting the group to hold meetings at the college in the summer of 1949: "We have enough Jim Crow institutions and organizations to last us for a long time. . . . We expect to land a second heavy blow on this Jim Crow scheme sponsored by the American Legion and a few 'white folks Negroes.'" Spencer may not have included Jackson in his list of "white folks Negroes," but he had no compunction about criticizing the state's leading African American college for its complicity in segregation. He was also prepared to upbraid the American Legion in an editorial for the *Richmond Afro-American,* an unusually bold move for an African American in the vulnerable position of school principal. Spencer went beyond African American papers, castigating segregated "regional schools" in the pages of the *Richmond Times-Dispatch.* Like Jackson, his editorial ventures and his support for political education were part of a "civic crusade to arouse the so-called sons and daughters of Ham to become vote-conscious in our local and State communities." The salary equalization cases, the crystallization of the VTA as a vehicle of racial protest, and the movement to elevate the political consciousness of Virginia's teachers may not have been the sole factors in Spencer's increased militancy, but they certainly interacted with other forces in encouraging black middle-class impatience with racial accommodation.[18]

Spencer was enthusiastic about voting instruction, but he was not alone. Lutrelle Palmer believed that Jackson's initiative would reinforce existing programs of political instruction. As principal of Huntington High School in Newport News, Palmer assured him that a schoolwide program of instruction on the requirements and rubrics of voting had been in place for several years. The students applied their knowledge in annual elections for student council representatives, paying poll taxes, and registering to vote in polling booths supervised by judges and clerks. George Binford, principal of Central High School in Charlotte, Virginia, notified Jackson that social science teachers had offered students instruction on voting and had achieved some success in persuading their parents to vote. In these schools, students absorbed a sense of the electoral process and reduced the mystery that surrounded voting. In staging elections, civics teachers also exposed students to the idea that voting was not a function of political dependency reminiscent of the plantation South but rather an exercise of civil rights under the authority of national law. Classroom instruction on voting, government, and the implications of political involvement accelerated the process through which young African Americans detached themselves from a segregated worldview, one in which power and authority devolved almost uniformly on whites. What they began to appreciate was the notion of law as an equalizing rather than oppressive force. It was this appreciation that wore away at the mindset which consigned politics to the "better sort" of whites and subservience to all blacks. And yet, teachers offering civic instruction were in the minority and could be found for the most part in urban centers, not in the countryside, where the voting message had made considerably less headway.[19]

That began to change with Jackson's civic education program. Mary Carr Greer, principal of the Albemarle County Training School, held a faculty conference soon after receiving Jackson's appeal to consider voting and political instruction. Greer reported that the faculty would now cooperate "100% with you in your effort to get all the teachers in the Counties and Cities of Virginia to pay poll taxes, register, and vote." Greer became Jackson's steadfast ally and a proponent of political activity and pedagogy. In the coveted position of school principal, she demonstrated the political sensitivities that African American women had cultivated since the Reconstruction period. Responding to Jackson's annual call for teacher registration in 1944, Carr reported that political posters sent by the *Journal and Guide* had been distributed throughout the school and that the social studies classes had examined the question of black voting: "Several members of the classes were interested and promised to persuade their parents to register. As a result, many actually registered." By 1946, Greer and the teachers of the Albemarle County Training School had extended the voter mobilization program beyond the school and into the community; Jackson's teacher registration drive had become another channel for catalyzing political awareness in Virginia. The immediate incentive for voting in Char-

lottesville was the question of a bond issue to support local school improvement. "As you know," Greer confided to Jackson, "the Negroes are the ones who
will profit most by the program because we have the poorest school."[20]

Beginning as a drive for teacher registration, the suffrage movement spilled
over the walls of the training school and swept out into the community, cresting
in a political enterprise that featured nightly meetings and teacher involvement
in voter recruitment. In Albemarle as well as in other communities, the school
was becoming an agent of democracy, and women were playing a key role in
promoting it. By 1947, Greer could report that all of her teachers had registered
and were prepared to vote in an approaching election. Echoing Greer, Principal
James D. Washington of Tappahannock in rural Virginia reported that all of the
teachers in the Essex County Training School had registered to vote and paid
their poll taxes, while the remaining teachers had registered for the 1948 campaign. Aretha Fleming had not waited for Jackson's prompting: she and her
entire family had registered to vote for the 1948 election. More than this, she had
joined the Goochland Civic League, a voter mobilization group that had been
operating in the rural district for a year. Not surprisingly, then, voting activism
followed voting teachers, and in the aftermath of the war, that behavior was no
longer restricted to city sophisticates.[21]

The correspondence sheds light on the crucial role that female teachers
played in the movement to expand voter registration and advance civil rights.
It also suggests the critical role that Jackson's program played in heightening
political consciousness, particularly among the African American middle class.
Eunice D. Bundy, principal of Hanover County Training School, announced
that her school had conducted "an effective mock campaign and election," with
each civics class going through the steps of poll-tax paying, registering, and
voting. Janie Sims wrote to thank Jackson for the voting information he had
sent her, adding perceptively that, "If children become interested parents will be
influenced." Sims was a vigilant proponent of political activity who used her
classes to stress the idea that to be "worthy" of citizenship, African Americans
had to register to vote. Echoing Jackson's convictions, she argued that "there are
many rights the Negro could demand if he voted or more negroes voted." Detailing the electoral procedures taught in her social studies classes, Sims signed
her letter, "your teacher for better citizenship." Marie Hubbard, a Jeanes supervisor in Amelia County, informed Jackson that a woman in Amelia County not
only chaired the NAACP committee in charge of voter mobilization but also
functioned as president of the local teachers' association. Hubbard also con-

firmed that Jackson's relentless effort to expose the political lassitude of Virginia's black educators through registration and poll-tax surveys was having an effect: "I think that your survey will make more vote the next time because some seemed ashamed of not having voted when the question was asked." In fact, out of thirty-six teachers in Amelia County, only six had voted in the presidential election of 1944.[22]

Teachers responded in strength to Jackson's request for information on their voting status, often expressing gratitude for wrenching them out of political torpor. Letters such as the one from Rosa Carter in 1948 must have been immensely gratifying. With none of the dramatic flair of Janie Sims, Carter notified Jackson that she was "now a qualified voter because of your letter." Lazarus Bates echoed the sentiment, notifying Jackson that he and his wife had decided to register for the critical presidential election of 1948 because of his letter.[23] Maud Valentine informed the professor that although the teachers in her school had qualified to vote, the students had taken it upon themselves to interest their parents in electoral matters. T. A. Randolph, a school supervisor, declared that he held Jackson's program "in high esteem and I shall contact every teacher under my supervision to become a qualified voter." Eunice Bundy assured Jackson that his considerable investment of time and energy in the production of the *Voting Status of the Negro in Virginia* was paying off. "The handbooks are proving helpful," Bundy wrote, "not only individually but they are very valuable in connection with our civic classes and our voters league." Jeanes supervisor Mayme Coleman corroborated Bundy's observation and assured Jackson that his program had generated widespread interest: "Your booklet was received, this is just what we need. . . . I feel that each teacher will be able to help in each community. This will get it nearer to the people." As tools of political instruction and a touchstone for several groups involved in civic activism, Jackson's handbooks served the larger purpose of political mobilization. Using teachers as the medium, Jackson's voting instruction booklets established links between the middle-class activists and working-class citizens.[24]

Jackson's mass mailings and journalistic jeremiads opened channels of political communication blocked by the accumulated detritus of legal restrictions, social sanctions, and collective disillusionment. Several teachers wrote to Jackson for additional information, to supply data on the voting patterns of teachers in their school or district, to request additional booklets, to commend an article he had written in the *Journal and Guide,* or to invite him to address a community gathering. Catherine Holmes of Emporia, Virginia, wrote to request information on "citizenship," adding: "We have heard quite a bit about your interest in the Negro in Virginia. We read your article in the *Journal and Guide* every week and enjoy it very much." A former student turned to Jackson's column for guidance on conducting a registration and voting program for sixth- and seventh-grade history students. As Jackson promoted the program of the secretary of civic education, weaving it into the fabric of the Virginia Teachers Association, teachers made him the natural choice to lead local teachers in meetings focusing on political action. The VTA Speakers Bureau had already given Jackson the opportunity to disseminate the voting message, but as secretary of civic education, he solidified and expanded his political network. Miles Medford of the Richmond Parent Teacher Association (PTA) invited Jackson to address the group on "developing civic pride." He was ideal for the address, since the PTA branch intended to address civic pride in its broadest sense, including "registering, voting, public affairs, pride in home & community, citizenship responsibility, Negro history etc." His activity in the VTA only strengthened his reputation as a dynamic college educator and leading force behind the Association for the Study of Negro Life and History in Virginia. Mary Thompson certainly encapsulated the views of a majority of teachers who had weathered the salary disputes and internalized the connection between education and black political activity: "I think you are doing a wonderful job in trying to get our people to vote." Jackson was also doing a wonderful job in fostering a sense of community among educators founded on common notions of racial solidarity and political independence.[25]

Jackson's requests for information on the voting behavior of teachers also afforded African American women the opportunity to profile their own political odyssey. Offering insight into the political enthusiasm generated by wartime economic gains, favorable Supreme Court decisions, the Wallace campaign, and no doubt Jackson's own efforts, Margarette Brooks wrote excitedly that she had received Jackson's inquiry and felt it "much to [sic] important to sleep over tonight." Proudly, she informed Jackson that she was a qualified voter who had cast a ballot in 1947. Brooks not only voted but also did so at an advance polling booth "in Lawrenceville Va. a month before the election in Mr. Elmores [sic] office before him and two other persons in there at that time, as I was going away for the summer." It required considerable fortitude for an African American woman to pay the required tax six months in advance, register to vote, and then cast a ballot in the presence of a white male official representing a state that had spent the previous forty-five years policing the ballot box against African

American influence. Conscious of her accomplishment, she shared it with Jackson, himself a representative of African American males excluded for the longest time from political influence but often ambivalent about the public role of African American women. She then reviewed the candidates for state office and announced that she had been the "third person to vote by marking the ballot in present [sic] of the county clerk." For Brooks and others like her, voting was not a meaningless ritual, an inconsequential footnote to a chapter on the moderate civil rights movement. It required courage; it exemplified self-determination; and it expressed a basic alteration in consciousness. It was the moment African Americans exercised the moral imperative dictating racial equality. Whites might hope to neutralize black demands for equality by improving separate facilities and cordoning off access to power, but voting was an area where black expectations could not be segregated or channeled into unthreatening waters. By voting, Brooks exercised the social equality denied by the southern system of racial exclusion.[26]

Although Brooks absorbed the optimism spurred by a multiplying black electorate and the Truman administration's civil rights proclamations, she made it clear that for her, as for many middle-class African American women, political consciousness was nothing new. Brooks had been voting in Maryland "since Harding elections"; she understood the "importance" of voting for herself and to "all who cast the ballot." Thanking him for his interest in her "personal civic welfare," Brooks added eagerly that she had "used all the influence to bring many peoples with their civic duty and shall continue as long as I can for a better country state and nation." In the case of many African American women, particularly teachers who regularly confronted the consequences of political exclusion in the form of inadequate schools for African American children and inequitable pay for themselves, political involvement reflected circumstances, not will. Given the chance to vote in Maryland, Margarette Brooks cast a ballot; permitted to vote in Virginia, she exercised the franchise there, going through the paces of electoral qualification and negotiating the racial barriers that kept so many others away. Yet the tone that dominates Brooks's letter speaks not of individual courage in the face of adversity but rather of a sense of responsibility, of "civic duty"—her own and others'—because she recognized "its importance." Jackson's civic education campaign must have encouraged Brooks. The political developments that made the 1940s a democratic moment for workers and African Americans certainly created a hospitable atmosphere as well, but Brooks traveled to the voting booth alone on "July 3, 1947," casting a ballot "before him and two other persons." Brooks was particularly articulate, but she was not an exception. One of the persistent themes running through the correspondence is the political alertness of teachers even prior to Jackson's mailing campaign. Of course, nonregistered teachers were less likely to commit a confession of political indifference to paper. Several admitted to a political conversion of sorts at Jackson's promptings, while others proudly announced their status as active voters and attentive citizens. What is clear is that Jackson's campaign was solidifying the political commitments of those who were voting and prodding those who were not.[27]

By 1944, the progress in political activity among teachers was evident, a development related in no small part to the efforts of the civic education office. In November of that year, Jackson reported to VTA president C. W. Seay that his latest request for information on teacher voting patterns documented some "gratifying results." With data from approximately half of the state's principals, Jackson informed Seay that "three fourths or more" of black teachers had voted in the presidential election of 1944. Jackson was slightly more modest in the pages of the *Journal and Guide*; there, he claimed that "more than two thousand" out of approximately four thousand teachers voted in the presidential election of 1944, a remarkable improvement, nonetheless, over 1936, when fewer than five hundred teachers went to the polls.[28]

In a December column of the *Journal and Guide,* Jackson temporarily dropped his admonitory tone in favor of an upbeat celebration of "some very effective civic training" that had preceded the Roosevelt and Dewey contest of 1944. He congratulated the students and teachers who sponsored mock elections, campaigning and then casting ballots for their preferred nominees. Not surprisingly, Jackson reported that the students of Virginia State College gave Roosevelt a landslide victory over Dewey. He also applauded a principal who had arranged a bus trip for his senior class to witness African Americans voting. For Jackson, it was an encouraging sign that elite leadership really could racial exclusion of civil rights by setting the example of electoral participation and teaching the message of political awareness.[29]

In fact, a core of principals offered critical support for Jackson's civic education program. There is little evidence to suggest that principals acted as agents of the status quo, at least on the question of black teachers voting and instructing students in political participation. They tended to encourage civic education, and they supplied Jackson with information on teacher voting and poll-tax paying while offering a window on student responses to political instruction.[30]

In Campbell County, Principal Clyde Scott adopted the civic education department's political instruction program, which proved "very beneficial to the citizens of this county." During the war years, Scott and Lutrelle Palmer were among the few principals able to report that their schools were holding mock elections. With the expansion of the NAACP and the political excitement of the third-party initiatives in 1948, mock elections became a standard feature of civic instruction, at least in those schools that offered it. In Charlotte, Virginia, Principal George Binford presided over a mock election in 1948 involving all of the teachers and students. Again, women teachers took a leading role in the exercise, but they benefited from the active support of interested students. A. M. Binford, the principal's wife, and Eugene Wells, president of the student council, directed the project as part of a class on government. Encouraged by the exercise in civic equality, one of the teachers drove eighty-five miles to Richmond after school to cast his ballot. That year, Principal W. E. Friend of S. C. Abrams High School reported that Truman won the school's mock election. Enjoying newfound political consciousness, a group of students commandeered their families' cars to transport eligible African American voters to the polls. In a scene probably played out in countless rural villages throughout Virginia, a teacher from Friend's school traveled from "Fluvanna to Culpepper to cast her vote—a distance of 50 miles." But Friend would not be outdone, driving eighty miles from Fluvanna to Chesterfield to cast his ballot.[31]

Some principals and teachers chose alternative methods of political action, often coordinating voting and citizenship activities beyond the school campus. As teachers registered and taught electoral procedures to their students, they made the connection between individual political involvement and community action. Students in the government and sociology classes at Principal Caleb Gregory Brown's school in Alleghany County conducted surveys "to make the community vote conscious." Absorbing the theory of democratic participation in schools—one that made the pedagogical link between black history and civic education—young African Americans translated their knowledge into community activism, raising political awareness and setting an example of social concern for others. Citizens of Alleghany County subsequently organized a political club. Political energy also radiated from the Augusta County Training School, where, in 1948, most of the teachers were busy recruiting voters through the Staunton-Augusta County Civic League. Political enthusiasm followed naturally from Principal A. N. Jackson's efforts to encourage teachers "to emphasize the value of the ballot" and the responsibilities of citizens. Similarly, teachers at the Henry County Training School formed a committee to canvas the community and publish an honor roll of registered and active voters. Forming less than a broad-based movement, these students and their teachers nevertheless became the rivulets of political awareness that would build to a torrent of social protest less than two decades later.[32]

In some cases, teachers organized mock campaigns; in others, they converted school elections into arenas for political issues outside the classroom. Responding to Jackson's query about civic education at the Buckingham County Training School, Principal G. F. Harris noted that his students had substituted a "real election" to the student council for a mock presidential election. The elections, "patterned after that of our national and local governments," were particularly elaborate. Each class elected representatives for a planning convention and organized precincts in which students registered to vote once they had paid a poll tax of six cents. Harris was particularly pleased that in the election year of 1948, several students followed the national campaigns and "injected much of what went on throughout the country in their little campaign here." Just as lunch counters and school buses became the flashpoints of the later movement, voting, parties, unions, and electoral practices provided young people the touchstones for the civil rights movement in the 1940s.[33]

The elections were a moderate affair, reinforcing the status quo at the same time that they encouraged black self-determination. Although students "kept up with the national campaign," the election featured only the two major parties, not the Progressive Party, which unequivocally championed racial equality, an end to the Cold War, and a more equitable distribution of wealth. Learning the social importance of casting a ballot, students were also taught how to qualify to vote, meaning that they paid a poll tax in the one election where it could have been avoided, thus normalizing and legitimizing the practice. Students were also taught how "to be good citizens," a message carrying overtones of compliance and acceptance. Teachers, and Jackson of course, operated on the assumption that to change the system, African Americans had to work within it, even if that included paying a poll tax and limiting the electoral playing field to mainstream political parties. Although the student elections and the civic education program encouraged political involvement and confidence, they also transmitted a contradictory message: political liberation could coexist with racial control.[34]

Despite the accommodating subtext of the voting exercises, many African American teachers and principals championed a brand of political activism that fired the imaginations of young black students and challenged others to make a public commitment to racial equality. They forged links between political education in the schools and political awareness initiatives in the community. They vividly demonstrated their own commitment to voting, casting ballots as students looked on, pressuring teachers to register, and encouraging teachers to transform political sentiment into immediate political action. Jackson applauded the efforts of principals including Lutrelle Palmer, T. Roger Thompson, and J. Rupert Picott, "whose schools are veritable laboratories for the teaching of full fledged citizenship." He celebrated the accomplishments of teachers such as James W. Ivy, Eric Epps, and Ethel Pannell, each a representative "of the democracy for which this nation is now giving its blood and its wealth." The principals and teachers provided the support without which Jackson's message would have withered on the educational vine.[35]

Jackson accelerated the ideological momentum of the teachers' movement by extending the civic education program and using the pages of the *Journal and Guide* to focus attention on the "voteless" teachers. Examining the "non voting tradition" among African American teachers, Jackson claimed that politically disengaged educators were "non-reading teachers" who failed to educate themselves on current events and political developments. Acknowledging that teachers feared the retaliation of school supervisors, Jackson stubbornly reiterated his familiar mantra that things had changed, and that "[n]ot to vote is not to appreciate full-fledged American citizenship" or to "appreciate the contribution that the individual's race has made to his country." Voting and teaching civic participation was as much an exercise in nationalism as it was a demonstration of racial pride. He became increasingly militant on this point, probably as much out of frustration that a sizable minority of teachers remained unregistered as from a sense of urgency. In circular letters to teachers in 1948, he chided them for claiming nonresidency as an excuse for nonvoting. Boldly, Jackson announced, "We accept no such point of view." In fact, he added confrontationally, if teachers earning a living in Virginia did not register and vote in the state, "[they] should no longer accept employment in this state."[36]

Reaching beyond the elementary and high schools, Jackson appealed to college instructors to register themselves and train their students in the mechanics of voting. Criticizing the assertion that college instructors had no business in politics, Jackson observed that the same logic would require black institutions of higher education to abnegate responsibility for "any of the crying needs of Negroes." Jackson also targeted college summer school students, most of whom were teachers upgrading their qualifications. Since many of the summer school students were away from their voting precinct, he sent them detailed information on how to submit an absentee ballot in the upcoming gubernatorial election, which pitted the liberal Moss Plunkett against machine politician William M. Tuck. In addition to his relentless appeals for registration and poll tax payment, Jackson also called on high school principals to rally teachers to cast ballots in referenda on the poll tax. Reflecting his movement away from the official political neutrality that had governed his strategy with the Virginia Voters League, he called on principals to mobilize the teachers to vote against the Campbell suffrage amendments, which proposed to replace the poll tax with annual registration taking place four months prior to any election. The amendments also imposed literacy tests but left the General Assembly room to apply additional suffrage conditions at its discretion. Together with the Virginia Voters League, the NAACP, the Civil Rights Organization, and liberal Virginians, Jackson's voting teachers defeated the discriminatory amendments.[37]

Jackson used the civic education project to amplify the theme of social change through political power. He hammered away at the idea that racial progress would come when black professionals, particularly teachers, committed themselves to political activity, beginning with the decision to pay the poll tax and register to vote. Their example and conscientious instruction in political affairs would impel students to embrace political activity. His strategies remained consistent, but his notions of racial advancement evolved, although never beyond the basic liberal democratic precepts he had espoused since the founding of the Petersburg Voters League. When the VTA established the office of secretary of civic education, Jackson asserted rather vaguely that it would produce "vote conscious young people" willing to participate in the affairs of government. In 1943, he underscored the democratic and nationalistic implications of voting. By 1948, he had become more explicit about the meaning of the teachers' crusade, placing it in the larger context of race relations. Virginia's African American teachers were setting an example for other teachers and pushing back the boundaries of racial discrimination in a regionwide movement for social justice. By voting, they would "inspire pupils," but they would also "influence all teachers in the states to the south of us." Once Virginia's teachers could "announce to our fellow teachers in the Southern states that all or nearly all" had registered to vote, "then they too will awaken from their slumbers." Politically active teachers were involved in issues that extended beyond the Old Dominion: "The task in which we are engaged, then, is one of seeking to bring about reform in a whole region of our nation." By participating in a movement that had ramifications for all southern blacks, teachers would promote "political democracy" while also promoting the interests of the teachers' association.[38]

The election of 1948 (discussed in greater depth in chapter 7) had been a turning point, both for the nation and for the teachers. If the civic education program had entered the decade on shaky ground, it grew stronger in a climate that favored racial activism and the teachers' own appeal for fair treatment. In Jackson's estimation, the VTA had played a critical role in fostering political awareness among educators:

> By sponsoring a department of civic education through which individual teachers of the entire state are written to at least once a year concerning their voting status, and by providing them with literature dealing with the general subject of suffrage, this teachers association has developed a sense of civic responsibility among its members so strong that not many of them will openly confess that they see no value in exercising the American right of franchise offered by every state of the union to their qualified citizens.[39]

Getting teachers to vote and instruct their students in civic responsibility was a modest objective by later measurements, but a remarkable contrast with the political inertia of the early 1930s. Depression and war heightened the confidence of teachers throughout the state; Jackson and the VTA transformed that altered perspective into concrete action.

Changing Their Minds

If Jackson offered little in the way of a thoroughgoing critique of American capitalism, he avoided utopian schemes that bore little relationship to the needs of average African Americans. He chose to emphasize the ballot as well as the courts, the newspapers, and external forms of political pressure to advance reforms that expanded political and social opportunities for blacks. Like later civil rights activists, he recognized that the real hope for change lay with young African Americans awakened to their rights and to the possibility that concerted action, both collective and individual, could produce change.

What he did not understand was that the burden of racial uplift was too heavy for teachers to carry and too paternalistic for the majority of African Americans to accept. Enlightened teachers might promote equal salaries and better schools, but they paid little attention to the economic afflictions of most African Americans. Voting and court victories could reduce formal barriers to equality, but they also operated on the assumption that incremental change would eventually make racial separation untenable. As African Americans enjoyed greater economic mobility and political influence, they questioned the merit of a strategy that depended on patience and cooperation with liberal whites. Until teachers and their students embraced a philosophy of racial change that challenged segregation and made room for those outside the ranks of the traditional elite, there was little hope of building a mass movement. And although teachers functioned as part of an educational system controlled by adversarial whites, they continued to be susceptible to retribution, which limited their range of political action. Even so, it did not prevent them from inculcating civic consciousness.

It is easy to be lulled into the presentist mindset, judging past events by our own standards or those of the leaders that produced the victories we associate with the height of the civil rights movement. Since the grassroots campaigns of the 1960s—with their tactics of direct action and community mobilization— ushered in the new day for African Americans, surely the earlier strategies must not have worked? In the era before the monumental decision desegregating public schools, Jackson's strategy of relying on middle-class leadership—and in particular African American educators—made perfect sense. Black teachers enjoyed prestige and influence in African American communities. In an era before cohesive and regionwide civil rights groups mobilized young blacks, they were uniquely situated to reach students and mold their thinking about the racial landscape of America. And since Supreme Court decisions had produced change, and blacks were exercising considerable power within the Democratic Party, Jackson and the VTA were astute in believing that a strategy of black voting and litigation could overturn black proscription. Certainly, the Student Nonviolent Coordinating Committee, the Congress of Racial Equality, and the leaders who stood in front of these groups thought along similar lines, promoting ventures including the Mississippi Freedom Democratic Party, black voter registration, and voting rights legislation. Where Jackson and others miscalculated was in believing that elite leadership and a program of gradual improvement through conventional channels were enough to transform southern race relations. And they, like many African American activists of the period, overestimated the support of white liberals for a social order premised on genuine racial equality.

Even so, Jackson helped create an environment in which blacks could imagine freedom. Through the organizations, he established the groundwork for the intellectual transformation that was necessary for challenging the racial order. Through his speeches, his publications, and his appeals, he widened that revolution and convinced legions of African Americans that the democratic moment had arrived. As he wrote to Charles Wesley: "Our prospects for an awakening in voting among Negroes in the state are brighter than ever. *At least we now have the most effective organization for this purpose than ever before.*" Jackson was abundantly aware that political forces and black activism had converged.[40]

Although he admitted that it was "practically impossible" to determine how many teachers had registered to vote, he did try to measure his consciousness-raising efforts in quantitative terms, however imprecisely. In 1948, Jackson claimed that "more than one-half of the 4,500 [black] public school teachers in Virginia are qualified voters," while a "fair proportion" offered instruction on voting procedures, parties, and elections. In "Race and Race Suffrage in the South since 1940," Jackson pegged teacher registration rates in Virginia and Texas at "fifty percent or more" but noted disappointedly that "in the South as a whole the number drops to less than twenty percent." Depending on his audience, he would either emphasize the accomplishments of vote-conscious teachers or stress their persistent political indifference. He was probably the least equivocal in his reports to the Virginia Teachers Association executive, since they not only sponsored his office but also had a ground-level perspective on Virginia's black teachers. After detailing the handbooks and circulars distributed among schoolteachers, Jackson stated simply that "a growing number of teachers are becoming vote conscious, that they are giving instructions in suffrage and the affairs of government in their schools, and that a few are participating on a wider front by teaching voting requirements to adults in their communities." Clearly then, a majority of teachers had embraced the voting message and had become emissaries of the "cognitive revolution" that had sprouted in the era of Depression and war but would only achieve critical mass in the 1950s.[41]

It is not surprising, then, that Virginia and its schools would emerge as a central battleground of the struggle over segregation. Jackson and his vote-conscious teachers had been tilling the political ground since the late 1930s, teaching a generation of students that social change began with "civic consciousness." This was nothing less than teaching that education itself would lead students to question the world they inhabited and demand the rights that had been denied them. From that training, they began to understand the value of social engagement, not only through electoral participation but also through litigation and direct protest. It was a simple formula, one that W.E.B. Du Bois and likeminded activists had been espousing for years, but it only began to resonate when people such as Jackson taught it and lived it at the grassroots level. When teachers organized mock elections, registered to vote, joined the NAACP, and took students to witness democracy in action, the whole question of equality moved from the abstract to the tangible, supported along the way by social and political developments that only a war could generate. My teacher is voting, my principal supports it, and here we are imagining ourselves as full participants in a democratic society, students began to say to themselves. Demanding change no longer seems unreasonable, dangerous or *illegitimate*. More than this, it was the educators themselves, powerful authority figures, who were advocating political instruction and demanding equality for themselves. Jackson was particularly important in this process. He wielded the kind of influence that only a college professor (or a minister) could at that time. His civic education program, sustained by personal, immediate work in local schools, convinced students and teachers that schools should not be bastions of the status quo. If a prestigious historian, respected community leader, and prominent educator endorsed political action, and did so under the auspices of the teachers' own organization, then students could as well.

What began to emerge in the late 1940s in the schools was a movement culture located in the belief that civic participation could generate change. Voting, legal challenges, mass meetings, government instruction, and teacher activism were woven together by the growing confidence in public action over private resistance. Casting a ballot or taking a school board to court were not diametrically opposed strategies but complementary tactics stemming from this powerful insight.

Chapter 7

———•———

Years of Opportunity

Jackson and the Political Resurgence of the South

After my graduation from Virginia State University, I was employed in Char-
lottesville, VA as a music teacher. During that time, Afro-Americans were not
allowed to stay at white local hotels—so, a prominent black lady opened a small
hotel called Carver Inn where all notables of 'color' stayed and had their meals.
One day, as I was having dinner, several prominent lawyers were there discussing
their case—Swanson v. University of Virginia. Gregory Swanson, a black student,
had been denied admittance to the University of Virginia Law School. I was
introduced to them: Supreme Court Justice Thurgood Marshall, Spottswood
Robinson, etc. As they heard that I was Dr. Luther P. Jackson's son, Thurgood
Marshall said in a loud voice—Dr. Luther P. was my "idol". . . . Of course, this
team of lawyers won their case and Gregory Swanson was admitted to the Uni-
versity of Virginia Law School.

Edward Jackson to author, January 2002

The Second World War proved how quickly things could change for a country
that only years before had flown the banner of neutrality as the winds of war
whipped across the Old World once again. Massive military recruitment, the
expanded presence of women in the workforce, American intervention in a
second global conflict, unprecedented industrial production, the realignment
of domestic priorities, the expansion of American power abroad—each followed the decision to support the Allies and contain the Japanese. While southern impoverishment and illiteracy continued, defense spending in the region
brought money, jobs, and pavement into the region on a scale that would have
impressed Henry Grady. Machinery altered southern agriculture, but the rapid
migration of hundreds of thousands of black and white sharecroppers out of

the countryside and into the cities transformed it, leaving in its wake the remnants of the South's feudal plantation culture. As John Egerton explains: "America seemed on the verge of a great renewal, a reinvention of itself. With an air of invincibility, it was facing the future in an expansive, opportunistic, idealistic mood."[1]

This mood of hopefulness bolstered African American reformers, but it rang particularly true for optimist Luther P. Jackson. Surveying the racial changes precipitated by previous wars, Jackson confidently asserted that "our present global conflict should bring a degree of liberty to Negroes previously unknown."[2] In those few years before his death, Jackson cultivated and participated in a flowering of racial liberalism that would not appear again until the 1960s. This period saw Luther Jackson move beyond the limits of the tightly knit network of African American activists and academics into a world of interracial initiatives that opened up the possibility of broad social reform. Jackson moved beyond negotiating racial barriers to the belief that they had to be eliminated altogether. Jackson grew increasingly confident, even militant, and certainly more convinced of the connection between black civil rights and economic democracy. It was his personal zenith, but each success seemed to bring new frustrations and disappointment, an experience that reverberated with the tremors of liberalism in the 1940s.

Expecting a Turning Point

As wartime employment raised the prospects of a new day for working-class Americans, it generated enthusiasm for racial change. Blacks began to believe that combat service and mass industrial production might secure the entitlements denied by an almost implacable system of racial discrimination. Although most black soldiers harbored few illusions that military service would magically open the doors of racial exclusion, they did believe that it would create economic and political opportunities unimaginable in the prewar period. Southern blacks who wore the khaki returned to communities where activists such as Jackson had been translating the rhetoric of the Four Freedoms into action through voter registration and poll-tax drives.

The NAACP provided the principle vehicle of black political mobilization during the war. In the late 1930s, its membership hovered around 18,000 people; by the end of hostilities, it had reached almost 156,000.[3] Episodes of racial violence involving newly militant black soldiers defending their civil rights and whites defending their social privileges only confirmed that the war had released threatening forces. White southerners across the region struck out against black soldiers who acted on the civic entitlement that their uniforms implied.

It was this epidemic of racial violence against blacks in uniform that spurred President Truman to action. Truman already had his hands full with foreign policy issues that eventually led the United States into a power struggle with the Soviet Union over Europe, Asia, and Africa. An overheated economy that sent the cost of living skyrocketing and the growing disillusionment over Roosevelt's compromises with the Soviets sharply reduced public support for Truman. The substantial Democratic losses in the midterm elections of 1946 compounded the president's problems. Southern congressmen had obstructed poll-tax reform throughout the war and had made it clear that the Roosevelt legacy of social welfare—particularly the Fair Employment Practices Committee—would meet a swift end at their hands. It was against this grain of political conservatism and Cold War paralysis, which Truman himself aggravated through an increasingly hard-line policy toward the Soviets—that the president adopted a program of liberal reform, demonstrating his continued commitment to New Deal thinking.

But Truman was bolder than Roosevelt. While his predecessor vacillated on antilynching legislation and support for the anti-poll-tax movement, the former haberdasher from Missouri responded to the violence in the South—which included a race riot in Columbia, Tennessee, the lynching of three blacks in Walton County, Georgia, and the vicious maiming of GI Issac Woodward in South Carolina—by declaring "We've got to do something!" That something included the President's Committee on Civil Rights. In 1947, this committee issued the landmark report *To Secure These Rights,* an audacious manifesto for a country committed in principle to equality before the law but practiced in the art of denying it to the least powerful. The report, published in 1947, denounced the hypocrisy of the "separate but equal" doctrine and called for a national antilynching law, the elimination of the poll tax, the establishment of a permanent FEPC, the termination of segregation in the armed forces, the suspension of federal support to agencies practicing segregation, and the removal of remaining voting restrictions. In other words, the report advocated the political equality that Jackson and his contemporaries had championed since the 1930s.[4] Truman certainly responded to international pressures—the demand to reconcile American practice at home with American rhetoric abroad—as well as to the prospect of political support from a growing African American population in the North. But he could just as easily have built a winning combination in 1948 on strong southern support for racial exclusion, aggressiveness on foreign policy, and conservatism in social policy. That he did not suggests something about his support for the basic principles of the civil rights struggle.[5]

Jackson's political activism accelerated as labor leaders, civil rights proponents, as well as liberals on both sides of the Mason-Dixon Line struggled to capitalize on the political opportunities generated by the war. No agency was more important in connecting working-class organizations and racial amelioration than the Congress of Industrial Organizations (CIO). Having announced its unalterable opposition to racial discrimination in 1938, the CIO organized over four hundred thousand black and white workers throughout the South by the end of the war.[6]

Although the CIO sponsored segregated locals, it deliberately sought to include blacks in the organization and mobilize them alongside white workers in the drive for political influence. In some cases, it departed dramatically from southern social conventions. According to Carey Haigler, regional director of the CIO, the "dire forebodings" of those who wanted to maintain racial separation had not prevented black and white workers from cooperating on an equal footing in the local unions. Haigler was amazed by the willingness of white workers in one Alabama union to sit "of their own volition" in the same section as black workers: "It was hard for me to believe . . . that there were places in the Deep South where the two races lived in peace and harmony."[7] Unlike the NAACP, which white southerners disparaged as an agency of outside political agitation, the CIO could present itself as a voice of the southern working class and of liberal reform, a tradition stretching back to Jefferson and Madison. Jackson considered the CIO the leading opponent of racial exclusion in the South. During the war, he observed, the CIO "flouted the notion of white supremacy and, as far South as Birmingham, demanded that Negro workers be given a square deal."[8] CIO organizer Lucy Randolph Mason—a scion of the Virginia aristocracy and a tenacious advocate of working-class organization— marveled at the degree of racial cooperation in CIO unions throughout the region. Lamenting Agrarian poet Donald Davidson's racial conservatism, Mason commented that if he could accompany her to union meetings "where white and Negro workers sit together in meetings that provide a common ground for working out economic problems . . . forgetting to what race they belonged and sharing ideas and economic strength through union solidarity," he might abandon his retrograde notions about blacks.[9] Mason also poignantly captured the larger significance of the CIO's efforts in the South: "We need in the South to develop a South-wide movement, founded on labor, chiefly the CIO, and drawing to itself all the liberal forces that have courage to fight for democracy—democracy at home."[10] For Mason, Jackson, and liberals scattered throughout the South, the CIO organizing initiative represented an assault on the entire tradition of southern political and economic isolation. It offered the first genuine opportunity since the populist movement to cultivate a racially egalitarian, working-class democracy in the South.

The CIO pursued a strategy of political mobilization through its Political Action Committee (PAC). Established in 1943, the CIO-PAC coordinated the activities of local unions, state industrial groups, civil rights organizers, and liberals in the movement to wrench power from southern conservative and Republican opponents of the New Deal. The CIO-PAC focused on voter instruction and registration, activities that immediately appealed to Luther Jackson. Through its National Citizens Political Action Committee, designed to attract non-CIO supporters, the organization forged bonds with powerful elites in the nation's capital and other urban centers. The CIO also linked arms with leading liberal organizations in the region, the most important of which was the Southern Conference for Human Welfare (SCHW), an organization committed to dismantling economic injustice and political exclusion in the region. The SCHW distinguished itself by pursuing a progressive agenda focused on racial egalitarianism and the principles of the New Deal. In 1944, SCHW executives Clark Foreman and James Dombrowksi drafted a plan for the political revitalization of the region that called for financial support from the CIO. Through the efforts of Mason, Dombrowksi, and Palmer Weber of the CIO-PAC, the Southern Conference gained the official endorsement of the CIO in December 1944. The laying on of hands brought a financial reward as well: the CIO promised $35,000 to the SCHW to support the union in its drive to eliminate the poll tax and expand the electorate in the South. The concerted voter mobilization efforts of the CIO, SCHW, NAACP, and groups such as Jackson's Virginia Voters League, coupled with the ending of the white primary in 1944, produced monumental gains in black voting. In 1940, approximately two hundred thousand African Americans were registered to vote; in 1946, that number had tripled. That year, the CIO launched "Operation Dixie," an organizing initiative designed to strengthen southern unionism against an alliance of increasingly belligerent corporate managers and government leaders. In the context of growing political conservatism and hostility to labor unions, aggravated by a mass of paralyzing strikes in 1946, CIO organizers in the South had little interest in connecting a southern membership drive to wider questions of social justice. Although the CIO focused its energies on white workers in the textile industry—overlooking such sectors as lumbering, tobacco processing, and chemical manufacturing where the majority of African Americans worked —its campaign threatened the established order. By mobilizing even a fraction of the region's black industrial workers, Operation Dixie challenged the foundations of southern economic colonialism while fueling the growing civil rights movement.[11]

The CIO and the SCHW formed a mutually beneficial relationship that reached well beyond the Deep South and into Jackson's Virginia, where liberal elements challenged the Democratic oligarchy. In April 1945, the Virginia CIO Council followed national policy by creating a political action committee that fused local unions to liberal and labor reform groups throughout the state. The committee would achieve this broad appeal by purging the "CIO" from its label and flying under the flag of the "Virginia Citizens Political Action Committee" (VCPAC), a decision that reflected the growing antipathy of middle-class Americans toward union activism in the 1940s. Director Robert Johnson appealed to James Dombrowski, executive secretary of the SCHW, for financial assistance in the enterprise, assuring him that "[s]everal groups have already indicated their desire to become a part of such a movement." Johnson was specific: he wanted the Southern Conference to redirect the two thousand dollars they were considering for the Committee of 100—an ineffectual group of Virginia liberal elites—to the VCPAC. Through Virginia CIO president Boyd E. Payton, who had been in contact with the prominent organization, he had already learned of SCHW's interest in funding a political action group with connections to "a labor foundation." Johnson had reason to expect assistance: the CIO was SCHW's major contributor, and financial support would amount to a quid pro quo. Johnson's expectations were confirmed: the SCHW would send a monthly check of two hundred dollars for a year in return for a mailing list of VCPAC members who would receive the *Southern Patriot,* the Southern Conference's monthly publication. Just as Jackson's Voters League worked interdependently with the NAACP, the Southern Conference sought to maximize support and exposure through the political action committees it supported. For a brief period, these organizational networks provided circuits for the exchange of resources and ideas in the southern liberal reform movement.[12]

Jackson joined the VCPAC that year, paying the one-dollar fee to support an organization determined to "defeat the reactionary forces which threaten the existence of our American way of life."[13] The VCPAC was serious about building a coalition of liberal groups that included African Americans committed to voting and political change. Johnson appealed to Jackson to join the Richmond branch of the Political Action Committee and then recruited him along with other leading liberal figures onto the executive board of the VCPAC. Johnson's invitation was anything but random. As he explained to chairman Boyd Payton, the selection of Jackson reflected his stature in social reform circles: "Dr. Jackson, needless to say, is a very able man and has his finger on the Negro voting population in Virginia. He is an outstanding figure among his people and his opinions are respected." Jackson's connections to multiple civil rights groups and activists throughout the state represented a valuable asset for the VCPAC. He joined other liberal activists—including Brownie Lee Jones of the Southern School for Workers, Elizabeth Steptoe, a vigorous opponent of the Byrd organization, and lawyer Moss Plunkett—in bolstering local representation and diversity on the committee's executive.[14]

Jackson immediately launched into doing what he did best: generating support for reform through personal contact and persistent correspondence. At his first board meeting, he offered to contact organizations and individuals throughout the state who he believed might support the VCPAC.[15] He transplanted the idea of the voting qualifications booklet to the VCPAC, winning support for its distribution to union members and supporters throughout the state. The New Deal ethos of labor activism had rejuvenated the economic consciousness that Jackson first outlined in his 1937 article "Citizenship and Government Participation." He supported an increase to the minimum wage and lent his support through the *Journal and Guide* to fellow board member Brownie Lee Jones in her effort to rally Richmond workers to political action. His growing commitment to social democracy was already evident in 1944, when he endorsed Roosevelt as the candidate not simply for African Americans but for "common people" in their struggle to achieve higher wages, better schools, improved housing, social insurance, old age pensions, and collective bargaining rights. The VCPAC provided Jackson the organizational space in which he extended his understanding of the relationship between black civil rights, economic issues, and social reform. No doubt SCHW and other reform initiatives encouraged other African American activists to grasp the common interests uniting middle-class professionals and a biracial working class.[16]

But Jackson's evolving social consciousness had less to do with reflection than with the sense of crisis that pervaded the VCPAC in 1946. The organization confronted the formidable opposition of the Senator Harry Byrd machine, growing nationwide hostility toward organized labor, and divisiveness within the ranks of liberal reformers. At a meeting of the VCPAC in November 1945, State CIO Director Charles Webber spelled out the grim prospects for reform in Virginia. According to the recorder of the minutes, Webber believed that "we are in very deep trouble both state-wide and nationally." The House and Senate committees were stonewalling legislation, including anti-poll-tax measures, while the president failed to educate the public and lead the battle on Capitol Hill. Leading corporations were refusing to cooperate in plans for postwar reconstruction or in collective bargaining. No less disturbing, the president was apparently abandoning Roosevelt's conciliatory policies toward the Soviet Union. While an atmosphere of antilabor, Cold War militancy settled over the national scene, Virginia persisted in Pleistocene-era conservatism. "We have a straight rotten corrupt situation in every county in Virginia," Webber exclaimed. "The whole system of morality in Virginia is gone today." The central problem was the Byrd machine and its county ring, which thrived on a poll-tax system that severely restricted the state's electorate. Byrd controlled seventy county rings and conducted business as a "native fascist" and a "dishonest person." Webber appealed to the board members to field liberal candidates in the upcoming congressional elections and to "get the mass vote." He also believed, somewhat naively, that a letter-writing campaign might convince senators to vote for cloture on a pending anti-poll-tax bill, a measure that southern senators had consistently obstructed through interminable filibusters.[17]

But the political situation in Virginia was more complicated, as Elizabeth Steptoe pointed out. Senators Byrd and Carter Glass had the support of the major corporations, particularly Du Pont, and they exercised considerable influence over the major papers. Moss Plunkett identified popular lethargy and the ineffectiveness of the CIO, the AFL, and the Railroad Brotherhoods as the major factors preventing the formation of a united liberal front. Few liberals were ready to go into debt on what seemed like a quixotic assault against the Byrd machine. Even worse, the Republicans were now moving into the Byrd camp. Plunkett identified the NAACP as the best organized vehicle for challenging the Byrd oligarchy; Jackson agreed that the "Negroes are aroused, but not active enough." Black political activity held the key to turning the tide against the status quo in Virginia, which Jackson had known for some time.[18]

Webber's analysis was not inaccurate, nor for that matter were Steptoe,

Plunkett, or Jackson exaggerating the realities of the political landscape in Virginia. As political scientist V. O. Key explained, the Byrd machine conducted itself as an oligarchy reminiscent of nineteenth-century political machines and eighteenth-century Virginia aristocracy. Senator Byrd maintained party cohesion through efficient administration and a strictly circumscribed electorate. Between 1925 and 1945, only 11.5 percent of eligible voters cast a ballot in the state's Democratic primaries, the only elections that counted in the one-party South. Contemporary historians may wish to remember Virginia as a relatively progressive border state that remained on the margins of the civil rights movement, but Key reminds us that a "smaller proportion of Virginia's potential electorate voted for governor" than in any other state of the South. The machine exercised power through close supervision of the counties and cities. Its compensation board regulated the flow of money paid out to county officials; its circuit judges, selected by a Byrd-controlled General Assembly, determined the members of the electoral board that governed local elections; its clerks of the circuit court exercised near-autocratic control over county organizations. And in Virginia, corporations replaced rural planters as the economic interests most closely allied with political insiders. As Key explained, "The quid pro quo for support of the organization is said to be taxation favorable to corporations, an anti-labor policy, and restraint in the expansion of services, such as education, public health, and welfare." The policy of low-wage, paternalistic, anti-union conservatism prevalent throughout the South persisted in Virginia, militating against groups like the VCPAC that sought to institutionalize New Deal liberalism.[19]

The liberal forces that rallied around VCPAC had already challenged the Byrd machine, supporting the candidacy of board member Moss A. Plunkett in his run for the governorship in 1945. Plunkett, an ally of Jackson's in the struggle to repeal the poll tax, took up the political cudgels while serving as chairman of the Roanoke County School Board. From that vantage point Plunkett observed the Byrd organization's negligible concern for public education, not to mention public welfare. He had already made an unsuccessful bid for the lieutenant governorship in 1941. In 1945, he spent $50,000 of his own money in an effort to break the organization stranglehold. Grasping the rhetorical amulet offered by the war, Plunkett announced: "The central issue in this campaign is simple: Shall we continue to be ruled by a small political 'machine' with its silent, invisible government, or shall we establish in Virginia that democracy for which we claim to be fighting in this War?" Not surprisingly, organization candidate

William M. Tuck won the governorship, but Plunkett had earned the support of liberal and labor groups throughout the state. According to Plunkett, the NAACP—and quite certainly Jackson, operating through the association as well as the Virginia Voters League—delivered 25,000 votes to his candidacy, while 90 percent of the CIO and 47 percent of voters in Richmond cast a ballot for Plunkett. Leading the anti-organization forces were the areas where Jackson's voters' leagues, teachers' groups, and NAACP liaisons were the strongest. In the counties stretching from Richmond to Norfolk and the tidewater communities, Plunkett polled strongly. In Jackson's own Chesterfield County, as well as in Henrico, Prince George, Hopewell, Norfolk, Portsmouth and Newport News—areas covered by the *Journal and Guide* and by his extensive network of communications—the lawyer from Roanoke did extremely well. In industrial centers such as Norfolk, black and white workers turned out for Plunkett. In Petersburg alone, 44 percent voted for Plunkett. The campaign failed to dislodge the organization, but it reflected the growing momentum behind a liberal-labor coalition supported and in many cases led by African Americans such as Luther Jackson.[20]

Jackson supported Plunkett and the VCPAC, but in 1945 he was still devoting most of his time to the Virginia Voters League, to writing for the *Journal and Guide,* and to pushing the teachers ahead in the drive for registration and civic instruction. He also continued to maintain a full teaching load that included Saturday classes and summer courses while sustaining his scholarship and support for the ASNLH.

As the VCPAC metamorphosed into an extension of the Southern Conference for Human Welfare, Jackson's association grew stronger. In December 1945, not even a year after the VCPAC's founding, CIO headquarters decided to separate its political activities from those of non-union liberals. According to Jack Kroll, national director of the CIO-PAC following Sidney Hillman, organization leaders discovered during the election of 1945 that the National Citizens Committee "would not quite click." Presumably Kroll meant that the close connection between the CIO and the political action committee had alienated potential supporters and inhibited the liberal-Democratic campaign. As V. O. Key noted about the 1946 campaign, the "CIO-PAC often works undercover, for it realizes that its public endorsement may be the kiss of death to a candidate." But Kroll also argued that liberal and CIO entanglement encouraged insularity and redundancy since "CIO Representatives are out talking with progressives and liberals." Kroll noted that during the election the SCHW had become the spearhead of liberals in the South; the organization believed that an independent, progressive group would reach a wider spectrum of voters sympathetic to the democratic principles that the CIO championed.[21]

Clark Foreman of the SCHW agreed, notifying the VCPAC board that the Southern Conference would support a committee in Virginia. The Southern Conference had already set the precedent for state committees in Georgia, Alabama, and South Carolina. The liberal ferment and the reduced restrictions on voting in the state made Virginia appealing to the Southern Conference. The organizational framework provided by the VCPAC was also ideally suited to its objectives. Since the Southern Conference was moving aggressively in the direction of eliminating racial barriers and promoting black political engagement throughout the South, Virginia soil seemed fertile for change, tilled as it was by the NAACP, the Virginia Voters League, and the labor interests that coalesced around Moss Plunkett. Liberals needed to combine the energies of diverse reform groups while minimizing accusations of outside agitation. Jackson and others found that in the SCHW they had an organization that looked and sounded distinctively southern.

For their part, the SCHW executive believed that Luther Jackson was the ideal candidate. The organization wanted to hire a field representative to travel throughout the region and present the Southern Conference's message to the NAACP, the Urban League, businesses, professional organizations, and churches. More than propagating the Southern Conference's ideas, the field representative would activate potential voters and encourage them to support legislation directed at social and political reform. Jackson was a natural choice, even before the demise of the VCPAC. "Your work with the Virginia Voters League would be especially valuable and your achievements there would no doubt be heard with great interest," Dombrowksi wrote to Jackson. No less important, Jackson's example and leadership "would serve as a stimulus for political action elsewhere." By 1945, then, Jackson had become a figure of regional significance. His reputation for organization building and resourcefulness in advancing political revitalization had earned him the recognition of political reformers tied to national circles. As much as the opportunity appealed to him, he could not abandon Virginia State for a life on the road. He was certainly intrigued, discussing the issue in phone conversations with James Dombrowski and letters to Clark Foreman. The salary of $4,000 appealed to him, but Jackson wanted to know if the offer included travel expenses, since he was already earning $3,600 over a nine-month period. He was thinking of more than the salary; he was also concerned about the impact that extensive travel would have on a family already burdened by his persistent absences. In addition to his responsibility for a wife and four children, Jackson was particularly concerned about his daughter, Laura Frances, who "had been a great care on us for the past six years subject as she is to periods of emotional instability." His son Luther Jr. was "a member of the armed forces and is situated somewhere in the West Pacific at present." Although the position would give him "a wider field of responsibility and action," he had "family responsibilities of a varied character which I must consider in a venture of this sort." He also realized that Virginia State provided a base of operations and a hospitable environment for his political activism. The offer was a chance of a lifetime—to expand his reach, to foster political awareness, to usher in the changes that he had been struggling for over the past ten years—and he walked away from it, probably believing that his family and his academic career would not stand the strain.[22]

Jackson declined the SCHW, and South Carolina activist and nightclub owner Osceola McKaine accepted, becoming a dynamic promoter of the Southern Conference throughout the South. The offer had been a turning point for Jackson. Instead of regionwide responsibility, Jackson chose to focus his energies on Virginia, the place where he had spent the last fifteen years cultivating political awareness and civic responsibility. He chose to orchestrate civil rights initiatives tied to the larger movement but anchored in local participation. If anything, he became more deeply involved in the SCHW and its objectives.

Again, Jackson stepped to the forefront, mobilizing a wide variety of activists to sponsor the SCHW in Virginia. The reform network that Jackson had been building since 1935 provided the infrastructure for the most aggressive social reform movement in the South since the 1890s. To sponsor the group, Jackson appealed to insurance salesman Jewel Carrington, a "vigorous leader for voting in the black belt of Virginia"; to Reverend J. B. Henderson, "one of the leading ministers in the state for voting"; to Martin A. Martin, NAACP lawyer and critical figure in the salary equalization struggle; as well as to teacher activists J. Rupert Picott and Lutrelle F. Palmer. Jackson assured Foreman that they could win the support of more than five hundred African Americans for the new organization. Relying on his strategy for the Virginia Teachers Association, he planned a number of regional conferences to promote voter registration for the following year's primaries. The Virginia Teachers Association's voter education program would deliver votes to the movement. "I want you to know that I am extremely happy over the possibility of the organization of a Virginia committee of the Southern Conference for Human Welfare," Jackson ebulliently wrote to Foreman.[23]

Nearly one hundred Virginia liberals met at a YMCA in Richmond in January 1946 to launch the Committee for Virginia. Instead of the narrow interest groups that would dominate American politics after the 1970s, the committee represented the effort to "bring together all people in Virginia who believe in progressive democratic government." Even so, the organization operated on the timeworn assumption that social reform required the leadership of respectable middle-class elites. With a thousand dollars from the SCHW, the committee set out on a program of political education and voter registration. The Committee for Virginia now included such notables as Virginia Beecher, the group's executive secretary and vigorous civil rights advocate; Vivian Carter Mason, executive director of the National Council of Negro Women; Virginia Foster Durr, vice-chairman for the committee and sister-in-law of Supreme Court Justice Hugo Black; and P.B. Young, Jackson's long-time associate and publisher of the *Norfolk Journal and Guide*. It also included Jackson in the prominent position of vice-chairman. Interracial cooperation was nothing new to the South, but this was more than polite seminars on the "Negro problem." African Americans and women took leading roles in the organization, cooperating with liberals of the white middle class in a program of voter registration for political change. Now the key was to mobilize blacks and whites outside of the middle class.[24]

By June 1946, Jackson was reporting that the registration campaign was "shaping satisfactorily." He appointed a director for each of the counties and two cities in which the committee was focusing its activity. Form letters, pamphlets, analyses of Senator Byrd's voting pattern, and the platforms of liberal candidates circulated throughout the fledgling network of committee supporters. To transmit the message and organize voters at the county level, Jackson recruited Rufus Smith from the New York office of the NAACP and Eddie Lee of the Negro Organization Society (NOS). J. M. Tinsley, president of the Virginia State Conference, helped organize the registration drives while the NOS contributed financial assistance. Smith proved particularly helpful to the professor, traveling to nearly twelve counties and assisting local activists to increase the rolls of registered voters.[25] Characteristically, Jackson also went on the road for the Southern Conference, meeting Smith at Farmville, making arrangements to transport voters to the polling stations for the election, and delivering a lecture on the benefits of voting. Jackson's connections to local activists were particularly important to the committee. He was able to assess developments in the counties, evaluate the effectiveness of political organizers, and advise the SCHW on where it could maximize its financial support. Commenting on voting rights work in Prince Edward County, Jackson asserted that "the leaders there have done a commendable amount of preliminary work so that all in all the money spent in this county will pay greater dividends than in Buckingham." Plunkett also joined the ranks of traveling voting activists, appearing before African American audiences at Gloucester and Lawrenceville. Following his voting strategy for the Virginia Voters League and the Virginia Teachers Association, Jackson funneled literature onto the Virginia State campus and into the hands of sympathetic faculty members.[26]

In addition to voter registration, the committee participated in large meetings that reflected the increasingly militant, working-class character of the movement. Jackson urged Beecher to join him and Plunkett in attending a mass meeting in Suffolk where the Independent Voting League had recently registered as many as two hundred black voters. The meeting at Suffolk was particularly momentous for the SCHW, Jackson reasoned, since the Independent Voters League was "endeavouring to proceed on a biracial basis—on a basis of the common suffering of the laboring masses of whites and Negroes." Whites would be invited to attend the meeting at the Tynes Street Baptist Church, where "there will be no separate seating of the races."[27]

The city of Suffolk in Nansemond County offered a conspicuous example of the political awakening in the Black Belt South, the geographical stronghold of the region's traditional elite. In rural Virginia, the Byrd machine thrived on voting restrictions and the loyalty of party regulars. In Suffolk, as in areas throughout the South in 1946, labor unionists of both races cooperated in promoting political action. Jackson reported that Moses Riddick, a graduate of Hampton, "has moved out into the country where he has contacted all the registrars, made engagements with them, and carried loads of his fellow citizens to these officials."[28] Riddick benefited from the assistance of John C. Hunt, the white leader of the Amalgamated Local of the CIO. As Jackson explained to Beecher, Hunt had made himself "persona nongrata [sic] with A.F. of L. because of his labor views" and had fled Georgia and Tennessee for the comparatively hospitable racial climate of Virginia.[29] After a voter registration drive that had started only three months earlier, local activists could count almost two thousand people who had paid their poll tax and as many as one thousand who had registered out of a total population of approximately ten thousand African Americans. To Jackson, the efforts of the Independent Voters League's Leroy

Harris and Moses Riddick and of the CIO's John Hunt—which, according to the professor, had directly resulted in the registration of four hundred voters—offered the evidence of a developing social realignment. Jackson was ebullient, announcing that "[s]omebody in Suffolk has aroused the people of this city and county from their long sleep of many years." The hope lay in a forceful challenge to the Byrd machine in the upcoming primary.[30]

Anti-organization activists threw their support to Richmond lawyer Martin A. Hutchinson, a state capital employee who earned a law degree at night school. While Hutchinson offered Virginia liberals a choice for governor, African American candidates challenged elite rule at the city council level in Charlottesville, Norfolk, Danville, and Lynchburg, generating considerable political enthusiasm and participation among black voters.[31] For the first time in twenty-four years, the Virginia electorate would have a choice in the senatorial primary. The Committee for Virginia turned up the rhetorical heat over the summer, casting Byrd in the "negative" role of New Deal obstructionist and Hutchinson as the torchbearer for the Roosevelt administration's "creative ideas." Hutchinson may not have been the committee's ideal candidate, but he subscribed to the Keynesian fiscal principles that had found a home in New Deal policymaking. Hutchinson supported subsidies to farmers, federal aid to education, public housing initiatives—in short, the notion that "the spending of money by government produces those very products from which more wealth and more money can be derived." What unfolded in 1946 was less a struggle for the political inside than it was an ideological contest over the character of American public life. "Faced with two philosophies of government," Executive Secretary Virginia Beecher warned supporters, citizens were obligated to "make our own decision" by voting rather than "letting an efficient irresponsible organized political machine do it for us." Responding to criticism that the committee had sullied itself by explicit partisanship, Beecher insisted: "We feel that . . . when the average citizen and citizens' organizations take a fuller and more active share in the choice and election of politicians based on the politicians' relation to a social program in which they believe, then these citizens . . . are waking up to the responsibility absolutely inherent in and necessary for true democratic government." The Committee for Virginia advocated a form of participatory government that Cold War conservatism would banish but that New Left and civil rights activists would revive in the Kennedy era.[32]

Jackson adopted Beecher's sense of urgency, propelled by the prospect of a competitive election and the belief that liberal white support represented a turning point in the movement. SCHW organizer Osceola McKaine congratulated Jackson for "givin' 'em hell" through his column in the *Journal and Guide*. Jackson consistently believed that a sympathetic white middle class was at least as important as a conscious black electorate for dismantling racial inequality. His work with the Southern Regional Council, his effort to distribute voting surveys and black history to white educators and politicians, and his readiness to cooperate with influential whites including Moss Plunkett and Virginius Dabney exemplified his belief in the efficacy of a biracial coalition. Dabney, the editor of the *Richmond Times-Dispatch,* was an ambivalent liberal who at one time cautioned black activists against demanding immediate change and at another advocated for an end to segregation on Richmond's streetcars and buses. What Dabney never repudiated was the idea that the better class of whites should govern the pace and extent of racial change. When Jackson sought an outlet for his paper "Virginia and Civil Rights," which he had delivered to the Virginia Social Sciences Association at the University of Virginia in April 1949, Dabney's assistant editor declined on his behalf, citing the "present tension in race relations" that would prevent Jackson's article from finding "an entirely understanding audience."[33] Yet it was to these conditional liberals that Jackson and other black progressives appealed. Only they offered the hope that the white southern mind might be susceptible to reason, might be less intransigent than the weight of southern history and their own experience suggested. The advent of the Southern Conference for Human Welfare, the Southern Regional Council, and a phalanx of enlightened newspaper editors across the region confirmed the fracturing of the Solid South. Jackson applauded the "Silent South" for challenging the region's archaic political traditions by demanding the renewal of the Fair Employment Practices Commission against the virulent opposition of demagogues such as Theodore Bilbo, James O. Eastland, and John Rankin in 1945. The next year—the "year of opportunity"—Jackson extolled the CIO and the AF of L for bringing "division in the ranks of the former Solid South." These organizations, "which draw no color line in their efforts to defeat their enemies at the polls," provided battering rams against the walls of racial exclusion and political torpor. Thinking as a historian, he argued that the past offered the evidence that "whenever Southern white folk have divided among themselves, then the Negroes have had their day in court." The Readjuster movement in Virginia in the 1880s, the populist movement in the 1890s, and the organized labor drive of the New Deal era created the opportunities for African Americans to dismantle the southern racial caste system. Encasing his vision of racial change in a larger program of social reform—one that reflected the ethos of New Deal liberalism—Jackson asked black voters to scrutinize their congressional representatives' positions on a sixty-five-cent minimum wage, on federal aid to education, on a permanent FEPC, and on the poll tax. The question was not only racial liberalism but also whether a given congressman believed "in the principles of the late F. D. Roosevelt." It was a year of opportunity for African Americans, but it was also a chance to make elected leaders accountable for a quarter-century of obstructing "progressive measures" that were "designed to improve the lot of the poor man." By 1946, Jackson and most black progressives believed that the interests of the SCHW, the NAACP, organized labor, and African Americans had converged.[34]

Evidently the Byrd forces thought the same, responding to what seemed like a biracial, working-class front with traditional southern defensiveness. Byrd vilified the CIO-PAC as the "most sinister organization in the nation" and pointed to recent railroad and coal strikes as evidence that a "few powerful labor leaders" were determined to "halt democracy in its operation." Attorney General Watkins M. Abbitt was even more rhetorically resourceful, raising the specter of "carpetbaggers" descending on a helpless South. According to Abbitt, outside agitators once again threatened regional harmony: "The question now is, are the Democratic voters of Virginia going to allow these non-Virginians, self-appointed would-be dictators to invade our State, take over the electorate, throw out an able, well-trained, industrious, courageous public servant" and allow themselves to be "subservient to the will of a selfish minority pressure group?" For party regulars the answer was no, but many others dismissed the inflammatory rhetoric and identified the real issues at stake. Virginia was not threatened by "Communist domination," one reader of the *Richmond Times-Dispatch* explained, since the CIO was composed of "ordinary, hard-working citizens, practically all of whom are native born" and many of whom were veterans of every conflict from the American Revolution to World War II. CIO members came from the ranks of those living under "industrial serfdom" until the passage of the National Recovery Act and the National Labor Relations Act, both of which Byrd opposed. Another writer noted that Byrd's drift toward the Republicans in their opposition to the New Deal disqualified him as a Democrat. Condemning the "Nazis in the South," one commentator called on Virginians to lead "her neighboring Southern States out of the dark ages" by turning out to vote in strength against the "reactionary, Fascist tending politicians" that plagued the region. The opposition was never as united as the Byrd forces suggested, but it had found a political voice, one that disturbed the status quo in postwar Virginia.[35]

The campaign also forced Jackson to confront the limits of political activism for a professor at a public black college. It was one thing to be politically conspicuous, and another to be associated with an organization explicitly committed to purging the Byrd gang from power. Unlike the NAACP and the Virginia Voters League, the Committee for Virginia was a partisan operation and an adversary of the Virginia machine. It functioned as the extension of a region-wide political action committee with ties to organized labor and a membership that included a handful of communists and fellow travelers. Osceola McKaine understood the bind in which Jackson found himself. In selecting a coordinator to work full time on black political mobilization for the Committee for Virginia, McKaine chose Edgar Holt of Newport News, "just the type of person who would say the things you want said but which for certain reasons you cannot say."[36]

These "certain reasons" produced a firestorm of controversy when executive secretary Virginia Beecher publicized Jackson's position on the committee through an advertisement that assailed the Byrd machine and endorsed Hutchinson. Beecher soon wrote to Jackson, apologizing for "having exposed you to such a painful experience."[37] In an effort to defuse friction arising from his connection to the controversial left-wing group, and as part of a deal to keep his job after Byrd operatives tried to pressure Virginia State to dismiss him, Jackson wrote a letter to the *Times-Dispatch* praising Byrd's gubernatorial support of an antilynching law.[38] He contrasted Byrd's humanitarianism with the obstructionism of demagogues Eugene Talmadge and Theodore Bilbo. On the one hand, Jackson's letter echoed the moral indignation of those who condemned the reelection of the virulently racist Eugene Talmadge during a campaign of political violence that killed at least twelve people in July and August alone. The orgiastic violence culminated in the murder of four people, two men and two women, in Monroe, Georgia, on July 25, less than two weeks before the *Times-Dispatch* letter. As historian John Egerton explains, the rash of killings and brutalities in the South during the summer of 1946 was "fuelled by white fears that black veterans might become a revolutionary force, and that blacks in general would no longer stay 'in their place.'" At the same time, though, Jackson warmly applauded Byrd for having "performed so courageously as one of the most aggressive" opponents of lynching. He intimated support for Byrd's reelection by suggesting that voters "must now be grateful" for the Senator's stand on the issue. Jackson must have been additionally embarrassed to read a vigorous anti-organization letter, juxtaposed to his own, asking "Has Byrd fathered a major piece of progressive legislation in State or nation?" The public appeasement was not a particularly proud moment.[39]

Although the evidence is fragmentary, the letter was apparently a response to pressure from the administration, which in turn felt the heat from the Democratic power brokers in Richmond. Osceola McKaine seemed to confirm as much, consoling Jackson for the letter and assuring him that others understood that it was "the result of pressure." Jackson had been scorched by his proximity to the radical SCHW, and he would have to be cautious in the future. Thanking McKaine for his support during the two-week ordeal in August, Jackson admitted that as a state employee he would have to "guard against . . . involvement in partisan politics." Playing down the administrative censure, Jackson insisted that he benefited from a "liberal administration" at the college and said that it was in the effort to "save it from embarrassment that I wrote the letter in the Times-Dispatch."

Although the liberalism of Virginia State may have been in question, Jackson's position with the committee was not. He resigned from the board but maintained his commitment to it, working in an unofficial capacity to mobilize resources and supporters for the committee. As Jackson tellingly explained to board member Virginia Foster Durr:

> Kindly remember that my status with the Committee for Virginia is that of a mere member. In other words, if and when the group starts a fight on the governor of the state or on any of the top men in the Byrd machine, my name must not appear on any document or letter head. The situation might be a little different if more discretion had been exercised last summer. However, I am still glad to be of some service to the organization.[40]

Virginia Durr assured Jackson that she would not publicize Jackson's connection to the organization and would "be discreet myself in speaking of it," although the promise would be difficult to keep considering that Jackson had "done so much" for the group.[41]

Having criticized teachers for lack of political involvement, behavior that reflected their precarious position within a white-dominated education system, Jackson now found himself having to choose between career and political agitation. O. E. McKaine counseled Jackson on his predicament: "It is much better to keep you at Virginia State where you can still have access to the minds of our young people than have you lose that position and the opportunity it brings by not bending just a little bit."[42] Bend is precisely what Jackson did, beating a strategic retreat by resigning from the committee but continuing his support through energetic fund-raising and voting rights education. The episode illustrated the dilemma that African American educators active in the civil rights movement faced throughout the 1950s and 1960s. Schools offered valuable avenues of political instruction and sanctuaries for social criticism, but the very fecundity of political thought behind the ivy walls could make them targets of white hostility when thought became action. Jackson found himself under scrutiny at precisely the time that the movement became more vibrant, more progressive, and most threatening. The need to alternate between political activist and retiring, innocuous professor became even more urgent in the wake of the Committee for Virginia fiasco.[43]

The Committee for Virginia's exertions and the CIO-PAC were not enough to save the Hutchinson campaign. Bereft of financial support and facing an organization that denied opponents a foothold at the local level, Hutchinson went down to a predictable defeat in 1946. Despite the results and the low voter turnout, Jackson focused on the positive. In the city of Suffolk and in Nansemond County—where Moses Riddick, John C. Hunt, and James Lawrence had expended extraordinary energy in voter education, the same place where the NAACP, the Elks, a CIO local, and area ministers had cooperated in mobilizing citizens—the voting turnout was the largest in the past forty-five years. Almost a thousand voters had been awakened, and in three of the twelve precincts blacks cast more ballots than whites. As Jackson exulted in a letter to McKaine, "Hutchinson lost but he gave the machine a great scare." He won eight of twenty-four cities and "lost by a narrow margin in most of the other cities." Typically, the cities registered the strongest anti-organization sentiment; in the rural areas, for the most part, the Byrd machine operated smoothly.[44]

Although Jackson admitted that Virginia was "the deadest state in the union" on voter participation, he—along with civil rights activists and political reformers throughout the South—had good reason to celebrate developments in 1946. In Virginia, only 7 percent of eligible voters had met the qualifications in 1940; by 1946, 12 percent or 48,448 people had qualified to vote. The changes were not astronomical, but in a state that placed last among southern states in voter turnout for the Democratic primaries in 1937 and 1944, the improvement in black voting represented sizeable improvement. Though the Byrd organization was still able to ignore them, black Virginians were becoming active in a political culture rooted in elite control, aristocratic entitlement, and electoral suffocation. The *Times-Dispatch* blamed the "appalling political apathy" of Virginians on machine control and the limited number of directly elected offices. Jackson, in examining black voters, blamed inaction on a tradition of black political proscription. The notion that politics was the exclusive preserve of whites, and that the poll tax was a part of the rational order, pervaded the political atmosphere as strongly as magnolias in springtime. Noncompetitive elections combined with a tradition of biracial political exclusion produced an electorate that was, in every sense of the term, disfranchised. In this climate, the near doubling of black voters from 25,411 in 1941 to 48,448 in 1946 meant something.[45]

What seemed like glacial changes in the political landscape of Virginia appeared otherwise against the backdrop of developments throughout the South. In the position of field representative for the SCHW—the job that Jackson had turned down—Osceola McKaine witnessed the surging strength of black political consciousness across the region. Organizing voter education and registration initiatives in each southern state that year, McKaine discovered that "the Negro masses are demanding militant action, a complete break-away from the old methods." The black working class was beginning to make the connection between employment opportunities, school facilities, public services, and political action. They were internalizing the message that Luther Jackson had been advocating since 1937. This "progressive attitude," this "political sensitivity" was bridging the distance between African American intellectuals and the working class, a process simultaneously encouraging black leaders to greater levels of "boldness and courage." What McKaine described was Jackson's own ideological transformation, as escalating black militancy "moved forward and to the left of center those Negro leaders wedded to the old order." Jackson had never been the hat-in-hand supplicant that McKaine portrayed as the typical "upper-crust" African American, but he tended to subordinate economic issues in the quest for political inclusion. Now Jackson was breaking away from the middle-class perspective and was emphasizing working-class interests in a broader program for social and economic reform. Now political action became more than a vehicle for acquiring improved public services; it was the weapon for achieving social justice across the racial spectrum. Jackson never lost his focus on black civil rights; he did not follow Du Bois or Robeson or Ralph Bunche in advocating a radical restructuring of American society. But he did believe that biracial political action could produce a social order cleansed of inequality and economic oppression.[46]

Equally promising was the fact that black candidates had entered the field and were activating black voters in a way that Hutchinson or Plunkett never could. Throughout the 1940s, African American hopefuls ran for city council positions in Richmond, Roanoke, Charlottesville, and Norfolk. Establishing alliances with progressive whites and organized workers, black political candidates tried to capitalize on the political opportunities that the postwar era presented. Attorney Oliver Hill came close to winning a primary for the Virginia House of Delegates in 1947, and William Lawrence did win a position on the Nansemond County Board of Supervisors, breaking the white monopoly on political office that had persisted since the Gilded Age. Supported by the Independent Voters League (IVL), local union organizers, and the NAACP—which in Suffolk counted 534 members—Lawrence excited the political hopes of blacks in this working-class district. He also captured the attention of local whites, who had become decidedly uneasy about the prospect of black political influence. While the White Voters Club of Suffolk and Nansemond County appealed to whites to stop the black and communist menace at the ballot box, more sinister elements expressed their displeasure by burning a cross at the intersection of the county's key highways. The reminder of genteel Virginia's capacity for racial hatred was, according to the *Journal and Guide,* a response to escalating black political activity in Nansemond County. Ugly displays of intolerance and hysterical appeals for white unity could do little to stop the transformation of blacks into politically active citizens. Transporting black voters to the county hall to register to vote, the Independent Voters League played a critical role in galvanizing support for William Lawrence. In his typically prescient fashion, Luther Jackson submitted that "here in one county in the South are people who have awakened to a sense of their own strength simply by exercising the right of suffrage." By 1948, local activists operating through the Independent Voters League and the NAACP had given Nansemond County the highest number of African Americans registered in any county in Virginia. That year, Oliver Hill also won a seat on the Richmond City Council, a watershed moment for the civil rights movement in Virginia.[47]

The Southern School for Workers provided Jackson another critical channel for promoting voting rights activism and labor organization in the state. The Southern School joined the Committee for Virginia and the CIO-PAC in an expanding network of biracial organizations committed to racial egalitarianism and southern democratization. Like the Highlander Folk School, the Southern School offered workers instruction in political affairs and labor organization, but it also provided adult education to people who had attended little if any elementary school. Eliminating illiteracy was no academic exercise, though. Nonreading workers were nonvoting workers, particularly after Virginia adopted blank forms for voter registration. White workers had been reluctant to attend the Southern School for fear of having to admit to their illiteracy. Jones was convinced that after the 1948 ruling, workers would overcome their insecurities by recognizing that only training would permit them to vote.[48] The Southern School was mobile, offering political instruction to union locals throughout the region. The Southern School attracted the support of leading reformers including Robert Johnson, Lucy Randolph Mason, Virginia Foster Durr, and Lillian Smith, but the leading force behind the school was Brownie Lee Jones, a tenacious political activist and vocal member of Richmond's liberal network. In 1944, Jones, who would serve with Jackson on the Committee for Virginia, recruited the professor to function as an expert at an upcoming Workers' Education Conference on the poll tax. Their association provided a remarkable measurement of how far biracial progressive reform had advanced since the United States went to war.[49]

Jackson became Jones's expert on voting behavior in the state. She relied on his annual voters reports to document the political lethargy of Virginia's workers and inform them of the dramatic progress made in other states. In return, Jones provided him with financial assistance and a wider field of activity for generating black political activism. He featured the school in an article for the *Journal and Guide* and contributed annually to its operation. In recognition of his support, Jones and the board for the Southern School appointed him vice-chairman of the organization. As had the ASNLH, the NAACP, and the SCHW, the Southern School found in Jackson a stalwart fund-raiser and dedicated supporter.[50]

In addition to exposure and advice, Jackson lent the school his services. In July 1948, he addressed a meeting of unionized textile workers, woodworkers, and steelworkers. Jones wanted Jackson to "get these people to actually wake up and do a job politically." She regretted that she would not be able to pay him an honorarium for his work but comforted herself with the assurance that "you are as interested as we are" in promoting working-class political engagement. In late August and early September, Jackson sacrificed his holiday to undertake voter registration field trips for the Southern School. He canvassed Emporia, Franklin, and the Windsor District of Isle of Wight, meeting with labor leaders and workers and inculcating them in the fundamentals of voting. He also met with registrars and reported to Jones on their tolerance of black applicants. He was anguished to find that in Franklin almost two hundred African Americans had paid their poll taxes while only 45 had registered to vote. Determined to correct the imbalance, he collected the names of the 155 nonregistered poll-tax payers, called at some of their homes, held a meeting, and trained local union members to continue the registration work. The work harmonized effortlessly with Jackson's program for political revitalization. "I want you to know that I have enjoyed this job very thoroughly," he wrote to Jones. "It happens to join in perfectly with the program I have been engaged [in] under the banner of the Virginia Voters League." Enthusiastic about the convergence of the two organizations, Jackson decided to subsidize the correspondence of Southern School–related organizations through the Virginia Voters League.[51]

Mutual self-interest brought them together, but mutual respect maintained the alliance. They related as intellectual equals and as friends, in the process welding together a limited but promising agenda of reform, proving that the racial divide could be bridged. Jones visited Luther and Johnella Jackson on the campus of Virginia State in the summer of 1946, and Jones reciprocated, inviting the Jacksons and Southern School assistant Helen Baker to dinner the following year. In planning a board meeting in December 1947, Brown felt "triumphant" about having arranged an interracial dinner at a restaurant in downtown Richmond, an event to which Jackson and his wife were both invited. After the completion of a printing job that he had arranged for the chronically underfunded school, Jackson reported that it "represent [ed] in a small way my intense interest and concern for your school." On another occasion, he confided his increasing "appreciation for the work you and Helen are doing. In comparison with you two I suspect we public school teachers are merely scratching the surface." Jones appreciated the praise, but assured Jackson that "[i]t takes the combined work of all of us to make any dent in this part of the world." The Southern School, like the Southern Conference for Human Welfare, offered a space in which blacks and whites, both men and women, could operate on a level of social and intellectual equality, concentrating their energies on common issues that temporarily erased invidious gender and race distinctions. In a region that habitually excluded blacks and working-class whites from the political system, the school sought to instruct both in their democratic inheritance, in the notion that social change required racial cooperation. They did so on a racially egalitarian basis, challenging the southern proscription on integrated education and interracial working class unity. Southern School activists preached political reform and practiced racial inclusion, a combination that won them Jackson's unflagging support.[52] It was this dedication that made him indispensable to the Committee for Virginia, particularly as it found itself rattled by mismanagement and blown about by the gale winds of anticommunism.

Since the New Deal era tied the fortunes of southern reform and black civil rights to national politics, southern activists were bound to experience the ideological turbulence generated by the Cold War. In the context of hardening opposition to Soviet domination in Eastern Europe—a posture encouraged by diplomat George Kennan's aggressive "Long Telegram" calling for containment of Soviet expansionism, by the failure to establish a system of international atomic control, by Winston Churchill's apocalyptic "Iron Curtain" speech, by communist insurgencies in Greece and Turkey, and by Truman's conviction that the Soviets were abrogating sacred agreements ratified by Stalin and Roosevelt—the latitude for political dissent afforded by the hardscrabble years of the Depression diminished drastically, inflicting internal damage on groups like the SCHW that championed fundamental reform.

As the Byrd campaign suggested, opponents of the Truman administration's liberal policies stood to gain from tarring labor unions and reform organizations with the brush of communist sympathy. While the Republicans saddled the Democrats with the economic aftershocks of demobilization—inflation, continued price controls, general strikes, and product scarcity—they also played the tune of communist subversion that would soon become Joe McCarthy's favorite number. Republicans applied the strategy of guilt by association, insinuating that support from the left-leaning CIO-PAC meant Democratic complicity in an ever-widening communist insurgency. The strategy worked, leading the GOP out of the political wilderness imposed by the New Deal and into a majority in both houses of Congress. In the effort to rebound from the losses, Truman and party strategists set out to forge a Cold War consensus built on national security through external aggressiveness, internal conformity, and a social welfare program that would neutralize the party's left wing.[53]

The Democrats' move to the center triggered a CIO ideological realignment that excluded the SCHW and the Highlander Folk School. CIO locals would be permitted to finance only organizations approved by the national office, and neither of these allegedly communist-infested organizations qualified.[54] Severed from CIO financial support, the organization redoubled its efforts to supplement its already exiguous revenues.[55] As if to dispel any lingering doubts about his commitment to the SCHW following the *Times-Dispatch* letter, Jackson notified Durr in January 1947 that he had collected $120 for the organization. He also offered to tour the state and drum up support through personal contacts. He wanted Durr to understand that his interest in the Southern Conference was "very deep" and that he would work for the organization despite its limited membership and the inhospitable political climate. He followed through on his promise, exceeding his target by eventually collecting $402 for the committee. From October 1946 until August 1947, Jackson raised a total of $625 for the Committee for Virginia. His efforts probably kept the committee financially solvent throughout those two years. Durr complimented Jackson's "remarkable" fund-raising, while Anne Gellman, devoted committee activist and part-time secretary, confessed, "Were it not for your untiring efforts the maintenance of the State office would be impossible." As the committee struggled for its financial survival, Jackson did what he had been doing for civil rights organizations since the 1930s: raised money and political awareness. Activists such as Jackson transformed the aspirations of southern liberalism into tangible realities, creating the institutional framework and reformist example for the later civil rights movement.[56]

Jackson consistently believed that the Committee for Virginia was one phase of the Southern Conference's larger agenda for progressive reform. He routinely updated executive secretary James Dombrowski on his financial activities for the organization, on litigation against unequal educational facilities in Virginia, and on strategies for increasing black voter activity in the South. His work for the Committee for Virginia expressed his "deep interest in the Southern Conference" and his determination to sustain its program in "these trying times." As much as Jackson devoted himself to the NAACP and the ASNLH, he looked to the SCHW as the weapon to break the conservative grip on power in the South. As a biracial organization that endorsed black voting and liberal reform, Jackson, who had grown increasingly impatient with the counsels of delay, could hardly think otherwise. Yet banking on the SCHW and the Southern Regional Council, Jackson and other reformers insulated the movement from outside pressure, the key forces in eradicating repressive southern institutions from slavery to segregation. Despite the tendency to separate the Southern Regional Council and the SCHW from national streams of political reform, Jackson remained convinced that interracial action would provide the entering wedge for racial democracy. The accusations, the financial weakness, and the internecine disputes would not distract him. Jackson assured Dombrowksi that his "heart is in the Southern Conference" and that he would "continue to strive for its upbuilding," a commitment he maintained for the rest of his life.[57]

Were the energies of people such as Luther Jackson, Virginia Durr, and Anne Gellman enough, organizations like the Committee for Virginia would have weathered the storms of the postwar period. Instead, they imploded under external political pressure and internal weakness. The specter of communism visited the Committee for Virginia at a board meeting in April 1947. Only weeks before the meeting, the Truman administration had adopted a loyalty program authorizing the investigation of all federal employees. It also permitted the attorney general to compile a list of potentially subversive organizations, a list that would eventually include such clear and present dangers as the Cervantes Fraternal Society, the Nature Friends of America, and the Committee for the Protection of the Bill of Rights.[58] Two weeks before the loyalty program, the president promulgated what came to be known as the Truman Doctrine, the pledge to universalize containment by extending assistance to any nation struggling against communist subversion. The Republican Congress had already set the anticommunist tone for 1947, declaring its intention to purge the communist menace from public institutions and unleashing the House Un-American Activities Committee (HUAC) on Hollywood, higher education, and organized labor.

Into this electrified atmosphere executive board member Henry Fowler introduced a resolution calling on the group to denounce communism and protect itself from further suspicion. Fowler believed that the committee was "vulnerable and likely to become a tool for the communist party which leaves no stone unturned" in its campaign to infiltrate liberal organizations. Other board members supported the resolution, pointing out that continued suspicion of the committee as a "communist front organization" deterred potential members and desperately needed revenues.[59]

Yet it was not simply a question of expediency, Virginia Durr and others argued, but also a matter of principle that went to the core of what the SCHW represented. Since the SCHW had been founded on the principle of inclusion, any decision to limit participation based on ideological stripes would involve a repudiation of Southern Conference ideals and set a dangerous precedent for further exclusion. In staking out this position, Durr followed the Progressive Citizens of America (PCA), the most uncompromising national liberal organization and the vehicle for Henry Wallace's presidential challenge in 1948. The PCA would not prohibit membership on the basis of ideological or political affiliation. Durr asserted that authorities were wielding the scepter of anticommunism against any group that protested or "believed that the status quo could undergo improvements." The communists may have represented an extreme perspective, she later confided to Jackson, but stigmatizing them endangered the civil liberties of all citizens and democracy itself. Jerry O. Gilliam, president of the NAACP branch of Norfolk, agreed. He argued that the communist scare was "artificial" and motivated by those who "wanted to squelch all liberal movements and frighten people into saying and doing nothing." As African Americans had learned during the Scottsboro affair—in which nine blacks had been unjustly convicted of raping two white women—the communists had also promoted black civil rights when few others would. As Gilliam observed, communists had "given a big push" to the issues that the Southern Conference considered essential to its mission.[60]

Following intense debate, the board voted twelve to five to rescind the loyalty declaration, but it was a hollow victory. Three board members resigned over the dispute, and Virginia Beecher would soon join them, citing the committee's declining finances. Durr was elevated to the chairmanship of the committee after Jackson volunteered to raise the money to pay its office rent, twenty-five dollars of which he would contribute himself. "I wish I could tell you adequately how much your support means to me and to the Conference," Durr wrote to Jackson. "I think you have done more than anyone to save it thus far." Durr understood better than most how important Jackson's contributions had been to sustaining the faltering group.[61]

If the loyalty question strained the group, the political developments of 1948 tore it apart. This was the year of political fragmentation, the year that the New Deal coalition split apart on the craggy rocks of southern intransigence and anticommunism, altering in the process the character of national politics. A States' Rights Party coalesced around defiance of the Democrats' adoption of a solid civil rights plank at the national convention in 1948. The party became the precursor of Massive Resistance, the intransigent southern opposition to court-ordered integration that manifested itself first in Virginia under the leadership of Senator Harry Byrd. The States' Rights Party was also the harbinger of the southern Republican insurgency. At the same time, left-wing liberals and radicals transformed the Progressive Citizens of America into the Progressive Party and nominated maverick Henry Wallace—former vice-president and secretary of commerce turned vigilant critic of containment and U.S. militarism—for the presidency. Clark Foreman, who had worked for the SCHW since its inception, resigned from the presidency to become treasurer for Wallace's campaign. The progressive liberal movement that had found a home in the Democratic Party would rupture over Wallace's campaign and the larger question of Cold War confrontation.

Party alignment became the central question at the committee's executive board meeting in February. The board adopted a resolution opposing the endorsement of any presidential candidate, a decision subject to confirmation by the membership at a subsequent general meeting. The board then laid out the possibilities for future action. Should the group operate as a political action committee, endorsing local and national candidates? Should it function as a legislative pressure group and educational agency (an option no doubt patterned after the example of the Southern Conference Education Fund, which had been separated from the SCHW in 1945 in an effort to preserve the organization's tax exempt status)? Or should it preserve the "present structure," allowing members and local chapters to endorse their own candidates? The options were loaded, since the Committee for Virginia had always functioned as a political action organization rallying support for the antimachine forces in Virginia and liberal Democrats at the national level. Now that there was a clearly progressive option in the field, one that was drawing the support of high-ranking SCHW officials, Durr and other Wallace supporters pushed the committee to endorse it and dump Truman.[62]

Only twenty-one members attended the meeting, eleven of whom voted to support Wallace's candidacy. The decision drove Brownie Lee Jones, Charles Webber, and Anne Gellman out of the committee. Jackson voted against aligning with Wallace, believing, as he suggested to Dombrowski, that he owed it to those who had contributed money to the organization. He explained his thinking in an impassioned and wounded letter to Virginia Durr: "I deem it regrettable that our organization is one which has so many schisms and resignations." For the sake of endorsing Wallace, a position that the attending members would not "advertise . . . to the world," the committee had forced a situation in which "our most dependable members were probably driven away from our organization." Jackson found himself in the same predicament, alienated from the committee and uncertain about where he would direct his energies as well as the contributions of people who considered Jackson their link to the SCHW.[63]

Gellman echoed Jackson's disillusionment at the disintegration of the committee and the SCHW: "The world is in a frightful condition these days and to split America to splinter parties will never help attain a broad liberal medium on the national scene and ultimately for world peace." Gellman had identified the major weakness in the liberal movement—the failure to create a wide-ranging movement for social reform that could absorb ideological divisions and offer an alternative to Cold War militarism. More than this, she criticized the committee for losing its focus on the problems in their own backyard: "We have one big job in Virginia and that is to arouse our Negro and white workers to vote and throw out the Reactionary, dead leadership that strangles every-thing the people attempt for progress." In her estimation, and probably Jack-son's as well, Wallace could offer little in accomplishing this objective. Gell-man—like Jackson and others frustrated by the inability of the left to sustain a grassroots, liberal coalition—had little interest in devoting "energy to causes creating more chaos and confusion." Power struggles between James Dom-browski and Clark Foreman, confusion over the functions and financing of SCEF and SCHW, persistent accusations of communist collusion, and the di-visive impact of the Wallace campaign finally ended the SCHW's troubled ex-istence.[64]

While Gellman and Jackson lamented the Wallace endorsement, Durr wel-comed it and served as coordinator for the Progressive Party in Virginia. At the same time, she tried to salve the wounds and explain her position. "I know you are a realist and perhaps I am a Romanticist," she admitted to Jackson. She could not in good conscience support a party that traded in "empty promises" and supported "corrupt fascist-reactionary governments" in the name of anticom-munism. Certain that they differed only in strategy, not on ultimate objectives, Durr wanted the opportunity to convince Jackson of her position. She accu-rately assessed their divergent ideas on political strategy. When committee members tried to organize a Wallace rally in Richmond, Jackson notified Gellman that he "recoiled" at the thought of a Wallace meeting at that time. In Jackson's view—one that would persist throughout 1948[9]—the committee should have focused on groups that could support the organization in its finan-cial crisis. Although the group had disintegrated, Durr hoped to "salvage" the educational function of the committee through a "Citizens Educational League" that would pull together the nonpartisan voters leagues and civil rights groups throughout the state.[65]

What Durr failed to understand and what Jackson instinctively grasped was that the Committee for Virginia had offered the most effective vehicle for mobilizing organized labor, civil rights advocates, and voting rights activists in the state. The organization had never transformed itself into a mass movement, but southern liberals had also never encountered a federal government more willing to eliminate legal barriers to racial equality. In the wake of wartime political gains, the President's Committee on Civil Rights, and Truman's decision to desegregate the armed forces, the nonpartisanship of voting rights groups such as Jackson's Virginia Voters League was an illusion at best. They functioned to mobilize voters for Truman at the national level and anti-organization candidates in the state. By diverting support from a president who had made desegregation a possibility and from a party that offered the only stable shelter for organized labor, the Wallace campaign exacerbated the divisions that would untangle the New Deal coalition. Oddly enough, Durr realized the possibilities inherent in the Truman program: "I think this issue of the President's Civil Rights Report is one around which we should rally. There is a grass root movement in Virginia. These scattered voters' clubs and civil rights groups are the beginning of it." Jackson would have agreed on the strength of the "grass root" movement, but abandoning a viable medium for a political untouchable seemed decidedly unwise.[66]

In casting his support to the devil he knew, Jackson paralleled the strategy of Aubrey Williams and the Southern Conference Education Fund (SCEF). Following the Committee for Virginia debacle, Jackson attached himself to the SCEF, assuring Dombrowksi of his support for the organization and his commitment to fund-raising. Williams admired Wallace, but he fervently believed that southern progressives would find a forum in the Democratic Party, particularly since the national convention had adopted an unequivocal civil rights plank. While countless liberals abandoned the party for the Wallace train, SCEF endorsed the civil rights program that the president outlined in his State of the Union address in 1948. As the SCHW disintegrated after the election, the Education Fund consolidated its resources and focused on assailing segregation.[67]

But Jackson was ready to do more than support another public education group, however enlightened. Following the election, he encouraged Harry T. Penn, president of the Virginia Civil Rights Organization (V-CRO), to consider transforming a Truman reelection committee that both had joined into a permanent political action organization. What he envisioned was a group committed to Truman and the Democrats and complementing the educational Virginia Voters League and the V-CRO. The proposal represented a major departure for Jackson and anticipated the direction that the civil rights movement would take in the 1960s. Educational agencies, operating under the thin veneer of nonpartisanship, had played a critical role in forging the infrastructure for voter education and in raising awareness of political questions. Now the time had arrived, Jackson optimistically believed, to drive the wedge further into a fractured Solid South by forging a political action group that would get the vote out for Truman and anti-organization Democrats. While Virginia Durr hoped for a resurrected Committee for Virginia comprised of educational and political action wings, Jackson focused on coordinating the energies of existing groups. His plan was to connect the Virginia Voters League and the African American–led Virginia Civil Rights Organization with a vehicle dedicated to mobilizing support for the Truman Democrats. More than this, Jackson expected to fashion an interlocking directorate for the groups. "In short," he explained to Penn, "I wish to greatly strengthen the rather loose voters leagues we have been maintaining the past seven years." Both Durr and Jackson were groping for mechanisms to forge the weak reform coalition into an effective front for racial liberalism. The difference was that Jackson would not support third-party panaceas or new and improved voter education schemes that contributed to factionalism and confusion. If anything, he returned to the Virginia Voters League, focused on the Democrats, and lowered his expectations for social reform. Ever the pragmatist, he campaigned for the biracial Education Fund while solidifying black initiatives in the state. Without fanfare, he had started to move toward a civil rights agenda led and determined by African Americans.[68]

But while Truman offered the practical choice, it was the Wallace campaign that reflected the democratic awakening that swept across the region in the 1940s. To be sure, African Americans voted for a president who boldly went before Congress to announce a civil rights program based upon the landmark report *To Secure These Rights* and later ordered the desegregation of the military and the federal bureaucracy. To diminish Truman's decisive impact on the direction of national civil rights policy is to ignore the historical record for historical romance. Yet Wallace ignited southern black and white liberal hopes in a way that the incumbent—who sought to balance New Deal liberals against southern conservatives—could not. Campaigning throughout the South, appearing only before integrated audiences, and denouncing racial discrimination in all its forms, often at considerable peril to himself, Henry Wallace answered African American hopes for a political leader who lived the democratic principles he espoused. Here too was a candidate unapologetically committed to keeping alive the flame of New Deal liberalism, the kind of social democracy that had seemed so promising in the Roosevelt years. The Wallace campaign accelerated the voter participation that Jackson, McKaine, and Jones had championed, and it was a movement that the NAACP would advance despite a political environment poisoned by hysterical anticommunism. Howard University law professor Charles Houston articulated the larger significance of the campaign: "He pioneers a movement toward freedom that has implications far more significant than the ballot count in the coming election." Houston was only partially correct, though, since Luther Jackson, J. M. Tinsley of the Virginia NAACP, Osceola McKaine of SCHW, and others had cleared away much of the undergrowth of political disenchantment before Wallace's arrival.[69]

As much as Wallace's tour captured the imagination of southern liberals, the Declaration on Civil Rights Conference held in November 1948 at the University of Virginia enshrined the egalitarian principles that infused the embattled movement. Led by James Dombrowski, the Southern Conference Education Fund (SCEF) launched a spirited campaign against segregation that included conferences and publications focusing on higher education. The SCEF conducted surveys of university professors in eleven states that seemed to suggest that a majority favored an end to segregation in graduate and professional schools. Dombrowski and President Aubrey Williams raised the stakes, arranging for a conference of civil rights activists to sign a declaration previously endorsed by two hundred liberals throughout the South.[70]

Jackson, now a member of the board of directors, took the lead in mobilizing African American participants for the conference. On November 20, fifty signers met at Thomas Jefferson's Monticello—symbol of the paradox of American slavery and freedom—to adopt the uncompromising civil rights manifesto. Appealing to the Enlightenment ideals embedded in the Constitution, it reminded Americans that "Truth and justice are not bounded or divided by parallels of latitude." The drafters highlighted the incongruity of racism and democracy and underscored the contradictions between America's bid for world leadership and its discriminatory practices at home. By invoking the memory of Jefferson's Declaration of Independence, the drafters sought to anchor modern southern liberalism in the soil of the region's past and in its greatest contributions to the nation's traditions. By appealing to Judeo-Christian precepts, the group fused the declaration to the nation's religious heritage, which enjoyed enthusiastic vitality in the South. Through individual initiative, political action, and the combined efforts of labor, civic, professional, religious, and other groups—evidence that the search for a united liberal front continued—the signers called for "freedom from any discrimination bolstered by law." In the effort to strengthen ties between liberals, to direct and encourage those seeking "a democratic solution of race problems," and to build a public consensus in support of a Supreme Court case against segregation, the SCEF printed one hundred thousand copies of the declaration for distribution across the United States.[71]

For a brief moment, the declaration united activists from across the spectrum of the political left in defense of the ideals they had championed since the 1930s. If the Declaration on Human Rights encapsulated American hopes for a more humane and just world order, the Declaration on Civil Rights expressed the enduring dream of a more egalitarian social order at home. Freed of partisan or organizational constraints, they enunciated the basic precepts of racial liberalism at precisely the time when most American elites were abandoning them. After the "pilgrimage" to Monticello, Jackson led the signers in a discussion of how to apply the principles in practice. Virginia's leading liberals attended, including attorney Oliver Hill; Marvin Caplan, editor of the *Southern Jewish Outlook*; Charles Webber of the CIO, Brownie Lee Jones, and Virginia Durr. Here were ideals that Jackson and Durr could agree upon, and here were the essential tenets that would guide the later civil rights movement under the leadership of a new generation of democratic activists. Despite the growing antipathy toward anything that looked remotely like communism—which to southern conservatives meant anything that looked like racial equality and to the rest of the country anything that resembled progressive reform—those in attendance would have agreed with Aubrey Williams that, "in a real sense a new day was dawning in the South." Jackson reinforced Williams' optimism. The developments of the past decade had given him the opportunity to mediate between white and black liberals and to build the NAACP as an effective vehicle of political activation: "Together these organizations should bring about great changes in our Southern way of life and that in the not too distant future." For Luther Jackson, it seemed as if the fight had just begun.[72]

Chapter 8

—————•—————

The Clock of Time Will Not Be Turned Back

I want to tell you about a visit I made with Uncle Luther. . . . The campus had a mailbox and this was Sunday. We walked over there and he said he hadn't picked up his mail from the day before, so he opened up his mailbox and had several letters in there and one of them he opened quickly and smiled and said "I got a check." Now I'm not sure if this was money from the Association or voter's campaign or what but he showed me and [it read] the "Southern Youth Conference" or something. Now during this period was Senator McCarthy's campaign in Congress to search out Communists and people involved with [the] Communist cause. They had red lists of all kind of people who were assisting the Communist Party and there was a list of black people that they accused of that and so I said to Uncle Luther, "Wait a minute, this is on McCarthy's list. Aren't you afraid you might get in trouble of cooperating with them?" And he turned that smile on me and said I don't care and I'm not a communist. . . . And so I talked to him a little bit more about it and he was just fearless. He said we can't afford to have anything like that keep us from saying what we're thinking or writing what we're writing and so I'm just not worried about it. At that time they were persecuting Du Bois and Paul Robeson and other outspoken people but that's the way it was. That was the last time that I talked to him in person.

Dorothy Hodge Davis Johnson, niece of Luther P. Jackson[1]

Now a prominent activist and scholar, Jackson was a likely candidate for an invitation from a conference on economic and social life in Virginia. Held at the University of Virginia on April 30, 1949, the conference was a high-water mark of Jackson's public career. As former student Thomas J. Sellers recalled, "Prolonged applause greeted him as he arose to deliver the first speech a member of his grouphad ever given before the Virginia Social Science Association in its twenty-two years of existence."[2] Addressing the conference on civil rights in Virginia gave Jackson the chance to connect to a broader community of academics. It also allowed him to further the link between his activism and schol-arship and to publicize the accomplishments and objectives of the movement.

By this point in his career, Jackson had little to prove. What he wanted was a forum, an arena for discussion and exchange, an opportunity to continue the interracial dialogue that the Southern Conference had once provided. More than interracial goodwill, the meeting would allow him to document what African Americans—the NAACP, the Virginia Voters League, the Virginia Teachers Association, the Elks—had achieved through steady and determined pressure. But his address also provides a unique perspective on the civil rights movement at this transitional period. It offers a glimpse of what seemed pos-sible to activists who could recall the hopelessness of the prewar period. It presents a resume of the civil rights movement in Virginia, encapsulating his life and work. At the same time, it highlights the limitations of his racial thought, as well as that of the black bourgeoisie. Yet Jackson and his generation stood on the cusp of momentous change, and they knew it.

A Colloquium of Hope

Political hope, he informed the group assembled at the University of Virginia—which included, among others, political scientist Alan Moger—lay with Presi-dent Truman's civil rights program and the national Democratic Party. The program would advance under the steady assistance of black voting, which operated in the Commonwealth "on practically equal terms with the whites." In sharp contrast to conditions at the beginning of the twentieth century, an "en-lightened public opinion"—one attributable to the work of Jackson and oth-ers—supported the expanded franchise and at least in theory a fair and impar-tial legal system. Jackson placed his faith in the "liberals of both races" who, over time, would persuade the conservatives to abandon their racist convictions. While Jackson cheered the growth of grassroots consciousness, he held on to the notion that a biracial, liberal front would finally crack the weatherworn mold of segregation in the South. It was a persistent theme for middle-class activists of the New Deal era, one that a later movement would relinquish in favor of direct action by people that white southern liberals would see as little more than a threat to their way of life.[3]

The open electoral system that Jackson had been striving for was within reach, at least in Virginia. The overwhelming majority of registrars accepted black applicants, which Jackson attributed to a shift in public opinion rather than to any change in suffrage regulations. The same story of progress applied to the other notorious mechanisms of black political exclusion. The poll tax—the injustice of which Jackson did not address—could be paid, since local officials would not refuse to collect it. The white primary—the pillar of the Solid South—had also crumbled, not simply because litigation had invalidated it in the state, or because Supreme Court decisions had suspended its use in the nation, but because of a change in "personal views." In fact, considering the limited education of most registrars, personal sentiments had more to do with who voted than arcane laws, most of which meant little in the rural South. What they did understand was the national mood, irrevocably altered by "two world wars for the preservation of democracy." Powerfully, Jackson suggested that in the struggle for racial justice, ideas did matter, and not just the ideas of those engaged in the struggle. Legal kingdoms could change but so too could people, driven to face the contradictions of a national ideology steeped in democratic egalitarianism and a society mired in pathological intolerance. The voting rights efforts of the NAACP, the teacher registration campaigns of the Virginia Teachers Association, the political action initiatives of the Southern Conference: each preceded the war, but each fed from the social energies it generated. The tumult of war had triggered a tectonic shift in southern thinking about race. Jackson alone had stared down more than one recalcitrant voting registrar, personifying for them the arrival of the South's altered consciousness. Douglass Southall Freeman, editor of the *Richmond News-Leader* and certainly no champion of black civil rights, attributed the growth of black voting to Jackson's "calm and vigorous leadership." As India Taylor Johnson, Virginia State University graduate and former student of Johnella Frazer, recalled, Jackson's voting message made such an impression on her that she recalls his injunction to vote at the approach of each and every state and federal election. More than a chronicler of events, Jackson was an author of change in the early civil rights era.[4]

But the changes were in their infancy, Jackson argued; most people were still weighted down by "forces of tradition and racial habit." Like other "suppressed people," African Americans needed more than new laws. And new laws did not mean assertiveness. For this polite audience of well-meaning academics, Jackson was at pains to discredit the "fallacy" peddled by opponents of civil rights that equalizing laws would lead blacks to "rise en masse and demand the exercise of their new born privileges." Nor would the abolition of Jim Crow transportation embolden African Americans to "immediately seek to sit beside white persons on the trains." No less disturbing was the image of blacks replacing whites "where white workers alone have been previously employed," a prospect that Jackson also dismissed. At this point in the civil rights movement, middle-class elites like Jackson sought to balance legal gains for blacks against white anxieties about social equality. This balancing act would give way to an ethic of self-determination that had never been absent from the African American freedom struggle, as David Walker, Marcus Garvey, A. Philip Randolph, and others had proven, but which in the generation after Jackson would become the zeitgeist to which Martin Luther King would famously seek to catch up.[5]

If Jackson downplayed the impact of desegregation on the old order, it was not the first time, having used the same tactic in his article for the New South. He was a strategist who sought to mobilize blacks while assuring southern whites—the primary audience for the New South and the Social Sciences Association—that the results would not be too shocking. Lacking the support of a mass movement, the attention of the national media, and the interest of most whites outside of liberal circles, Jackson and his contemporaries could do little else. A product of a middle-class environment that privileged civility over confrontation, he was ill-disposed to sponsor protest that failed to respect these constraints. He was a product of his time, but he was not its prisoner; voting and political agitation rattled white political manhood, the very foundation of black subservience. Harry T. Moore, Medgar Evers, and countless voting rights activists whose stories still need to be told attested to this: black voting threatened the southern way of life.

And voting promised measurable change in the lives of African Americans, an argument that Jackson had made since the 1930s and revisited in his address that night in Charlottesville in 1949. Equal opportunity employment, education, decent housing, adequate health care, efficient (or existent) public services: these goals depended not on white beneficence but on the extent to which African Americans organized to eliminate racial inequalities. "Zealous people at the top must be joined together in order to overcome the apathy of the multitude below." Those who had a modicum of economic independence and the capability to articulate collective grievances, in other words, needed to organize.[6]

Instead of wishful thinking, Jackson identified the organizations that were transforming racial consciousness, "even though such efforts may take considerable time." With a membership of thirty thousand, the NAACP stood ahead of the rest and was "reaching the masses in ever growing numbers." His own Virginia Voters League (VVL) was not far behind, circulating literature on voting and the poll tax, holding rallies, connecting civic organizations throughout the state, and "provid[ing] them with speakers," which usually meant Jackson himself. Through the VVL, almost twenty thousand people were contacted annually about voting rights and the poll tax. It was hardly the evidence of a mass movement, but it was the groundwork for a challenge to segregation and the myriad indignities it had sustained.

If the VVL and the NAACP cleared a path for action, the Virginia Civil Rights Organization (V-CRO) was following it into a head-on attack against segregation. Jackson probably drew his greatest encouragement from the V-CRO, which he joined as a member of its executive committee. Here was an organization spearheaded by African Americans, supported by the state's leading civil rights groups, and committed to overturning segregation ordinances in Virginia. The V-CRO capped Jackson's public career. It incorporated the NAACP, the Virginia Teachers Association, the fraternal order of the Elks, the Negro Organization Society, as well as the myriad business and professional groups enlisted in the black freedom struggle. Coordinating for action rather than education, the V-CRO pointed the way toward future protest, anticipating the improvement associations that sponsored social protest in the 1950s and the Committee of Federated Organizations (COFO) of Mississippi Freedom Summer fame. The V-CRO infused Jackson with hope: it seemed to represent the triumph of concerted action over isolated protest.[7]

In February 1948, the V-CRO struck out against segregation. It submitted bills to the General Assembly for the repeal of segregation on common carriers and at public events. Here was evidence of the self-determination that Jackson, P. B. Young, J. Rupert Picott, and J. M. Tinsley had been advocating. Instead of following the lead of the cautious editor of a Richmond newspaper, black activists challenged Virginia's tradition of racial paternalism. The bills, Jackson noted proudly, were "the first of their kind to strike a blow at racial segregation by the Negroes themselves." He testified at the hearings, as did "liberal white citizens" who "spoke as loudly for their repeal as did the Negro leaders of the Commonwealth." Not surprisingly, organization stalwarts defeated the bills. Despite the defeat, the episode demonstrated the duplicity of states' rights politicians who claimed that civil rights matters were a state prerogative but then denounced V-CRO as an example of "outside interference in southern affairs." Jackson's point was that born-and-bred Virginians and southerners, not "outsiders," staffed the V-CRO. The failure of the state legislature to play by the rule of "southerners only" in racial matters amounted to a betrayal of trust.

He could only conclude that the states' rights defenders had little interest in dismantling segregation, regardless of who supported it. The bill's defeat exposed the nexus of race and power underlying the façade of paternalist civility in Virginia. It also forced Jackson to question one of the basic assumptions of his own public career. Since the beginning of the Virginia Voters League, he had operated on the conviction that black and white southerners had to resolve racial issues on their own. It informed his decision to support the Durham Conference, the Southern Regional Council, the Southern Conference for Human Welfare, and the Southern School for Workers. A vigorous supporter of the NAACP—the great bugaboo of "outside agitation" for white southerners of the 1950s—Jackson saw it as a vehicle of southern black advancement, not nationwide racial protest. The failure of the antisegregation measures made him question this assumption, and it was one that black activists of the later civil rights movement would jettison entirely.[8]

But Jackson's historical consciousness would not let him abandon legislation altogether. As a historian, he took the long view, recognizing that failed legislative maneuvers did not render conventional methods of change useless. "We did not fail," he assured readers of the *Journal and Guide,* since American history was littered with failed legislative appeals against "some evil in society." As he explained, "[b]ills to abolish Negro slavery, the whipping post, imprisonment for debt, and those to legalize labor unions" suffered the same fate. If Jackson was unusually optimistic about the legislative process, he had the historical precedent to corroborate it. The Wilmot Proviso, antislavery petitions to Congress, appeals to end lynching at the state level, and bills to open the franchise to women had demonstrated that legislative appeals could increase public awareness and pressure decision-makers to respond. Jackson also understood that political circumstances determined the effectiveness of these appeals. Voting strength more than anything would force lawmakers to pay attention.[9]

While the legislative route proved frustrating, the legal system yielded hope that concerted action could produce results. Six years before the *Brown* decision, the Supreme Court and the lower courts began adjusting to the altered racial atmosphere by responding to NAACP litigation. The NAACP's escalating legal challenge to racial inequalities in higher education—the Sweatt case in Texas, the McLaurin case in Oklahoma, the *Gaines* decision in 1938 compelling the state of Missouri to equalize education or admit the plaintiff to the state university—dramatically illustrated the potential for progress. But the civil rights movement was not something happening to someone else, somewhere else. It was moving ahead in Virginia, where Richmond attorneys Spottswood Robinson and Martin A. Martin brought the Irene Morgan case against segregation on interstate carriers to trial. Appealed to the Supreme Court and argued by William Hastie and Thurgood Marshall, the *Morgan* decision prohibited segregation on interstate transportation, setting the precedent that the Freedom Riders would test in 1961. And that was not the extent of the legal victories. Attorneys Robinson, Martin, and Oliver Hill also won cases for the equalization of school facilities in King George, Chesterfield, Gloucester, and Surry Counties. Jackson supported these efforts through fund-raising, letters to state education officials, and editorials in the *Journal and Guide*. While he told his readers that the *Morgan* decision had removed the "badge of racial inferiority," he confidently announced to the Social Science Association that the Supreme Court now understood that the doctrine of "separate but equal" was "nothing more than a myth."[10]

This was the pivotal point of Jackson's own intellectual odyssey, the admission that segregation and equality were incompatible. Like most African Americans, he had resented segregation from an early age. "I have been sick of the situation all of my days," he told representative Armistead Boothe, the sponsor of a bill to end to segregation on public transportation in Richmond.[11] Yet his personal antipathy for segregation did not register as public protest before 1942. From his early timidity about questioning legalized segregation, to his endorsement of the equivocal Durham Conference statement, to his demand for an end to segregation, Jackson had followed the intellectual journey of his generation. Of course, black activists from Frederick Douglass to W.E.B. Du Bois had attacked segregation. But Jackson belonged to the southern black middle class, a group caught between heightened racial consciousness and the discipline of Jim Crow. He was also an instructor at a state college, which made him vulnerable to reprisals. The ability of whites to retaliate against black subversives militated against direct action. Taking a stand against racial proscription in the South meant abandoning the masks and circumlocutions that blacks had used to negotiate segregation. It meant challenging the necessary myth that southern middle-class blacks accepted Jim Crow, understood it, and benefited from it. His changing consciousness mirrored the policies of his beloved NAACP. As J. M. Tinsley, president of the Virginia State Conference, explained rather circuitously in 1949: "we are not asking to be segregated anymore—that is why we are not asking for separate schools, no matter how much the buildings cost. If these Negro monuments are built to keep the races separated, it will not be our choosing."[12] Tinsley's and Jackson's altered perception of racial possibilities paralleled the moment when colonial agitators dropped the facade of fraternal dissent and called for independence; the moment when President Lincoln relinquished conciliation and mobilized the mititia against a defiant Confederacy; the moment when the Populists threw down the gaunt-let to the political status quo and demanded a new antimonopoly party; the daunting moment when principles became action. The philosophers of racial inequality had interpreted America in different ways; Jackson and his followers were now starting to change it.

The social and economic forces unleashed by the Depression, the New Deal, and the war disrupted the givens of southern life and created a sphere in which black political imaginations could flourish. In his classes at Virginia State, Jackson voiced his cynicism about American nationalist mythology. He stressed that emancipation had led to segregation rather than freedom and that segregation was anything but a question of social convenience. At its core, it was a system that perpetuated the denial of "genuine democracy" to African Americans. He believed that the pattern of inequality was not the product of the post–Civil War restoration of southern white authority but rather a tradition stretching back to 1619, when blacks first arrived as coerced labor on American shores. He was encouraged in the years following World War II by the advent of white-dominated groups that denounced segregation—including the Federal Council of Churches—and by the international embarrassment that segregation had become for a nation claiming the mantle of global democratic leadership. But he emphasized that blacks would have to demand change, and not simply through the ballot box. Achieving equality was more than a question of voting; it also required the repudiation of a mentality premised on racial inferiority. Will segregation last another 250 years, he asked his classes? "It will not if Negroes can only manage to shake off the spurious doctrine taught them by the white man that they belong to an inferior race." Segregation was not a cumbersome legal arrangement but rather a system designed to reinforce racial distinctions to the detriment of the black "mind and soul." Instead of voting for piecemeal reforms, he called on African Americans to fight against segregation in order to "save the soul of our nation."[13]

His aggressive posture influenced his perception of groups involved in the civil rights struggle. The "little band of white southerners" that staffed the SCHW was "fighting racial segregation with all the zeal of the NAACP." Trying to attract Southern Conference Education Fund (SCEF) supporters after the collapse of the Southern Conference, Jackson described it as a "militant organization" that was building a new South. Appealing to supporters a year later, he reminded them of the group's agenda: "The spirit and aims remain the same [as SCHW], namely, a frontal attack on racial segregation much after the pattern of the NAACP." The NAACP had become the standard by which he measured the commitment of other civil rights groups. He recommended the SCEF not because it conducted surveys like the Southern Regional Council, or because it promoted interracial understanding as had the Commission on Interracial Cooperation, but because it "embraces only those white Southerners who are willing to move along militant lines." In the early years of his relationship with Johnella Frazer, it was she who had been "red hot" for Du Bois, and Jackson who had orbited in the Washingtonian cosmos. By 1948, W.E.B. Du Bois was inviting Jackson—along with St. Claire Drake, John Hope Franklin, Lorenzo Greene, Rayford Logan, and Charles Thompson—to participate in a lecture series on "The Negro in American History" at the New School for Social Research. That year, the Virginia Conference of the NAACP awarded him a bronze plaque for his distinguished service in the field of civil rights. Declining recruitment to the presidency of Virginia State College after Luther Foster's death, Jackson made it clear what kind of candidate he did *not* support: an accommodationist. "You will do me and every body here a personal favor," he wrote to J. Rupert Picott, "if you will spread the word among rooters for this gentleman [Archie Richardson] that we are certain he is lacking in the qualities necessary for running Virginia State College in these hectic times of NAACP. agitation, a stand on civil rights, and other questions affecting the welfare of Negroes everywhere." In 1949, an anticommunist crusader included Jackson in a report on African American subversives for publicly opposing the smear tactics of the House Un-American Activities Committee. By 1950, Luther Jackson had become a militant.[14]

In an aside attached to a letter to Charles Johnson in November 1949, Jackson mentioned Carter G. Woodson's declining health: "Like so many people he has a bad heart and he shows it in his face and body as a whole." Ironically, Jackson himself belonged to this group. He had been suffering from cardiac irregularities, a condition that he dutifully kept from Johnella and his family. On April 8, Jackson sent a telegram to the SCEF executive informing them that he would not be able to participate in the Atlanta conference since he would be attending the funeral for Carter G. Woodson. A week later, on April 13, 1950, he died of a heart attack in his sleep. It was a devastating blow to his family, to his children who had competed with Jackson's public life for his private attention and time, and to the legions of students who admired and loved him. Tributes poured in from colleagues, former students, fellow activists, and from people who simply knew, admired, and loved him. His loss deprived the Virginia movement not only of a great organizer but also of a great spirit, the kind that drew people to him out of the magnetism of his personality and the strength of his ideas.

A Life for Something Larger

Any assessment of Luther Jackson must begin with his life's work, the effort to generate black political activity. Above every conceivable strategy, he fixed his sights on voting as the antidote to racial inequality. This singular focus tended to obscure the layers of informal racial control that reached into the social fabric of postwar America. And yet, if Jackson seemed to consider voting a panacea, he never lost sight of the connection between social and political advancement. Nor did he consider voting a harmless exercise in interracial friendship. As he explained to a graduating class at Fisk University in 1939, voting would allow blacks to "reward your friends; punish your enemies. Southern Senators in Congress may filibuster forever on the anti-lynching bill. They may do it forever because there are no reprisals coming from their Negro constituents." To college professors who preferred the status quo, he asserted that "a certain amount of precaution is necessary in Southern race relationships; yet by no means can the school faculty be the most conservative element in the community." It was precisely this willingness to test the limits of a black institution dependent on white authority that earned Jackson the censure of the college administration.[15]

He repeatedly stressed the concrete benefits of political action and placed the voting campaign in the historical currents leading to black freedom. The consciousness-raising effort, he argued in 1943, might "sound visionary and impossible of attainment," yet it was the only method for achieving genuine social reform: "It was by such methods that Negro slavery was abolished, that women won their rights, that public school education was attained, and that universal suffrage was inaugurated throughout the land."[16] He imagined that voting would give African Americans the tools to exercise a measure of control over their lives. In his vision, segregation would fall, inequitable education would end, and racial cooperation would replace the gulf separating whites and blacks. He had few illusions that racial antipathies would evaporate when blacks began to vote in strength. He did believe, however, that political action could build a framework of rational governance stronger than the racial prejudice that infected the southern white mind.

More than vague optimism, he imparted to his students, fellow teachers, and black Virginians an example of political consciousness that endured after his death in 1950.[17] As his colleague and friend James Hugo Johnston wrote shortly after his death in 1950, Virginians would remember Jackson as the person "who did most to develop an appreciation among his people of their rights and duties as citizens. In this respect his influence for positive good *extended far beyond the boundaries of Virginia.*" (emphasis added.) His work with the Virginia Teachers Association gave him a platform to convince teachers that education could not float above the gritty world of political struggle. Methodically overturning obstacles to voting registration, the Virginia Voters League chipped away at the foundations of political exclusion. The league also forged links between voters' clubs and gave direction to the campaign for political involvement. The voting status of African Americans became a matter of public concern, an issue that demanded the attention of opponents and supporters alike. Black political activity disturbed the stagnant political waters of modern Virginia. Jackson helped build and then mediate between several civil rights organizations. In the process, he created the institutions and ideological momentum that encouraged the mass movement of the post-1954 period. Most important, he offered an example of political responsibility for those accustomed to indifference. His example was founded on steady resistance to racial discrimination and an abiding confidence that blacks had it within their power to take control over their lives. At a time when African Americans lacked visible leadership, his work lent authority and a voice to the struggle for equality in Virginia and the South.

His was one of the most powerful voices encouraging African Americans to take action, local action, the kind of action that produced a student revolt against segregation and launched Virginia into the forefront of the drive against Jim Crow. It is not difficult to imagine a connection between Luther P. Jackson's appeals to teachers, his ambitious civic education program, his magnetic presence in Virginia's black educational world, and the emergence of Prince Edward County as one of the test cases in the momentous *Brown v. Board of Education* decision. There, in 1951, a sixteen-year-old student named Barbara Johns mobilized 450 students to go on strike for a school better than the tarpaper-covered, leaking, overcrowded, ill-equipped Robert Moton High that they inhabited. But the student strike quickly escalated into a more profound attack on the status quo. When a delegation of students tried to enlist the support of NAACP lawyers, they were informed that counsel would only be rendered on the condition that the Moton protesters demand an end to segregation, since the organization had abandoned the frustrating campaign of equalization. The lawyers who communicated the change in NAACP strategy and who would eventually take the case to court were none other than Spottswood Robinson and Oliver Hill, the lawyers responsible for the salary equalization cases in Chesterfield County, Gloucester County, and dozens of counties across the state. These were the same lawyers whom Jackson had supported through the NAACP and the *Journal and Guide*. Chesterfield was also the same county in which Jackson had unequivocally demanded that the school superintendent abide by a federal circuit court ruling mandating salary equalization for black teachers. Years of litigation, of voting activism, of Negro History Weeks and appeals by activists like Jackson and the teachers, parents, and students who listened to him, had cleared a path for even bolder, younger activists like Barbara Johns. When the *Brown v. Board of Education* case went to the Supreme Court in 1952, it did so on the strength of a "cognitive revolution" to which Jackson had contributed mightily.[18]

Jackson challenged academics of his day and continues to challenge scholars of ours. At a time when historians lament their isolation from a public eager for historical perspective but ignored by most academic practitioners, his life offers an example of professional responsibility. Against the resistance of Carter G. Woodson, he sought to redefine the historian's public role. He believed that the historian could write analytical narratives that balanced professional standards and the public demand for historical guidance. Admittedly, he did not always succeed in this effort. Even so, he recognized that the relationship between historical inquiry and public consciousness was too vital to sever by academic obfuscation. He understood that the analysis of the past should not be carried on within the boundaries of an exclusive professional caste. The reconstruction of the past was not a unilateral process: Historians had to address the concerns of those who turned to them to make sense of their present. In responding to this public voice, they would help refashion their world-view by defying historically conditioned indignities. Jackson believed that the past was not a museum of curiosities but rather a repository of lessons for the present.

In the same way that he challenged historians to reach out to a wider audience, he encouraged academics of all stripes to look beyond the campus and address the social problems that afflicted the people they taught. Understand-

204 · Luther P. Jackson and a Life for Civil Rights

ing and lecturing on the injustices of the past was the start; the next step was to correct them in the present. For an era vexed by the disintegration of civic culture, the triumph of a consumer ethic powered by the fantasyland of cyberspace, and the allegedly inexorable forces of globalization, Jackson and his period stand as a testimony to the capacity of people to stake out a version of community based on social responsibility. Entangled in circumstances that often seem beyond our control, we cast about for a sense of autonomy amid market-driven forces that leave little room for values, let alone virtues, that do not respond to the imperatives of global competitiveness and the free market economy. Jackson's work and that of his contemporaries provide a stunning example of the power of small groups to foster solutions that drive against the grain of social conformity, of disinterest toward complex social problems, intellectual banality, and the decisions of remote and unresponsive power brokers. His call for civic responsibility provides a compelling alternative to the prevailing dogma that we are first and foremost consumers, not citizens. In other words, his period provides a profile of what local democracy has meant and could mean again in the American experience.

Ultimately, Jackson could not offer a program broad enough to contain the moral energy of people opposed to the entire system of racial exclusion. Voting was crucial, but ballots alone could not extirpate the customs, bi-laws, community-sanctioned indignities, and reflexive violence that preserved the racial hierarchy. Sadly, Jackson died in 1950, far too early to witness the forces set in motion by the activists of his generation. Yet one is left to wonder if Jackson would have endorsed the confrontational protests of young people grown weary with the counsels of patience. His was a protest born of tremendous optimism about the potential for change through conventional institutions. He espoused a message of self-realization, but the vision that transformed the racial landscape was not his. In that vision, voting was a piece of a larger and, for the time being, scattered puzzle.

Despite the limitations of his program, he became an exponent of authentic democracy at a time when the lights of republican government were going out across Cold War America. When the marginalized black civil rights struggle of the 1950s emerged in large-scale protest, it did so under the aegis of democratic inclusion, the intellectual foundation of Jackson's worldview. The core of the civil rights movement had always been the democratic inheritance guaranteed by the very people who had constructed a society based on racial coercion. Despite the undulations of black nationalism, Pan-Africanism, armed resistance, economic independence, cultural pride, and the messianic liberation of a later period, the struggle for equality had persistently spun on the pivot of American democratic egalitarianism. Jackson implicitly understood this. "Some of us feel the coming of a renaissance in the Southern region," James Hugo Johnson wrote in his obituary for Jackson. "If so, Jackson's contribution is a part of that renaissance."[19] This is all that Luther Jackson had really hoped for—to stimulate an awakening, a "renaissance" that would lead to change. He accomplished this more than he could realize.

In an era that has witnessed the resegregation of America, the continued impoverishment of working-class blacks, the entanglement of countless young African American males in a legal system that metes out police brutality and disproportionately harsh penalties, and the persistence of an educational bureaucracy that fails to offer black children anything resembling an equal opportunity, we have good reason to question Jackson's optimism about the American democratic tradition. But we also have reason to listen to his injunction against political disenchantment. If for no other reason than that the alternatives of comfortable indifference and self-congratulatory color-blindness have failed to resolve the racial divisions at the center of American life, we might benefit from listening to Jackson's call for civic involvement. We might benefit from an honest confrontation with problems that hypernationalist flag-waving will not resolve. Americans have good reason to follow his lead in seeking public solutions for social inequalities that the private marketplace cannot address. In doing so, they will rediscover the full meaning of the democracy that Jackson championed.

Notes

Chapter 1. That the Hope Might Become a Reality

1. Palmer, "He Left a Lonesome Place," 198.

2. An important revision of the conservative mythology of the NAACP is Meier and Bracey's "The NAACP as a Reform Movement, 1900–1965: 'To Reach the Conscience of America,'" For a study of the NAACP's struggle against lynching, educational inequalities, and political disfranchisement in the 1920s, see Schneider, *"We Return Fighting": The Civil Rights Movement in the Jazz Age.*

3. This is beginning to change, with the recent publication of J. Douglas Smith's *Managing White Supremacy: Race, Politics, and Citizenship in Jim Crow Virginia*, and Larissa Smith's doctoral dissertation, "Where the South Begins: Black Politics and Civil Rights Activism in Virginia, 1930–51." As Robert Pratt writes, "One facet of Virginia history that has long been ignored is the commonwealth's place in the black civil rights movement of the mid-twentieth century." Virginia "played a significant part in it," Pratt acknowledges, but developments there have been overshadowed by events in Montgomery, Birmingham, Selma, and Little Rock. Despite the fact that the Virginia experience was not "in the national spotlight," it was "no less pivotal in the remaking of an American society committed to the ideals of social justice and racial equality" (Pratt, "New Directions in Virginia's Civil Rights History," 149). This study takes its lead from Pratt's injunction to examine this neglected period. At the same time, it seeks to answer in part Ronald Heinemann's appeal for an "examination of the life of the black community" that includes "the fight against discrimination." Commending recent studies of black leaders in Virginia, Heinemann hoped that additional studies of "notable black Virginians, particularly the lawyers of the NAACP" would follow (Heinemann, "Virginia in the Twentieth Century," 150, 152).

4. Tuck, "Black Protest in the 1940s."

5. And Jackson was not alone in this venture, as a growing number of historians have recognized. Recent works have stressed the importance of local activists in advancing a civil rights movement that materialized earlier than the conventional narrative suggests. One of the earliest to underline the Second World War as a decisive factor in stimulating black protest was Richard Dalfiume in a chapter titled "The 'Forgotten Years' of the Negro Revolution." Important recent studies of black activism and its connection to New Deal liberalism in the South include Sullivan, *Days of Hope: Race and Democracy in the*

New Deal Era; Reed, *Simple Decency and Common Sense*; and Egerton, *Speak Now Against the Day: The Generation before the Civil Rights Movement.* Two studies that illuminate the diversity of black activism and the importance of the NAACP—an organization in which Jackson played a decisive role—at the state level include Fairclough, *Race and Democracy: The Civil Rights Struggle in Louisiana, 1915–1972*, and Dittmer, *Local People: The Struggle for Civil Rights in Mississippi.*

6. Charles Eagles makes this point precisely, while also pointing out that historians need to explore the continuing civil rights struggle after the fateful disintegration of the liberal coalition and the Vietnam conflict. Reconceptualizing the chronology of the civil rights movement is essential to recovering the voices and contributions of those who operated without the benefit of an aroused national audience or, like Luther Jackson, did not live to see the dramatic events that his work facilitated (Eagles, "Toward New Histories of the Civil Rights Era"). For a historiographical essay emphasizing the significance of grassroots studies and their importance in addressing the question of continuity between the earlier movement and the post-1954 period, see Lawson, "Freedom Then, Freedom Now: The Historiography of the Civil Rights Movement."

7. Most studies continue to emphasize the period after 1954 to the exclusion of voting rights activism, biracial political initiatives, and legal challenges in the period from the New Deal to the Brown decision. Examples include Sitkoff, *The Struggle for Black Equality, 1954–1980*; and Weisbrot, *Freedom Bound: A History of America's Civil Rights Movement.*

8. Moore's voting rights activity and his close involvement with the NAACP closely paralleled Jackson's (see Green, *Before His Time: The Untold Story of Harry T. Moore, America's First Civil Rights Martyr*).

9. Raymond Gavins lucidly mapped out this pragmatic approach, which combined Washingtonian themes of self-reliance and Du Boisian notions of protest and inclusion, and which characterized Gordon B. Hancock, P. B. Young, and by extension most middle-class activists in Virginia during Jackson's period, in *The Perils and Prospects of Southern Black Leadership: Gordon Blaine Hancock, 1884–1970* and in "Hancock, Jackson, and Young: Virginia's Black Triumvirate." Recognizing the depth of white hostility to black equality, they applied as much pressure against segregation as circumstances and resources allowed. Focusing on P. B. Young, Henry Lewis Suggs arrived at much the same conclusion, emphasizing the "Bookerite" themes that pervaded his efforts to negotiate the political and economic challenges of the Depression. He opposed segregation but followed the Durham Conference by accepting it as a current reality that few white liberals were ready to abandon. Cautious optimism more than aggressive confrontation marked Young's career as publisher of the *Norfolk Journal and Guide* (see Suggs, *P. B. Young, Newspaperman: Race, Politics, and Journalism in the New South, 1910–1962*; "Black Strategy and Ideology in the Segregation Era: P. B. Young and the *Norfolk Journal and Guide*, 1910–1954"; and "P. B. Young of the *Norfolk Journal and Guide*: A Booker T. Washington Militant, 1904–1928"). Although Jackson is accurately described as a pragmatist, he was not a conservative, a description that invariably reflects current sensibilities but distorts historical conditions. Jackson was also more consistently committed to an egalitarian view of African American political life and to the possibilities of liberal-labor reform than were Young and Hancock.

10. The argument that black middle-class activists unconsciously accommodated themselves to political exclusion by advocating a "racialized" version of black uplift is found in Kevin Gaines, *Uplifting the Race: Black Leadership, Politics, and Culture in the Twentieth Century*, xiv–xvi, chap. 3. Certainly Jackson struggled with the claims that middle-class values made on his understanding of black progress in America. What is probably more remarkable than the black elite's internalization of dominant social norms is the capacity of some of its members, Jackson included, to articulate a political program in a society that had all but reconciled itself to the notion that political entitlement was the prerogative of white males. When the question was what ideals should provide the standard of African American public life, Jackson would have answered in a way that reflected his middle-class status. When the issue was who should be entitled to vote, be elected to government, and achieve the full equality before the law, Jackson would have answered all people. In other words, middle-class morality was not a precondition of citizenship.

11. Author cited as "T.D.P.," "Jackson, Luther Porter: Educator, Historian, Virginia Civic Leader," folder 1, box 1, Jackson Papers; Luther P. Jackson Jr., "Lute and Miss Johnny: A Memorial Tribute to Luther Porter Jackson," in author's possession courtesy of Edward Jackson, 1–2.

12. Luther P. Jackson Jr., "Lute and Miss Johnny," in author's possession courtesy of Edward Jackson, 3–6; Jackson, "The Call for the Highly Educated," 39.

13. Author cited as "T.D.P.," "Jackson, Luther Porter: Educator, Historian, Virginia Civic Leader," folder 1, box 1, Jackson Papers; Meier and Rudwick, *Black History and the Historical Profession*, 85–86.

Chapter 2. Jubilee Days: Luther Jackson, Johnella Frazer, and African American Life

1. As the authors of a new collection argue, "Black resistance, not white supremacy, was continuous, while white supremacy remodeled itself to meet any challenge." Jackson and Frazer were part of a "long tradition of African American activism" that limited and mediated the impact of white supremacy after emancipation (Dailey et al., eds., *Jumpin' Jim Crow*, 5; see also 3–6).

2. Lewis, *In Their Own Interests*, 89–101. As Lewis suggests, Frazer and Jackson participated in a rich cultural life that flourished within the boundaries of segregation but was not exclusively defined by those limits. Religion, food, visiting, entertainment, fraternal groups, sporting events, and casual, day-to-day interactions: these were the materials of a culture that offered a sense of purpose and even power to average African Americans of the twentieth century. Mingling the secular and the sacred, the rural and the urban, African American culture thrived behind the "veil" of segregation.

3. Egerton, *Speak Now Against the Day*, 148–50, 284–85.

4. Franklin, *From Slavery to Freedom*, 272–73.

5. Quoted in Litwack, *Trouble in Mind*, 77.

6. "Obituary," folder 8, box 1, Luther P. Jackson Papers, Virginia State University Archives, Petersburg, Virginia. Hereafter abbreviated as Jackson Papers.

7. Ibid; Wilkerson, interview; Lee, interview; India Taylor Johnson, interview; Spaights, interview.

8. Frazer to Luther Jackson, March 23, 1921, folder 10, box 1, Jackson Papers. For Frazer's musical activities, see Frazer to Jackson, June 29, 1921, folder 11; Frazer to Jackson, August 9, 1921, folder 13; Frazer to Jackson, April 13, 1921, folder 10, box 1, Jackson Papers.

9. Jackson to Frazer, October 30, 1920, folder 9, box 1, Jackson Papers. As Grace Elizabeth Hale explains in *Making Whiteness*, many southern blacks were "self conscious" about the cultural traditions of the slavery period: "Certainly, the patronizing attitudes toward the folk traditions of slavery expressed by southern and northern whites, from amateur travelers to professional educators and anthropologists, as well as the educational and civic programs of the rising class of African American leaders and reformers, made many self-conscious about the slave past" (19). Although this may have been the case, Luther Jackson and Johnella Frazer showed little sensitivity about the Jubilee songs, and at least at the Virginia Normal and Industrial Institute, they found a receptive audience. Considering the school's precarious financial position and President Gandy's determination to restore it to college status, the political overtones of performing the spirituals for white audiences is clear.

10. See, for example, Frazer to Jackson, September 4, 1920, folder 9, box 1; Frazer to Jackson, April 13, 1921; Jackson to Frazer, October 29, 1920, folder 9, box 1; Jackson to Frazer, April 19, 1926, folder 49, box 3, Jackson Papers.

11. Frazer to Jackson, April 13, 1922, folder 21, box 1; Jackson to Frazer, June 11, 1926, folder 57, box 3, Jackson Papers.

12. Frazer to Jackson, August 21, 1921, folder 13, box 1, Jackson Papers.

13. Frazer to Jackson, September 21, 1921, folder 19, box 1, Jackson Papers.

14. J. Douglas Smith, *Managing White Supremacy*, 4, 27–28.

15. Gavins, "Urbanization and Segregation," 267–68; Randolph, "The Civil Rights Movement in Richmond," 63–64; Smith, *Managing White Supremacy*, 28–29, chap. 9.

16. Jackson to Johnella Jackson, May 10, 1925, folder 39, box 2, Jackson Papers.

17. Frazer to Jackson, April 13, 1921, folder 10; Frazer to Jackson, September 4, 1920, folder 9, box 1, Jackson Papers.

18. Quoted in Fairclough, "Being in the Field of Education," 72.

19. "Colored Musicians Entertain Legislators," *Richmond Times-Dispatch*, February 9, 1922, folder 19, box 1, Jackson Papers.

20. Frazer to Jackson, February 8, 1922, folder 19, box 1, Jackson Papers.

21. Frazer to Jackson, April 27, 1922, folder 21, box 1, Jackson Papers.

22. Ibid.

23. As Patrick Miller has argued, African American promoters of college athletics often couched their justifications of varsity sports in terms of racial uplift. Advocates believed that athletic excellence would cultivate the virtues necessary for material success while at the same time constructing "significant platforms for proving equality." Many assumed that, having demonstrated their skill and thus their character on the football field, blacks would enjoy acceptance on an equal political and social playing field (Miller, "To 'Bring

the Race along Rapidly,'" 111). For additional insight on sports as testing ground for African American assimilation of middle-class virtues, see Captain, "Enter Ladies and Gentlemen of Color."

24. Jackson to Frazer, May 10, 1925, folder 39, box 2, Jackson Papers.

25. Frazer to Jackson, June 29, 1921, folder 11, box 1, Jackson Papers.

26. Frazer to Jackson, May 30, 1921, folder 11, box 1, Jackson Papers.

27. Fraser to Jackson, May 18, 1921, folder 11; Frazer to Jackson, September 22, 1921, folder 19, box 1, Jackson Papers.

28. Frazer to Jackson, May 4, 1921, folder 11, box 1, Jackson Papers.

29. Jackson to Frazer, October 30, 1920, folder 9, box 1, Jackson Papers.

30. Frazer to Jackson, May 4, 1921, folder 11, box 1; Frazer to Jackson, April 5, 1922, folder 21, box 1, Jackson Papers.

31. Lewis, *In Their Own Interests*, 99.

32. Frazer to Jackson, April 13, 1921, folder 10, box 1, Jackson Papers.

33. Frazer to Jackson, November 12, 1925, folder 44, box 2; Frazer to Jackson, April 27, 1922, folder 21, box 1, Jackson Papers.

34. Frazer to Jackson, February 15, 1933, folder 67, box 3, Jackson Papers.

35. Frazier, *Black Bourgeoisie*, 216–24; Gilmore, *Gender and Jim Crow*, xix, 3–4, 13–15; Myrdal, *An American Dilemma* 645–47; for a discussion of the class distinctions within African American society and the cultural ideals of the black elite, see Gatewood, *Aristocrats of Color: The Black Elite, 1880–1920*.

36. Dittmer, *Local People*, 25.

37. Kluger, *Simple Justice*, 464.

38. Dittmer, *Local People*, 75.

39. Frazer to Jackson, August 30, 1923, folder 27, box 1, Jackson Papers.

40. Frazer to Jackson, March 23, 1921, folder 10, box 1, Jackson Papers.

41. Sherman, "The 'Teachings at Hampton Institute,'" 279, 277–79, 298.

42. Jackson to Frazer, July 26, 1925, folder 30, box 2, Jackson Papers; Sherman, "The 'Teachings at Hampton Institute,'" 281, 287, 295–96, Du Bois quote on 283; see also Sherman, "'The Last Stand.'"

43. Frazer to Jackson, March 23, 1921, folder 10, box 1, Jackson Papers; Luther P. Jackson Jr., interview.

44. Jackson to Frazer, September 13, 1925, folder 42, box 2, Jackson Papers.

45. Jackson to Frazer, October 4, 1921, folder 15, box 1, Jackson Papers.

46. Ibid.

47. Jackson to Frazer, August 10, 1921, folder 13, box 1, Jackson Papers.

48. Meier, *Negro Thought in America*, 193.

49. Du Bois was notoriously inconsistent in his views, never more so than in the 1930s, when he vigorously endorsed socialism, black cultural nationalism, and separatism as necessary response to implacable white racism. As John B. Kirby explains in *Black Americans in the Roosevelt Era: Liberalism and Race:* "W.E.B. Du Bois' denial of interracial cooperation, whether of a radical working-class variety or of the kind envisaged by a southern liberal like Will Alexander, his affirmation of distinctive cultural and social characteristics

and the necessity of black self-help and race unity, and his assertion that race prejudice was not on a decline as a result of the Depression crisis or liberal reformism but remained a permanent feature of American life challenged the basic assumptions of most black and white thinkers of the period" (196). Oddly enough, Du Bois and Jackson moved closer together on the ideological spectrum as Du Bois gradually endorsed economic self-reliance. This was the position that Washington had advocated and to which Jackson subscribed, particularly through his encouragement of the Petersburg Negro Business Association. It might be argued, however, that while the means became similar, the ends remained worlds apart. Du Bois imagined a much more radical separation, while Jackson and many others like him saw it as a resourceful expedient and a bridge to the larger society they inhabited (see Kirby, *Black Americans in the Roosevelt Era,* 196–97).

50. Jackson to Frazer, October 30, 1920, folder 9; Frazer to Jackson, May 18, 1921, folder 11, box 1, Jackson Papers.

51. Frazer to Jackson, September 22, 1921, folder 19, box 1, Jackson Papers.

52. Frazer to Jackson, February 15, 1933, folder 67, box 3, Jackson Papers; Luther P. Jackson Jr., interview.

53. Meier, *Negro Thought in America,* 166–67. As Meier cogently explains, "White hostility called forth a defensive philosophy of self-help and racial solidarity, frustration of political ambitions caused a redirection of energies toward economic accumulation, and the closing of economic opportunities strengthened the ideology of a segregated economy championed by the newer business and professional men" (166). Political activism consistently set Jackson apart from this characterization, but to varying degrees and at different times he represented each of these tenets.

54. Wilson Jeremiah Moses has argued that Marcus Garvey, founder of the Universal Negro Improvement Association, combined hostility toward segregation and moderate civil rights organizations with an abiding admiration for certain features of Western civilization and its American representations. Admitting the differences between Garvey and many of his contemporaries, Moses nonetheless identifies a continuum between nineteenth-century black nationalism—which stressed racial uplift and the civilization of Africa along Western lines—and Garvey's racial program. This might be the case, but Garvey's position on segregation was anything but clear. His fixation on racial purity and his bizarre endorsement of the Ku Klux Klan gave his critics plenty of fodder (see Moses, *The Golden Age of Black Nationalism,* 262–68, 197–98).

55. Jackson to Frazer, October 30, 1920, folder 9, box 1, Jackson Papers.

56. Meier, *Negro Thought in America,* 134–35; Franklin, *From Slavery to Freedom,* 321–22.

57. Jackson to Frazer, October 30, 1929, folder 9, box 1, Jackson Papers.

58. Goggin, *Carter G. Woodson,* 59–60; Tindall, *The Emergence of the New South,* 268–69.

59. Form letter, Petersburg Civic Association to the Ministers of Petersburg, April 3, 1938, folder 511, box 18, Jackson Papers.

60. Ibid.

61. Jackson to Frazer, October 30, folder 9, box 1, Jackson Papers.

62. Jackson to Frazer, October 3, 1921, folder 15; Frazer to Jackson, October 4, 1921, folder 15, box 1, Jackson Papers.

63. Meier and Rudwick, *Black History and the Historical Profession,* 84.

64. Frazer to Jackson, March 7, 1922, folder 20, box 1, Jackson Papers. All of the quotations in the paragraph are from this letter.

65. Ibid.

66. Frazer to Jackson, March, 1922, folder 20, box 1, Jackson Papers.

67. Frazer to Jackson, August 30, 1923, folder 27, box 1; Frazer to Jackson, folder 49, box 3, Jackson Papers.

68. Jackson to Frazer, May 10, 1925, folder 39, box 2, Jackson Papers.

69. Jackson to Frazer, November 8, 1925, folder 44, box 2, Jackson Papers.

70. Jackson to Frazer, July 26, 1925, folder 30, box 2, Jackson Papers.

71. Jackson to Frazer, March 19, 1926, folder 48, box 2; Jackson to Frazer, May 16, 1926, folder 49, box 3, Jackson Papers.

72. Jackson to Frazer, July 26, 1925, folder 30, box 2.

73. Frazer to Jackson, October 20, 1928, box 3, folder 57, Jackson Papers; Luther P. Jackson Jr., interview.

74. Luther P. Jackson Jr., interview.

Chapter 3. Jackson, the Association, and the Meaning of Black History

1. On the international focus of African American historians and Woodson's contribution to this perspective, see Kelley, "'But a Local Phase of a World Problem': Black History's Global Vision, 1883–1950," and Goggin, *Carter Woodson: A Life in Black History,* chap. 6. As Woodson explained, the growing popularity of works on black history had developed out of the realization "that the public cannot depend upon the oppressors of a race to give a true picture of those whom they despitefully use" ("Negro History Week— The Eighth Year," 108). For additional insight into the struggle to introduce the black experience into a historiographical field dominated by assumptions of black inferiority and the immutability of race, see Lewis, "'To Turn As on a Pivot': Writing African Americans into a History of Overlapping Diasporas."

2. Goggin, *Carter G. Woodson,* 32–39; Meier and Rudwick, "J. Franklin Jameson, Carter G. Woodson, and the Foundations of Black Historiography." For a brief overview of Woodson, the formation of the association, the historians who benefitted from it assistance and contributed to its work, as well as Woodson's philosophical emphasis on scholarship over "race agitation," see Janette Hoston Harris, "Woodson and Wesley: A Partnership in Building the Association for the Study of Afro-American Life and History," *Journal of Negro History* 83 (Spring 1998): 109-119.

3. Jackson to Frazer, April 19, 1926, folder 49, box 3 (first quote); Jackson to Frazer, November 29, 1925 (second quote); Jackson to Frazer, March 14, 1926 (third and fourth quotes); for plans to bring historian Benjamin Brawley to the Virginia Normal and Industrial Institute campus, see Jackson to Fraser, July 11, 1926, folder 52, box 3, all in Jackson Papers. Jackson was not the only historian that Woodson inspired. Rayford Logan attended the high school where Woodson taught, and he went on to earn a Ph.D. at Harvard,

returning to work as his mentor's research assistant. Woodson also cultivated the likes of Charles Wesley, Lorenzo Greene, James Hugo Johnston, and Alrutheus A. Taylor (see Meier and Rudwick, *Black History and the Historical Profession*, 74–75). Woodson inspired through his scholarship but also through his stimulating and erudite lectures. As Jacqueline Goggin explains in *Carter G. Woodson*, "Woodson overwhelmed his audiences with a wealth of information in his speeches, starting with African history and working his way through all of African-American history, and he frequently electrified them with his oratorical skills" (42).

4. Jackson to Frazer, n.d., 1928, box 3 (first quote); Jackson to Frazer, January 29, 1929, folder 60, box 3 (second and third quotes); Jackson to Frazer, March 28, 1929, folder 62, box 3, Jackson Papers.

5. Jackson to Frazer, n.d., 1928; Jackson to Frazer, November 27, 1928, (first quote); Jackson to Frazer, December 9, 1928, (third quote), all in box 3, Jackson Papers.

6. For Craven's influence on Jackson, see Meier and Rudwick, *Black History and the Historical Profession*, 86; for Frazer's query about Dodd's racial views, see Frazer to Jackson, March 20, 1929, folder 62, box 3; Jackson to Frazer, November 19, 1928 (including quote); Jackson to Frazer, November 27, 1928, box 3, Jackson Papers.

7. Jackson, *Free Negro Labor and Property Holding in Virginia, 1830–1860*, 10, 11. See also the introduction and chap. 1.

8. Jackson to Woodson, January 15, 1942, folder 989, box 35, Jackson Papers

9. Jackson to E. Franklin Frazier, March 1, 1940, folder 136, box 6 (first two quotes); Jackson to E. Franklin Frazier, December 19, 1942, folder 152, box 6 (third quote); Jackson to Charles S. Johnson, September 3, 1943; Jackson to Charles S. Johnson, November 20, both in folder 166, box 7; Jackson to Woodson, February 27, 1944, folder titled "ASNLH Jackson-Woodson 1944," box 35, Jackson Papers. Jackson corresponded with other academics in search of and willing to provide documents related to African American history. See, for example, Jackson to George Woody, November 15, 1941, folder 191, box 6; and Jackson to Garnet Ryland (University of Richmond), August 9, 1942, folder 148, box 6. Jackson's assistance to Woodson preceded his enrollment in the doctoral program at the University of Chicago. See his letter disclosing information about James H. Colson Jr., principal of Dinwiddie Normal School until 1912, and William Colson, an "adventurer" to Liberia. Jackson to Woodson, September 4, 1925, folder titled "ASNLH Jackson-Woodson 1925." (Subsequent citations from this part of the collection appear without folder references since the letters are organized according to the years of the correspondence.) Each is found in the Jackson Papers.

10. Jackson, "Unexplored Fields in the History of the Negro in the United States," 65.

11. Goggin, *Carter G. Woodson*, 78–80.

12. Charles H. Wesley to Jackson, January 27, 1936, folder 974, box 35, Jackson Papers; Goggin, *Carter G. Woodson*, 111–14. Wesley's analysis reflected Woodson's belief that the foundations refused to support the ASNLH because Woodson insisted on maintaining the association's intellectual autonomy (see Goggin, *Carter G. Woodson*, 112).

13. Jackson, "The Annual Negro History Drive in Virginia," *Virginia Teachers Bulletin*, 13.

14. Woodson to Jackson, November 1, 1934, box 35; Woodson to John Gandy, president of Virginia State College, March 20, 1935, box 35; Jackson to Woodson, April 4, 1935, box 35, Jackson Papers.

15. Jackson to Woodson, November 18, 1936; Jackson to Woodson, January 6, 1936, both in box 35, Jackson Papers. To distribute Negro History Week materials, Jackson recruited A. G. Richardson—his associate from the days of the Petersburg Voters League—and Curtis Crocker. The ASNLH and the NAACP grew into popular organizations in the 1930s, but each depended on networks of communication and support operated by middle-class blacks (see Jackson to Woodson, January 7, 1942, box 35, Jackson Papers).

16. Jackson to Woodson, January 6, 1936; Woodson to Jackson, May 17, 1937; Jackson to Woodson, September 30, 1944; ibid., September 1, 1944, all in box 35, Jackson Papers.

17. Jackson to Woodson, May 15, 1937, box 35, Jackson Papers.

18. Jackson to Woodson, June 26, 1944, folder 990, box 35, Jackson Papers.

19. Jackson to Woodson, September 30, 1944, box 35, Jackson Papers.

20. Jackson, "The Annual History Drive in Virginia," 13; Jackson to Woodson, February 16, 1937, box 35; Jackson to Woodson, April 16, 1946, box 35; Jackson to Taylor, June 14, 1949, folder 247, box 12, Jackson Papers.

21. Grossman, "A Chance to Make Good," 397–400. Jackson also consistently appealed to the Jeanes supervisors to expand association memberships and distribute historical literature—particularly his own—to Virginia's black teachers (see Jackson to Jeanes supervisors, May 10, 1944, box 35, Jackson Papers).

22. Levine, The Unpredictable Past, 116. Levine makes the point that Garvey did not create racial consciousness, since African Americans could hardly avoid it in a climate of racial hostility and legal restrictions. What he did was articulate those sentiments at a time when African Americans yearned for control over their own destinies. Similarly, Jackson expressed a sense of racial awareness that average people had forged out of a tradition of perseverance and community self-reliance. Although Jackson did not invent racial consciousness, he directed aspirations for change into political avenues that had been blocked by official sanction and pervasive skepticism about voting. He and Woodson both realized that fundamental changes required a reconceptualization of the African American experience in history.

23. Trotter, "From a Raw Deal to a New Deal: 1929–1945," 423; for Randolph, black union organization, and increasing support for socialist alternatives, see Grossman, "A Chance to Make Good," 404–6.

24. Goggin, "Countering White Racist Scholarship," 361.

25. Kelley, "'But a Local Phase of a World Problem,'" para. 9.

26. Marcus Garvey, quoted in Levine, The Unpredictable Past, 120; Jackson, "The Annual Negro History Drive," 13; on the tendency of leaders to ascribe indifference to the masses while exalting their own roles in cultural renewal, see Levine's "Marcus Garvey and the Politics of Revitalization" in The Unpredictable Past, 107–36; Randolph quoted in Klinker (with Smith), The Unsteady March, 156.

27. Jackson, "Negro History Week," Norfolk Journal and Guide, February 1943.

28. Jackson, "The Work of the Association and the People"; for the importance of the

Negro History Bulletin, see Goggin, *Carter G. Woodson,* 114–15; as Meier and Rudwick point out, the NAACP started to focus on economic questions during the hardscrabble years of the Depression. The organization also doubled its membership between 1929 and 1939. Other civil rights organizations emerged, several adopting a leftist perspective that reflected a growing tolerance for radical alternatives in difficult times. The National Negro Congress, which supported communist-aligned groups, like the Communist Party itself, provided one of the more prominent destinations for African American political wanderers in the 1930s (see Meier and Bracey, "The NAACP As a Reform Movement" 16–18).

29. Woodson, "Negro History Week—The Twelfth Year," 142–43.

30. W. P. Bayless to Jackson, March 2, 1943, folder 156, box 7; Wellington Beale to Jackson, January 17, 1938, folder 133, box 5, Jackson Papers.

31. Virginia Southerland to Jackson, April 7, 1943, folder 158, box 7; see also Peggy Pender to Jackson, February 16, 1944, folder 172, box 7, Jackson Papers

32. Claude Ruffin, February 19, 1944, folder 172, box 7, Jackson Papers.

33. "Mrs. Gibbes," quoted in Jackson to Woodson, April 16, 1943, box 35, Jackson Papers.

34. Jackson to Woodson, March 26, 1943; Jackson to Woodson, April 4, 1943,, box 35, Jackson Papers.

35. February 6, 1943, box 35, Jackson Papers. For additional correspondence on teacher support of the association, see Jackson to Woodson, March 13, 1943; Woodson to Ruby Vaughan, March 15, 1943; Jackson to Woodson, January 31, 1943; Jackson to Woodson, July 1, 1943; Jackson to Woodson, January 15, 1947; Woodson to Sadye J. Yates, January 11, 1947, all in box 35, Jackson Papers.

36. Woodson to Jackson, December 13, 1937, box 35, Jackson Papers.

37. Woodson, "Negro History Week—The Twelfth Year," 145–46.

38. Fulz, "African American Teachers in the South," 411. The theme of self-confidence through historical rehabilitation continued into the 1930s and resonated among people other than professional historians. As W. F. Savoy, an ASNLH chairman, explained in "The Negro in the Curricula of the Schools": "The schools should fuse into the study of the development of our country the accomplishments of this ethnic group in the same way that other peoples and individuals are included. Self-esteem and emotional security are thus developed" (56). A history that included black exploits meant more than a broadened perspective on the past. It also meant the elimination of at least some of the intellectual barriers between blacks and self-actualization. This tendency to place blacks in the role of hapless victims and to minimize racial resilience materialized powerfully in the sociology of E. Franklin Frazier, who located the fragmentation of the black family in the trauma of slavery. Although this assumption came under attack in the 1960s, it enjoyed considerable currency in Jackson's period (see also 55–56).

39. Zimmerman, "Each 'Race' Could Have Its Heroes Sung," 92–93.

40. Reddick, "Racial Attitudes in American History Textbooks of the South," 264; Woodson, "Negro History Week—The Eighth Year," 108; Beale to Jackson, January 17, 1938, folder 133, box 5, Jackson Papers.

41. Woodson to Jackson, April 5, 1937, box 35, Jackson Papers.

42. Jackson to Woodson, October 9, 1943, folder 989, box 35, Jackson Papers.

43. Ibid; Jackson to Woodson, November 24, 1943, box 35, Jackson Papers.

44. Woodson to Jackson, January 11, 1944, box 35 (first quote); Jackson to Woodson, February 27, 1944, box 35 (second quote); Woodson to Jackson, March 18, 1944, box 35; Jackson to Woodson, March 8, 1944, box 35; Woodson to Jackson, March 4, 1944, box 35; September 30, 1944 Summary Statement of Drive for 1943–44, box 35, Jackson Papers. Though it might be hazardous to infer too much from it, Woodson initially responded to the project by stating: "In the main I agree with you on your proposals. The idea is a good one. After the annual meeting has passed I shall be in a position to give more time to it." Woodson was evidently distracted by preparations for the association meeting, but his response does seem to suggest that, even at this point, he had reservations about the proposal. Quite conceivably, he and Woodson were operating on different assumptions about the booklet's content (Woodson to Jackson, October 20, 1943, folder 989, box 35, Jackson Papers).

45. Jackson, *Negro Office-Holders in Virginia,* xi.

46. Woodson to Jackson, February 23, 1946, folder 994, box 35, Jackson Papers.

47. Jackson to Woodson, March 21, 1946, folder 994, box 35, Jackson Papers; on Woodson's proclivity for control, see Goggin, *Carter G. Woodson,* 126–27, 139.

48. Meier and Rudwick, *Black History and the Historical Profession,* 81. Greene thought seriously about abandoning Woodson but decided against it, convinced that "the Association and the *cause* is *bigger* than the *man*" (82); Jackson to Taylor, June 14, 1949, folder 247, box 12, Jackson Papers.

49. Jackson to Woodson, March 21, 1946, folder 994, box 35, Jackson Papers.

50. Jackson to Woodson, March 31, 1946, folder 994, box 35, Jackson Papers. As Goggin points out in *Carter G. Woodson,* "In the twilight of his life, Woodson devoted all of his languishing energies to popularizing black history among a mass audience, the cause that had always commanded the lion's share of his attention" (179).

51. Jackson to Woodson, May 20, 1944, folder 990, box 35, Jackson Papers.

52. Ibid.

Chapter 4. Voting for Freedom: Jackson and the Movement for Black Political Participation

1. Quoted in Litwack, Trouble in Mind, 370.

2. Glenda Elizabeth Gilmore explains disfranchisement in terms of the loss of political manhood. Whites of the Reconstruction era tried to restrict political leadership to the "Best Men" of both races. White elites expected that by monopolizing the definition of the "Best Men," they could limit political authority to white property holders as well as the least threatening and the fewest middle-class blacks. The Populist crusade, which brought working-class blacks and whites into a powerful anti-Democrat coalition, as well as the advent of imperialism and its ideology of worldwide white dominance, convinced younger whites to abandon their fathers' "Best Men" definition. To them, manhood meant the burden of whiteness and the obligation to dispel the darkness of allegedly backward civilizations. Despite the efforts of North Carolina's "best" black men to maintain class as the litmus test for political inclusion, elite whites cast political manhood in racial terms

that excluded even middle-class African Americans from political life (see Gilmore, *Gender and Jim Crow*, 61–89).

3. The historiography on Jackson is very thin, but Raymond Gavins suggests that Jackson and contemporaries such as P. B. Young and Gordon Hancock were racial moderates. Yet he also points out that opposing white racism, promoting racial autonomy, and encouraging black voting "were anything but conservative endeavors." Although Jackson espoused economic self-reliance and hard work—the values normally associated with Booker T. Washington—he also endorsed protest and political action, the virtues of W.E.B. Du Bois and the Niagara Movement (see Gavins, "Hancock, Jackson, and Young"). Although labels do little to elucidate Jackson, he is probably best described as a political realist who combined a number of strategies in the search for racial equality. He opposed disfranchisement but called for payment of the poll tax. He encouraged racial self-reliance yet cooperated with whites in a number of interracial initiatives. Confronted with racial exclusion, Jackson sought inclusion before all else. If anything, Jackson sought the fulfillment of the democratic promises made during Reconstruction, promises that took as their basic premise civic and political equality before the law (see Jackson, "New Year's Resolutions," *Norfolk Journal and Guide*, January 2, 1943). Jackson's liberal democratic beliefs mirrored those of other prominent southern blacks, including Charles Johnson, Gordon B. Hancock, and James Weldon Johnson. In an analysis of Fisk sociologist Charles Johnson, Matthew William Dunne writes that "the heart of the southern liberal program was a solid belief in the crucial elements of the American creed—in democracy, in equality, in freedom, in the pursuit of happiness—and in the institutions of American government" (Dunne, "Next Steps," 2).

4. John Douglas Smith, "Managing White Supremacy." In addition to racial violence and intimidation, Earl Lewis notes the pervasive "cues" that reinforced racial distinctions in Norfolk, Virginia. Derogatory terms, police interrogation, and paternalistic assertions of black inferiority entered into the "collective memory" of Norfolk blacks, convincing them that "full participation hinged on their ability to promote their own interests" (Lewis, *In Their Own Interests*, 66–67; see also chap. 3).

5. Goldfield, *Black, White, and Southern*, 2–6. As Goldfield explains, the code of racial behavior distorted white perceptions of African Americans, creating a "stage Negro" that reflected the characteristics that whites ascribed to the entire race. The southern racial etiquette fostered a range of beliefs that validated black subordination (see also Litwack, *Trouble in Mind*, 3–51). For the psychological dimension of racial control at work in the Jim Crow South, see the intriguing oral history featured in Chafe, "The Gods Bring Threads to Webs Begun." For African American opposition to segregation in the New South, see Hale, "'For Colored' and 'For White,'" 163–66. Robin D. G. Kelley argues that episodes of black resistance on public transportation were often in response to the flagrant attempt by bus drivers and white passengers to humiliate black travelers. Routine confrontations and breaches of the color line demonstrated black willingness to challenge white domination of public space (see Kelley, "'We Are Not What We Seem,'" 102–10).

6. Goldfield, *Black, White, and Southern*, 25–27; Kennedy, *Freedom from Fear*, 208–10; Sullivan, *Days of Hope*, 3–5, 177–78.

7. Rubin, *Virginia: A Bicentennial History,* 160–61; J. Douglas Smith, *Managing White Supremacy,* 31–32.

8. Heinemann, *Depression and New Deal in Virginia,* 185.

9. Gavins, "Hancock, Jackson, and Young," 476; Suggs, "Black Strategy and Ideology in the Segregation Era," 179–80; Rubin, *Virginia: A Bicentennial History,* 170–71; Dabney, *Virginia: The New Dominion,* 493–96, 503.

10. Goldfield, *Black, White, and Southern,* 28.

11. Roosevelt's appointments included Mary McLeod Bethune to the post of special advisor on minority affairs, as well as Robert Weaver and William Hastie to the Office of Negro Affairs, a division of the Department of the Interior. Ickes, like other New Deal reformers, operated on the assumption that federal policy should incorporate African Americans into an expansive industrial economy that would soften class barriers and racial distinctions. For Ickes and many others in the Roosevelt cabinet, economic opportunity would dilute the racial animosities that had grown thick in the atmosphere of Republican negligence (see Kirby, *Black Americans in the Roosevelt Era,* 18–35).

12. Fairclough, *Better Day Coming,* 195–96.

13. As a number of historians have pointed out—David Kennedy most recently—Hoover was far from the curmudgeonly defender of laissez-faire portrayed in many earlier accounts. Hoover encouraged businesses and local governments to generate recovery in 1929, a strategy that reflected the diminutive size of the federal government and the limited fiscal tools available to it. Nevertheless, the Hoover administration's preference for solidifying the banking system and avoiding large-scale relief programs sealed its political fate (see Kennedy, *Freedom from Fear,* 47–49, 70–91).

14. Buni, *The Negro in Virginia Politics,* 90–91, 106–7, 124–125; Moon, *Balance of Power,* 156.

15. Key, *Southern Politics in State and Nation,* 20.

16. Bass and Devries, *The Transformation of Southern Politics,* 339–40.

17. Lawson, *Running for Freedom,* 15–16.

18. Jackson to Rayford Logan, May 10, 1943, folder 160, box 7, Jackson Papers.

19. Gavins, *The Perils and Prospects of Southern Black Leadership,* 87.

20. This struggle over the meaning of race and its relationship to issues of class, social reform, and political power is effectively illustrated in John Kirby's *Black Americans in the Roosevelt Era: Liberalism and Race,* chap. eight.

21. "League of Negro Voters Constitution," in folder titled "Virginia Voters League Constitution," box 18, Jackson Papers.

22. Jackson to "Fellow Citizen," April 26, 1937, in folder titled "Virginia Voters League Main Office 1937–39," box 1, Jackson Papers.

23. Ibid.

24. "Local Fraternities Support Voters' League," n.d., folder 524; form letter, Jackson to "Fellow Citizen," March 22, 1935, folder 509; Jackson to the Faculty of Virginia State College, November 25, 1935, folder 509, box 18, including quote; form letter, Jackson to "fellow citizen," April 26, 1937, folder 511, box 18, Jackson Papers.

25. Jackson to D. A. Wilkerson, April 4, 1935, folder 509, box 18, Jackson Papers.

26. Ibid. Jackson, "The Deadline for All Citizens," April 17, 1943, *Norfolk Journal and*

Guide; Jackson to Reverend Richard Bolling, December 10, 1943, folder 167, box 7, Jackson Papers.

27. Jackson, "Failing to Embrace Political Opportunities," *Norfolk Journal and Guide,* November 14, 1942; see also "The Deadline for All Citizens," *Norfolk Journal and Guide,* April 17, 1943; "Ministers of the Gospel and the Voting Movement," *Norfolk Journal and Guide,* December 4, 1943; Jackson to Reverend Richard Bolling, December 10, 1943, folder 167, box 7, Jackson Papers.

28. "Why Negro Should Vote in Petersburg and How They May," in folder titled "Virginia Voters League Report #5," box 18, Jackson Papers.

29. Madden, interview.

30. Buni, *The Negro in Virginia Politics,* 142.

31. Ibid., 124–26. Jackson and his contemporaries vigilantly intervened in reported cases of registrar discrimination, but undoubtedly many cases went unreported and unopposed. Buni's suggestion that "unfair questioning" persisted only in a handful of counties—and then only until the NAACP or the Virginia Voters League challenged it in the courts—is a little dubious. Just as documenting the myriad cases of racial discrimination in the lives of average southern blacks is next to impossible, so too is it difficult to pin down when a given disqualification was in fact an informal application of the southern racial code. Probably the safest conclusion is that the frequency and conspicuousness of "understanding" questions declined significantly. This point is important to keep in mind as a balance against Jackson's assertion that blacks suffered primarily from self-disfranchisement after 1940.

32. "What the People Think of Voting in Petersburg, Virginia," 1, folder 524, box 18, Jackson Papers.

33. Ibid; Sullivan, *Days of Hope,* 106–7.

34. Hale, *Making Whiteness,* 284; quotes from "What the People Think about Voting in Petersburg," 2–3, folder 524, box 18, Jackson Papers.

35. "What the People Think about Voting in Petersburg," 2, folder 524, box 18, Jackson Papers.

36. Gilmore, *Gender and Jim Crow,* 147–49.

37. Sullivan, *Days of Hope,* 107. In 1940, Virginia Durr of the Southern Conference for Human Welfare accompanied thirty women from the organization to Washington, where they signed a statement of protest against the poll tax. The event commemorated the twentieth anniversary of the Nineteenth Amendment, but it was less a celebration than an admission that barriers still prevented women from voting. A Department of Labor report estimated that four million American women could not vote because of the poll tax. The report also identified the special burden the tax placed on working-class families. After a senator and two congressional representatives took up the matter, the women's initiative gained national media coverage and added momentum to the drive to abolish the poll tax (see Reed, *Simple Decency and Common Sense,* 72–73).

38. Ibid.

39. "What the People Think about Voting in Petersburg," 3, folder 524, box 18, Jackson Papers.

40. Ibid.

41. Jackson, "Citizenship Training," 481.

42. Curtis, "Luther P. Jackson and the Virginia Voters' League," 22–23.

43. Jackson, "Citizenship Training," 481; Curtis, "Luther P. Jackson and the Virginia Voters' League," 24–25.

44. Jackson, "Citizenship Training," 481; Buni, *The Negro in Virginia Politics,* 127–28; minutes of the Virginia Voters League, November 28, 1948, folder 522, box 18; Jackson form letter, April 26, 1941, in folder titled "Virginia Voters' League Main Office, 1940–41," box 18, Jackson Papers.

45. Jackson, "Instructions to County Chairmen," June 21, 1941; "Citizenship Survey of New Kent County," n.d.; Jackson to "Eighty Chairmen of the Virginia Voters' League," June 26, 1941, folder titled "Virginia Voters League Main Office, 1940–41," box 18, Jackson Papers.

46. Jackson form letter, August 4, 1941; Jackson form letter, August 27, 1941, box 18, Jackson Papers; Buni, *The Negro in Virginia Politics,* 128–29.

47. Jackson, "Citizenship Training" 483–84.

48. Ibid., 484–85.

49. Higgins to Jackson, April 18, 1941, folder 138, box 6, Jackson Papers.

50. V. O. Key to Jackson, September 14, 1948, folder 239, box 12,; Du Bois to Jackson, August 4, 1948, folder 238, box 12; Hugh and Mabel Smythe to Jackson, August 4, 1948, folder 238, box 12, Jackson Papers.

51. Jackson to Evans, September 20, 1943, folder 164, box 7, Jackson Papers.

52. Buni, *The Negro in Virginia Politics,* 127–28; Jackson to the city chairmen of the Virginia Voters League, September 25, 1942, in folder titled "Virginia Voters' League, Main Office, 1942–3"; "Instructions Relative to Voting Requirements," n.d., folder 516; Jackson, "The Role of the NAACP," *Norfolk Journal and Guide,* April 3, 1943; see also "Rules Governing the Virginia Voters League," which explicitly endorsed the effort to affiliate with the State Teachers Association, the Negro Organization Society, and the NAACP. Folder titled "Virginia Voter League Rules," box 18, Jackson Papers; exemplifying Jackson's support for the NAACP was his address on "Lining up the Virginia Negro to Vote," given at the Virginia State Conference in 1941. There, Jackson emphasized that the Virginia Voters League was "supplementary" to the NAACP, functioning as a "clearing house" for stimulating black political participation (see "Proceedings of the Evening Session—Virginia State Conference," November 9, 1941, Reel 25, Selected Branch Files, 1940–1955, NAACP Papers).

53. In a recent review of Neil McMillen's *Remaking Dixie,* Roger Lotchin warns against easy assumptions about the war's alleged transformation of the South. Although segregation, disfranchisement, and poverty continued after the conflict, many historians insist on a "foundations theory of war" in which World War II becomes the "delayed fuse" for the civil rights movement of the 1960s. Since the war did not immediately set in motion events that eradicated formal racial discrimination, Lotchin recommends a more rigorous accounting of cause and effect relationships between the war and the black freedom struggle (see Lotchin's review of *Remaking Dixie: The Impact of World War II on the American South,* ed. Neil McMillen, in *Journal of American History,* 1131).

54. Egerton, *Speak Now Against the Day,* 213; Foner, *The Story of American Freedom,* 242,

55. Sitkoff, "African American Militancy in the World War II South," 79, see also 70–92. Richard Polenberg contends that the federal government pressured the black press into dropping their vigorous support for the "Double V"—victory abroad and at home against segregation. By threatening to withhold newsprint or even prosecute offending newspapers, the administration was able to derail serious criticism of racial inequalities (Polenberg, "The Good War?" 306–7).

56. Buni, *The Negro in Virginia Politics* 84 (December 1997): 146.

57. Minutes of the Virginia Voters League, August 17, 1941, in folder titled "Virginia Voters League Minutes—1941," box 18, Jackson Papers.

58. Jackson to Virginia State University staff, December 1, 1941, folder titled "Virginia Voters League Main Office, 1940–41," box 18, Jackson Papers.

59. Jackson to D. A. Wilkerson, April 4, 1935, folder 509, box 18, Jackson Papers.

60. Picott, *History of the Virginia Teachers Association,* 111–17; Tindall, *The Emergence of the New South,* 564; for the salary equalization drive in Louisiana and its importance for strengthening connections between the NAACP and the Louisiana Colored Teachers Association, see Fairclough, *Race and Democracy,* 99–102.

61. Established in 1915, Carter Woodson's association became the most important vehicle for promoting black history in the pre–World War II period. Jackson was largely responsible for expanding the association's presence in Virginia and for promoting the observance of Negro History Week among its teachers. Disseminating the history of black cultural and political accomplishments was central to the association's efforts to challenge the racial discrimination that filtered into textbooks and classrooms across the country. Encouraged by the Harlem Renaissance and the association's example, the Virginia Teachers Association endorsed this pedagogical orientation in the 1930s. According to Jackson, they became its leading proponents in Virginia thereafter (see Jackson, *A History of the Virginia State Teachers Association,* 95–112). For Jackson's invaluable work on behalf of the association in Virginia, see Goggin, *Carter G. Woodson,* 116–17. On Jackson's often stormy relationship with Woodson, who resented the former's ability to combine popular appeal and scholarly undertakings, see Meier and Rudwick, *Black History and the Historical Profession,* 86–88.

62. Jackson to the chairmen of the Virginia Voters League, December 16, 1941, in folder titled "Virginia Voters' League Main Office, 1940–41," box 18, Jackson Papers.

63. Fairclough, *Race and Democracy,* xviii.

64. Appealing to teachers was one of Jackson's main strategies for preserving the league during the war. As he put it to the chairpersons of the Virginia Voters League, "Cooperate with the Jeanes Supervisor or your high school principal.... In recent weeks every Jeanes supervisor and high school principal has been reached with several pieces of mail asking that we get our teachers qualified, and that we place special stress on voting in class room instruction" (emphasis added). Jackson to the one hundred chairmen of the Virginia Voters League, April 9, 1942, in folder titled "Virginia Voters' League, Main Office 1942–43," box 18, Jackson Papers.

65. Janken, *Rayford W. Logan and the Dilemma of the African American Intellectual,* 99–106.

66. Report on voting status of black teachers, 1948 (n.d.), folder 529, box 18, Jackson

Papers. Jackson had prepared a similar report in 1944, which covered 110 high schools. That year, he credited the Virginia Voters League with increasing the number of teachers voting from 15 percent in 1936 to over 50 percent in 1944 (see Jackson, "Citizenship Training," 485–86).

67. Jackson, "Citizenship Training," 485–86; Madden, interview; Luther P. Jackson Jr., interview.

68. Howell to Luther P. Jackson Jr., March 2, 1984, in author's possession.

69. Ibid.

70. Report on the voting status of black teachers; Jackson to I. A. Derbigney, October 26, 1941, folder 140, box 6, Jackson Papers. In addition to classroom instruction, Jackson also took his classes to witness government in action at Washington, Richmond, and Petersburg. Students returned ready to write letters to congressional representatives and sign petitions to end the scourge of lynching.

71. Jackson to Derbigney, October 26, 1941.

72. In fact, P. B. Young had been advocating the organization of voter leagues since 1921. Paralleling Jackson, Young favored an active electorate over mass protest. Again, like Jackson, Young was a longtime proponent of classical Washingtonian values, but he deviated from his mentor on a number of *Journal and Guide* issues, particularly the question of political participation. While Washington accepted disfranchisement, Young, like Jackson, insisted on political engagement (see Suggs, "P. B. Young of the Norfolk" and "Black Strategy and Ideology in the Segregation Era").

73. Plunkett to Jackson, August 26, 1941, folder 138, box 6; Jackson to Plunkett, August 29, 1941, folder 138, box 6; Plunkett to Jackson, December 1, 1941, folder 142, box 6; Plunkett to Jackson, May 6, 1942, folder 14, box 6; Jackson to Congressman Dave E. Satterfield, October 13, 1942, folder 150, box 6; Plunkett to Jackson, October 13, 1942, folder 150, box 6; Jackson to Senator Harry F. Byrd, November 4, 1942, folder 15, box 6, Jackson Papers; Barnard, ed., *Outside the Magic Circle: The Autobiography of Virginia Foster Durr*, chap. 9; Lawson, *Black Ballots*, 83–85. For Jackson's support of the national anti–poll-tax campaign, see "Abolishing the Poll Tax," *Norfolk Journal and Guide*, June 5, 1943.

74. Hancock to W.E.B. Du Bois, September 12, 1942, box 1, Hancock Papers; Hancock to Jackson, June 15, 1942, folder 147, box 6, Jackson Papers (quote).

75. Hancock to Du Bois, September 12, 1942, Hancock Papers; Gavins, "Hancock, Jackson, and Young," 479–80. Hancock, obviously on the defensive about the intentions behind the Durham Conference and his role in it, rendered another account of its origins to the Southern Regional YWCA in 1944. There, he reiterated the argument that the conference organizers sought to deflect southern white reactionary criticism, but he added that the tension of the war years were more a direct threat to southern blacks and that, in the end, they wanted "the same things as other Negroes throughout the nation" (see "The Southern Regional Council: Its Origins and Purpose," box 1, Hancock Papers).

76. "A Basis for Inter-Racial Cooperation and Development in the South: A Statement by Southern Negroes," in Johnson et al., *To Stem This Tide*, 132–39.

77. Jackson, "A Program of Political and Civil Rights," *Norfolk Journal and Guide*, March 11, 1944, Jackson Papers.

78. "A Basis for Inter-Racial Cooperation and Development in the South: A Statement

by Southern Negroes," 132–39; form letter, Virginia Conference on Race Relations, July 27, folder 147, box 6, Jackson Papers; Gordon B. Hancock to Jackson, June 15, 1942, folder 147, box 6, Jackson Papers.

79. Gavins, "Hancock, Jackson, and Young," 470–86; historian Numan Bartley describes the SRC as "the most traditional of mainstream liberal organizations." Dominated by whites, the organization sought to ameliorate segregation through "behind the scenes" appeals to political and business notables in the South. According to Bartley, the organization had grown to only 3,500 members by the end of the 1940s (Bartley, *The New South*, 29–31).

80. Quoted in Sullivan, *Days of Hope*, 149.

81. Lawson, *Running for Freedom*, 26.

82. Jackson to Frazer, August 31, 1947, folder 68, box 3, Jackson Papers.

83. Jackson to Johnella Frazer, September 4, 1947; Jackson to Frazer, August 31, 1947, folder 68, box 3, Jackson Papers.

84. Jackson, "Race and Suffrage in the South," 1, 18.

85. Ibid., 9, 18, 25.

86. Hugh and Mabel Smythe, August 4, 1948, folder 238, box 12; Jackson to W. C. Hueston, December 7, 1948, folder 242, box 12, Jackson Papers.

87. See "A Program of Political and Civil Rights"; "The Role of the N.A.A.C.P.," *Norfolk Journal and Guide*, April 3, 1943.

88. Jackson, "Within the Walls of Segregation," *Norfolk Journal and Guide*, March 27, 1943.

89. Lawson, *Black Ballots*, 124–26.

Chapter 5. Teachers Struggle for a Voice: From Professionalism to Political Action

1. Chafe, "The Gods Bring Threads to Webs Begun," 1544–45.

2. Figures for male teachers are comparable. In 1940–41, African American schoolteachers were paid on average $726 annually, while white men were paid $1,272. Figures from superintendent of public instruction, Commonwealth of Virginia, *Annual Report*, 1940–1950, as cited in Wilkerson, "The Negro School Movement in Virginia," 19.

3. Ambrose Caliver, "Education of Negro Teachers," in U.S. Office of Education Bulletin Number 10, cited in Fultz, "Teacher Training and African American Education in the South," 198.

4. Fultz, "Teacher Training and African American Education in the South," 199–200; Adam Fairclough has recently restated the case that black education, in whatever form, was intrinsically subversive of white supremacy. Certainly a good many white southerners never made the subtle distinctions between Booker T. Washington's industrial education and the liberal-classical brand practiced at countless African American schools, including colleges, throughout the South. To these, education of any sort destabilized a social order premised on racial exclusion. Whether or not Washington's ultimate but deferred hope for racial equality leavened his accommodationism is another question (see Fairclough,

"'Being in the Field of Education,'" 71; see also Anderson, *The Education of Blacks in the South*). For a study that emphasizes the cultural and intellectual vitality of black schools despite the disadvantages of segregation, see Walker, *Their Highest Potential,* particularly chapter 6, which stresses the idea that teachers encouraged their students to excel despite racial intolerance.

5. Anderson, *The Education of Blacks in the South,* 101, 153–56; Jackson, *A History of the Virginia State Teachers Association,* 43–49. Anderson makes the point that blacks had been supporting schools through taxes as well as private contributions since Reconstruction. The practice of "double taxation" simply reflected the realities of a biracial school system in which public officials could funnel African American taxes into white institutions with impunity.

6. Jackson, *History of the Virginia Teachers Association,* 34–35; Talbot, "History of the Virginia Teachers Association."

7. Fairclough, "'Being in the Field of Education,'" 72. The Negro Organization Society—a vehicle of the Hampton Institute and a proponent of industrial education—absorbed the local improvement league movement after 1917. Jackson describes it variously as a "tidal wave" and a "machine"—accurate metaphors for the Tuskegee-Hampton program and its juggernaut of northern philanthropy. Whatever the limitations of the Tuskegee philosophy in advancing civil equality, the Negro Organization Society sponsored local leagues willing to "erect better buildings, create longer terms, increase the salaries of teachers, and effect a more regular attendance on the part of pupils." The progress was limited, but it suggested that efforts in this direction made a vital connection between educational reform and the professional advancement of teachers, both of which required popular mobilization (see Jackson, *History of the Virginia Teachers Association,* 61–62).

8. Fulz, "African American Teachers in the South," 410. Lester Lamon and others have made the point that as whites devoted more attention and resources to their own education, blacks struggled to keep pace. They challenged the increasing discrepancies in "the quality and quantity of school buildings, student-teacher ratios, teacher pay, school terms, provisions for secondary schooling, and legislative appropriations." For the most part, African Americans failed to convince white administrators that black schooling mattered. As Lamon points out, the deliberate isolation of black schools provided white officials justification enough to ignore any appeals to improve them (Lamon, "Black Public Education in the South," 84).

9. Jackson, *History of the Virginia State Teachers Association,* 68.

10. Toppin, *Loyal Sons and Daughters,* 13–19, 53–55.

11. Jackson, *History of the Virginia State Teachers Association,* 69.

12. Colson, "The Teachers' College and Normal School," 294.

13. Toppin, *Loyal Sons and Daughters,* 79–83.

14. Jackson, *History of the Virginia State Teachers Association,* 92.

15. For example, Edna Colson gave an address on "Unsolved Problems in Negro Education" at the Norfolk annual meeting in 1925; Picott, *History of the Virginia Teachers Association,* 105–6; Jackson to Frazer, June 21, 1926, folder 49, box 3, Jackson Papers; Jackson, *History of the Virginia State Teachers Association,* 54.

16. Jackson, *History of the Virginia Teachers Association,* 90–91. By 1936, the membership had reached 3,500.

17. Ibid., 81–83.

18. Vivian F. Colter to Jackson, October 5, 1943, folder 164, box 7, Jackson papers.

19. S. D. Womack to Jackson, January 26, 1942, folder 143, box 6.

20. For VTA Speakers Bureau applications, n.d., see folder 725, box 28; for a sampling of additional requests for Jackson's services from schools and other organizations, see Seay to Jackson, January 22, 1942,; ibid., January 23, 1942; E. N. Talioferro to Seay, January 20, 1942; Seay to Jackson, February 13, 1942; Seay to Jackson, February 16, 1942; Seay to Jackson, February 25, 1942; Seay to Jackson, March 3, 1942; Seay to Jackson, March 11, 1942; Seay to Jackson, March 13, 1942; Seay to Jackson, March 19, 1942; Seay to Jackson, March 23, 1942, all folder 725, box 28, Jackson Papers.

21. E. N. Talioferro to Jackson, December 30, 1941, folder 142, box 6, Jackson Papers.

22. Jackson to C. W. Seay, April 7, 1942, folder 726, box 28, Jackson Papers.

23. Jackson to Seay, December 23, 1941, folder 724, box 28, Jackson Papers.

24. W. H. Budley to Jackson, February 6, 1942, folder 144, box 6, Jackson Papers.

25. As Lutrelle Palmer pointed out to school superintendents, the Virginia Teachers Association had tried over the past fifty years to professionalize teachers and convince them of their "obligation" to society, two objectives that had been advanced by sending "thousands of speakers to hundreds of localities to address parents and teachers on the great issues involved in education for democratic living" (Palmer to the superintendents of schools, September 27, 1941, folder 136, box 13, Jackson Papers).

26. Lessie Evans Hogart to Jackson, October 6, 1942, folder 150, box 6 Jackson Papers.

27. Wilkerson, "The Negro School Movement in Virginia," 17. Wilkerson points out that "[f]or a long time such activity centered chiefly in the maintenance of private Negro schools, pleas to public school authorities, and private money-raising to help improve the public schools—to lengthen the term, or increase the teacher's salary, or buy a plot of land to be donated to the county for the erection of a school building."

28. Quoted in Fulz, "African American Teachers in the South," 413.

29. Jackson, *History of the Virginia State Teachers Association,* 84, 93; Bullock, *A History of Negro Education in the South,* 181.

30. Grace Hays Johnson, "Phases of Cultural History of Significance for Negro Students," 34–35. See also Jackson, "Unexplored Fields," 57–58, 65–67.

31. Jackson, *History of the Virginia Teachers Association,* 103.

32. Zimmerman, "Each 'Race' Could Have Its Heroes Sung," 99; Fulz, "African American Teachers in the South," 411.

33. Picott, *History of the Virginia Teachers Association,* 96.

34. Figures from average monthly salary are taken from Bullock, *A History of Negro Education in the South,* 181; figures on decline in monthly salaries are from Mitchell, "The Economic Status of the Negro in Virginia," 11. The figure of twenty-one dollars applies to rural teachers; according to Mitchell, urban teachers experienced an average decrease of fifteen dollars for the same period.

35. Meier and Bracey, "The NAACP As a Reform Movement," 15–16.

36. Suggs, *P. B. Young, Newspaperman,* 158–59.

37. Meier and Bracey, "The NAACP As a Reform Movement," 15; Charles H. Houston, "Factors Involved in Salary Scheduling," n.d, Part 3, Series A, Campaign for Educational Equality, Reel 1; Houston, "Program of Attacks on Educational Discrimination," ibid., Reel 2, NAACP Papers. In the latter, attorney Charles Houston explained that the NAACP would focus on salary differentials since they were governed by law and "present[ed] a definite and concrete issue in which are implicated all the questions of school buildings, physical plant, curriculum, and length of term." The same report outlines the strategy against inadequate school transportation facilities and segregated graduate and professional education.

38. Bullock, *A History of Negro Education in the South,* 216–17.

39. Lewis, *In Their Own Interests,* 157.

40. Franklin, *From Slavery to Freedom,* 407–8; Roberts, "Some Background Factors in the Education of Virginia's Rural Negro Population," 16.

41. Lewis, *In Their Own Interests,* 158–60. For a more complete treatment of the early salary equalization cases in Norfolk, see *In Their Own Interests,* chap. 6, as well as Suggs, *P. B. Young, Newspaperman,* chap. 10.

42. Lewis, *In Their Own Interests,* 161–64; Suggs, *P. B. Young, Newspapersman,* 160–62.

43. Quoted in Lewis, *In Their Own Interests,* 165.

44. Quoted in Suggs, *P. B. Young, Newspaperman,* 164. Opposition to salary equalization was not limited to Virginia. As Gunnar Myrdal reported in 1944, the Alston decision did not sweep away salary inequities or the determination of local authorities to preserve them. Paralleling the Norfolk arrangement, local officials "that have shown any willingness to comply have usually contented themselves with plans for gradual equalization over a period of years." Myrdal added that the movement would have consequences outside the immediate material concerns of teachers: "The coming rise in the economic status of the largest Negro professional group will represent a change of no small importance. It is quite likely that it will have certain beneficial secondary effects on Negro education and on Negro leadership" (Myrdal, *An American Dilemma,* 338).

45. Lewis, *In Their Own Interests,* 160.

46. Jackson, "The Virginia State Teachers Association," *Norfolk Journal and Guide,* June 3, 1944. Establishing a clear sense of precisely how much support the plaintiffs received after Black was dismissed and after Alston's case failed in the district court of Norfolk is difficult. Certainly the upper echelon of the Virginia Teachers Association supported the litigation, considering the psychological and financial investment made in the salary initiative. According to Jackson, however, the period preceding the landmark Alston decision was filled with "dark hours." In Jackson's recollection, "they at first met with criticism and restraint from numerous people"—presumably even before Black's dismissal. Probably speaking about the turn of events in the Alston case—an ambiguity stemming from Jackson's deliberately breezy and rhetorical style—teachers "on all sides" sent up the cry of "Drop your suit." Jackson then recalls—in an example of journalistic melodrama —that he sent a letter to Black in which he assured her that "[r]eactionary forces may surround you, yet your cause is a just one . . . have plenty of

courage and remember that you are making history for all of us." Despite the regression, Jackson's point is clear: the salary equalization movement exposed the fissures in the ranks of African American teachers confronting the realities of a public power struggle over questions of race and class at the foundation of the social order in the South. The teachers' movement, like the voting initiative, was never a unified march to freedom (Jackson, "A Tribute to Melvin Alston, D. Ed.," *Norfolk Journal and Guide*, October 28, 1944).

47. Earl Lewis makes the point that since teachers enjoyed particular prestige in black communities, discriminatory salaries "affronted all blacks and underscored the pervasiveness of social inequality." Salary equalization for teachers might also have implications for other areas of the economy plagued by racial disparities (Lewis, *In Their Own Interests*, 160).

48. Suggs, *P. B. Young, Newspaperman*, 162. It is important to note the discrepancies between Suggs's, Lewis's, and Mark V. Tushnet's accounts of the Norfolk case. While Suggs asserts that the teachers approved a "settlement prepared by the NAACP" (162), Lewis believes that the teachers accepted a three-year phase-in scheme consistent with the city's proposal and opposed to the NAACP's counsel. Tushnet, on the other hand, contends that Marshall only "threatened to withdraw"—in Lewis's account, he did withdraw—which was enough to defeat the compromise and produce instead a "consent decree" rather than a dismissal of the case altogether. The consent decree, like the "compromise" in Suggs's and Lewis's accounts, provided for salary equalization over three years (see Tushnet, *The NAACP's Legal Strategy against Segregated Education*, 80).

49. Jackson, *History of the Virginia Teachers Association*, 108.

50. Jackson, "Citizenship and Government Participation," 10–11.

51. Jackson certainly approved of the legal counsel rendered in the Norfolk cases, writing to congratulate Leon Ransom, one of the members of the legal team. Ransom thanked him for the letter, suggesting that "it is expressions from friends like you that keep us heartened despite the disappointments and difficulties that we encounter.... We know you have a sincere and abiding interest in the work" (Ransom to Jackson, March 6, 1941, folder 138, box 6, Jackson Papers).

52. Jackson to E.S.H. Greene, superintendent of Chesterfield schools, February 2, 1941, folder 137 box 6; Jackson to E.S.H. Greene, superintendent of Chesterfield schools, December 6, 1948, folder 242, box 12, Jackson Papers.

53. Arthur Freeman and J. P. Spencer to J. Rupert Picott, September 19, 1946, folder 717, box 28, Jackson Papers.

54. Jackson to Picott, September 23, 1946, folder 717, box 28, Jackson papers.

55. Martin to Picott, September 26, 1946, folder 717, box 28; for additional background on the Equalization Committee's disappointment with the slow progress of the Chesterfield case, see J. M. Tinsley to Picott, September 27, 1946, folder 717, box 28, Jackson Papers.

56. Jordan, "The Impact of the Negro Organization Society on Public Support for Education in Virginia," 52–100.

57. James Spencer to Jackson, December 16, 1948, folder 242, box 12, Jackson Papers.

58. Jackson, "Rights and Duties in a Democracy," *Norfolk Journal and Guide,* February 6, 1943

59. Jackson to Greene, December 6, 1948, box 12, Jackson Papers.

60. Spencer to Jackson, December 16, 1948, box 12, Jackson Papers.

61. Jackson, "The Newport News Salary Case"; Gerald L. Smith, *A Black Educator in the Segregated South,* 129; Jackson, "Equalization of Salaries in North Carolina," *Norfolk Journal and Guide* August 7, 1943.

62. Jackson, "The Newport News Affair," *Norfolk Journal and Guide,* May 29, 1943.

63. Bullock, *A History of Negro Education in the South,* 219.

64. Jackson, "The Newport News Affair," *Norfolk Journal and Guide,* May 29, 1943.

65. Jackson, "Resorting to the Courts," *Norfolk Journal and Guide,* June 19, 1943.

66. Jackson to Palmer, August 11, 1943, folder 713, box 28, Jackson Papers.

67. Jackson, "The Newport News Affair—the Tragedy of 1943," December 23, 1943, unpublished manuscript, folder 1612, box 64, Jackson Papers.

68. Jackson, "Fighting Again in Newport News," *Norfolk Journal and Guide,* April 8, 1944; "The Teacher Salary Fight—The Hope for the Future," *Norfolk Journal and Guide,* January 13, 1945. For Jackson's coverage of the Newport News case and the salary equalization movement, see also "The Newport News Court Case," *Norfolk Journal and Guide,* August 14, 1943, and "The Teacher Salary Fight—The Hope for the Future," *Norfolk Journal and Guide,* January 13, 1945.

69. Jackson, "The Newport News Affair," *Norfolk Journal and Guide,* May 29, 1943.

70. Palmer to Jackson, May 21, 1943, folder 713, box 29, Jackson Papers.

71. Jackson to Wendell Walker, February 28, 1944, folder 172, box 7,; on his belief that the Palmer episode would continue to resonate among many of Virginia's black teachers, see Jackson to Arthur Davis, August 8, 1943, folder 163, box 7, Jackson Papers.

72. Palmer applauded Jackson for being "one of the first to recognize that this is no local affair merely." Palmer, of course, also cast the Newport News struggle in terms of a larger struggle against salary inequities and racial discrimination: "The action of the Newport News School Board far transcends the fate of the six teachers involved." Interestingly, Palmer suggested that the board's reaction was directed against the African American elite, the middle class that filled the ranks of the voting movement and the school equalization campaign. Palmer suggested the larger implications of the salary movement, which in conjunction with the voter registration drive accelerated the tempo of the civil rights movement: "This attack must be beaten down in its initial stages, otherwise we shall lose one of our greatest battles for the integration of Negroes into full American citizenship" (Palmer to Jackson, June 7, 1943, folder 713, box 28, Jackson Papers).

73. Jackson to C. W. Seay, June 5, 1943, folder 162, box 7, Jackson Papers.

74. Jackson to John B. Henderson, June 6, 1943, folder 162, box 7, Jackson Papers.

75. C. W. Seay to Palmer, May 26, 1943; Seay to Colgate W. Darden, May 26, 1943, folder 727, box 28, Jackson Papers.

76. Seay to members of the State Board of Education and Dr. Dabney S. Lancaster, May 26, 1943, folder 727, box 28, Jackson Papers (emphasis added). The dismissals certainly sent shock waves throughout the ranks of Virginia's black teachers. In one example, Jack-

son wrote a letter supporting the application of a former teacher at the Huntington High School for a position in Williamsburg. "I do not know why he wishes to change," Jackson commented, "except the uncertainty of tenure for any Negroes in Newport News under the iron rule of the present school board" (Jackson to Rawls Byrd, June 6, 1943, folder 162, box 7, Jackson Papers).

77. Jackson, "The Newport News Affair," *Norfolk Journal and Guide*, May 29, 1943. Although Jackson had a marginal role in the Norfolk case, he believed that the drive for salary equalization harmonized with his movement for political self-determination. Even before the Newport News case, Jackson wrote to Palmer that he was planning to pay attention to the teacher situation in the *Journal and Guide*: "After all, my aim is not simply voting but the larger program of participation in the affairs of government." To this end, Jackson proposed making the department of civic education a regular feature in the Virginia Teachers Association *Bulletin*. Jackson to Palmer, March 11, 1942, folder 712, box 28, Jackson Papers. In the *Journal and Guide,* he reinforced the idea that political action included more than casting a ballot: "The pastor, president, or head of a church, lodge, Greek letter society, civic association, voters league, or N.A.A.C.P branch may send letters and telegrams expressing the wishes of the group, or he may send in a petition signed by all the members of his organization." Regardless of the method, though, the end objective remained political influence for African Americans, not simply moral example or a return to white paternalism (see Jackson, "Exercising Pressure on Government," *Norfolk Journal and Guide,* October 31, 1942).

78. Seay to chairman, Newport News School Board, May 26, 1943; Seay to Jackson, June 7, 1943, folder 727, box 28, Jackson Papers.

79. Palmer to Jackson, November 24, 1943, folder 713, box 28, Jackson Papers; Jackson, "The Newport News Affair—The Tragedy of 1943," unpublished manuscript, folder 1612, box 64, Jackson Papers.

80. Palmer to Jackson, November 24, 1943, folder 713, box 28, Jackson Papers. Harvard Sitkoff notes that "[m]any of the African American educators and teachers, often the mainstay of the NAACP's southern branches, particularly feared the loss of their positions as a consequence of attacking and eliminating the segregated public school systems." Not until 1950 would the NAACP board of directors commit itself to a campaign explicitly directed against segregation rather than at the equalization of salaries and facilities (see Sitkoff, "African American Militancy in the World War II South," 79).

81. Tushnet, *The NAACP's Legal Strategy against Segregated Education,* 79.

82. Palmer to Jackson, October 18, 1944, folder 714, box 28, Jackson Papers. Looking at the salary initiative throughout the South, Patricia Sullivan concludes that "the slow, piecemeal nature of the legal campaign, along with the seemingly limitless capacity of local officials to evade rulings and harass plaintiffs in NAACP cases, was a continuing source of frustration and disillusionment" (Sullivan, *Days of Hope,* 142).

83. Bullock, *A History of Negro Education in the South,* 219; Wilkerson, "The Negro School Movement in Virginia," 19–20. Remarkably, Wilkerson's figures demonstrate that by 1949–50, the average salary for African American women teachers was $2,209, compared with the average salary of $2,160 paid to white women teachers. Male teachers still

lagged behind; for the same year, white male teachers earned on average $2,719, while African American male teachers took home $2,520. Disparities remained, but the gap had been reduced significantly. In 1940–41, for example, school boards in Virginia paid male African American teachers an average of $726 a year, while white male teachers pocketed $1,272, meaning that black men were paid 57.1 percent of what was paid to white male teachers. By significant contrast, black men took home 92.7 percent of what white male teachers made in 1949–50. Considering the changes corresponded to the progress of the NAACP legal challenges of the 1940s, this development must be attributed in large part to the equalization movement. Figures are drawn from the annual report of the superintendent of public instruction for Virginia (see Wilkerson, "The Negro School Movement in Virginia," 19).

84. Kluger, *Simple Justice,* 474.

85. Palmer to Jackson, October 11, 1944, folder 714, box 28, Jackson Papers.

86. Jackson, "Equal Salaries for Teachers in North Carolina," *Norfolk Journal and Guide,* August 5, 1944.

87. Palmer to Jackson, June 12, 1944, folder 714, box 28, Jackson Papers. Richard Kluger corroborates the importance of the salary cases for setting in motion a legal initiative that would eventuate in school desegregation: "In Virginia, the fight would escalate from a demand by blacks for equal pay for their teachers to insistence upon equal facilities and bus transportation for their children. It was a glacially slow process, but without doubt there was movement discernible now" (Kluger, *Simple Justice,* 216–17).

88. Jackson, "Winning Victories but Standing Still," *Norfolk Journal and Guide,* June 17, 1944.

89. Jackson, "Which Way Shall We Go—To the Polls or to the Courts," *Norfolk Journal and Guide*, February 22, 1947.

90. "Some Observations on the Rise of V-CRO to Wipe Out Certain Forms of Jim Crow," *Norfolk Journal and Guide,* January 3, 1948.

Chapter 6. The Curriculum for Change: Jackson, the Teachers, and Civic Education

1. Vincent Estill to Jackson, October 7, 1941, folder 140, box 6, Jackson Papers.

2. Jackson to the Jeanes supervisors and high school principals in Virginia, February 2, 1942, folder 705, box 28; Jackson to speakers on Speakers Bureau, February 14, 1942, folder 705, box 28,; Jackson to Moss Plunkett, July 7, 1942, folder 147, box 6. Writing to a voting activist in 1943, Jackson once again exhibited his elitist strategy for political action: "In order that we may stir up Accomac somewhat kindly furnish me the names and addresses of fifteen or twenty of your leading citizens." In Jackson's view, political mobilization would start with the elite and trickle down to the masses (Jackson to D. C. Rawley, May 6, 1943, folder 160, box 6,; quote from Jackson to Plunkett, October 2, 1942, folder 150, box 6, Jackson Papers).

3. Jackson actively encouraged chairpersons of the Virginia Voters League to coordi-

nate with Jeanes supervisors in promoting suffrage qualification. He also emphasized the importance of placing "special stress on voting in class room instruction" (see Jackson to One Hundred Chairmen of the Virginia Voters League, April 19, 1942, folder titled "Virginia Voters League, Main Office 1942–43," box 18, Jackson Papers).

4. McAdam, *Political Process and the Development of Black Insurgency,* 40, 73–86. Looking at the same time period, Jack Bloom emphasizes the impact that the New Deal had on the power of the plantation elite. While AAA parity payments encouraged the reduction of the rural labor force, federal relief programs such as the WPA drove up labor costs. Labor shortages exacerbated the problem of securing sufficient—and what planters considered affordable—help for harvesting cotton. Federal hydroelectric ventures and military spending encouraged industrial development and urbanization in the region, which further loosened planter control over poor blacks and whites. As Bloom points out, the Black Belt elite clung to the political system of racial exclusion while the economic and political order that had originally given rise to it changed (see Bloom, *Class, Race, and the Civil Rights Movement,* 63–70).

5. McAdam, *Political Process and the Development of Black Insurgency,* 43–48; Anonymous source, interview by Alexander Heard, May 6, 1947, Southern Politics Collection.

6. McAdam, *Political Process and the Development of Black Insurgency,* 48–51.

7. Ibid., 108.

8. Jackson, "Winning Victories but Standing Still," *Norfolk Journal and Guide,* June 17, 1944.

9. Ibid; "The False Beliefs of Most Teachers about Voting," *Norfolk Journal and Guide,* July 12, 1947. In a later appeal to the Jeanes supervisors for support in the effort to register teachers to vote, Jackson confidently claimed that "our race leaders" as well as "many white leaders" supported the voting campaign. Even more encouraging, Virginia's newspapers supported it, "the state department of education endorses it, and the local school boards and superintendents at least tolerate it. Why then should we be afraid?" (Jackson to Jeanes supervisors, October 1942, folder 705, box 28, Jackson Papers). His criticism of African American nonvoting may have had some merit, but his attack on teachers was dubious considering the developments in Norfolk over the salary disputes. In light of the dismissals and threats leveled by administrators at teachers throughout the South, African American educators had good reason to think twice about political activity, even something as apparently innocuous as registering to vote.

10. Jackson, "The Voteless School Teachers of Virginia," 12–13; "The Non-Voting Tradition among Teachers," *Norfolk Journal and Guide,* March 30, 1946. (He wrote two articles with the same title, the other appearing in the same periodical on March 13, 1943.)

11. Jackson to J. M. Ellison, president of Virginia Union University, March 19, 1942, folder 729, box 28; Jackson to "certain members of the Staff of Virginia State College," December 4, 1944, folder 707, box 28, Jackson Papers.

12. "Report of the Secretary of Civic Education at the Delegate Assembly," November 17, 1943, folder 706, box 28; Jackson to principals of Virginia high schools, March 23, 1943, folder 706, box 28, Jackson Papers.

13. "A Proposal to High School Principals for Class Instruction in Voting," Depart-

ment of Civic Education, State Teachers Association, April 3, 1942, folder 705, box 28; Jackson to L. F. Palmer, February 16, 1942, folder 713, box 28, Jackson Papers.

14. As he had explained in correspondence through the Virginia Voters League office, Jackson expected that civic instruction in the classroom would stimulate not only student awareness but also electoral participation on the part of reluctant parents. Classroom instruction would become an instrument of political education for an entire community. Quotes from Perlstein, "Teaching Freedom," 301.

15. Spencer to Jackson, April 7, 1942, folder 750, box 29, Jackson Papers.

16. Spencer to Jackson, December 20, 1940, folder 750, box 29; see also Spencer to Jackson, November 9, 1944, folder 750, box 29, Jackson Papers.

17. Spencer to Jackson, June 13, 1949, folder 750, box 29; in addition to applauding Jackson's confrontational letter to school superintendent Greene, Spencer also thanked Jackson for "the splendid [word indecipherable] job that you are putting over in our Virginia. Let me say "Carry On" (Spencer to Jackson, June 14, 1948, folder 750, box 29, Jackson Papers).

18. Spencer to Jackson, June 13, 1949, folder 750, box 29, Jackson Papers.

19. Palmer to Jackson, April 24, 1942, folder 712, box 28; Binford to Jackson, June 2, 1942, folder 746, box 29, Jackson Papers. For additional evidence of voting instruction prior to Jackson's efforts as well as expressions of support for his civic education program, see G. B. Ruffin to Jackson, May 21, 1942, folder 746, box 29; and M. H. Watson to Jackson, February 16, 1942, folder 762, box 29; Coleman to Jackson, April 1, 1942, folder 746, box 29, Jackson Papers.

20. Greer to Jackson, October 13, 1944, folder 733, box 29, Jackson Papers.

21. Greer to Jackson, April 30, 1946, folder 733, box 29; Greer to Jackson, June 4, 1947, folder 733, box 29; Greer to Jackson, December 1, 1948, folder 733, box 29; Washington to Jackson, May 10, 1948, folder 757, box 29; Fleming to Jackson, May 13, 1948, folder 766, box 29, Jackson Papers.

22. Bundy to Jackson, December 6, 1948, folder 770, box 29; Sims to Jackson, May 1, 1948, folder 73, box 28; Hubbard to Jackson, January 29, 1945, folder 735, box 29, Jackson Papers.

23. Rosa Carter to Jackson, May 10, 1948, folder 760, box 29; Lazarus Bates to Jackson, May 19, 1948, folder 770, box 29, Jackson Papers.

24. Maud Valentine to Jackson, June 12, 1948, folder 768, box 29; T. A. Randolph to Jackson, February 25, 1942, folder 773, box 29; Eunice Bundy to Jackson, April 26, 1944, folder 771, box 29; Mayme Coleman to Jackson, April 1, 1942, folder 746, box 29, Jackson Papers.

25. Catherine Holmes to Jackson, February 12, 1943, folder 769, box 29; for invitations from teachers' groups stemming from his work as secretary of civic education, see M. J. Spriggs to Jackson, October 9, 1946, folder 772, box 29, C. W. Seay to Jackson, February 25, 1942, folder 725, box 28; Miles Medford to Jackson, February 10, 1950, folder 252, box 12; Mary E. Thompson to Jackson, May 11, 1948, folder 760, box 29, Jackson Papers.

26. Brooks to Jackson, April 26, 1948, folder 742, box 29, Jackson Papers.

27. Ibid. For additional examples of teachers who were registered and active at the time

of Jackson's mail out, see R. L. Harris to Jackson, May 17, 1948, folder 235, box 12; Bettie Banks Jackson to L. P. Jackson, May 11, 1948, folder 746, box 29; Louise Owens Bell to Jackson, April 29, 1948, folder 742, box 29; Grace Robinson Shepard to Jackson, April 28, 1948, folder 742, box 29; Georgia E. Butler to Jackson, April 29, 1948, folder 775, box 29, Jackson Papers.

28. Jackson to Seay, November 13, 1944, folder 723, box 28; Jackson, "Civic Training in the Schools of Virginia," *Norfolk Journal and Guide,* December 23, 1944.

29. Jackson, "Civic Training in the Schools of Virginia," *Norfolk Journal and Guide,* December 23, 1944; the principal to whom Jackson referred was none other than James F. Spencer, Jackson's loyal ally. As he wrote in the letter that Jackson quoted, he arranged for students to visit the polls "whenever an election is held" (Spencer to Jackson, November 9, 1944, folder 750, box 29, Jackson Papers). In another gloss on teacher voting activity, Jackson wrote, "at long last a majority of our 4,000 public school teachers have awakened to the fact that the salvation of any people rests partly on their attitude toward elections and the affairs of government" (Jackson to S. H. Clarke, J. H Carey, and W. H. Willis, December 2, 1944, box 28, Jackson Papers).

30. Jackson made a direct connection between increased teacher voting and the activity of supportive school principals: "More than half the public school teachers in Virginia participated in the recent election partly because their principals urged them to do so" (Jackson to "certain members of the Staff of the Virginia State College," December 4, 1944, folder 707, box 28, Jackson Papers).

31. Clyde Scott to Jackson, May 28, 1942, folder 745, box 29; Binford to Jackson, December 17, 1948, folder 749, box 29; W. L. Johns of the Academy High School also informed Jackson that his school had held mock elections that were "carried out with a good deal of interest, with all high school pupils taking an active part" (Johns to Jackson, January 12, 1949, folder 741, box 29, Jackson Papers).

32. Caleb Gregory Brown to Jackson, June 11, 1948, folder 734, box 29; A. N. Jackson to Jackson, December 3, 1948; A. N. Jackson to Jackson, June 8, 1948 (second quote), both in folder 738, box 29, Jackson Papers. A. N. Jackson had already written to Jackson asking for assistance in developing a program for Staunton's civic association, which the former had hoped would be patterned after the program "outlined by the State Civic Organization of the Virginia Education Association" (see A. N. Jackson to Jackson, May 13, 1946, and Jackson to A. N. Jackson, May 15, 1946, both in folder 739, box 29; S. S. Trott to Jackson, April 30, 1948, folder 773, box 29, Jackson Papers).

33. Harris to Jackson, November 23, 1948, folder 744, box 29, Jackson Papers.

34. Ibid.

35. Jackson, "The Newport News Affair," *Norfolk Journal and Guide,* May 29, 1943.

36. Jackson, "The Non-Voting Tradition among Teachers," *Norfolk Journal and Guide,* March 13, 1943. (He wrote two articles with the same title, the other appearing in the same periodical on March 30, 1946.) Jackson used every source of information and influence he could to promote the civic education agenda. In 1944, Jackson appealed to executive secretary Rupert Picott to identify the number of teachers qualified to vote in any given town or city. Further adding to Picott's task, Jackson asked that Picott determine whether

teachers understood the Virginia voting requirements and if they studied his handbook on voting. He also asked Picott to educate any teachers he met in the mechanics of voting and to proselytize for civic education among teachers by suggesting "some of the exercises you had in your own school at Newport News" (Jackson to Picott, April 16, 1944, folder 715, box 28; Jackson to "Mrs. Gaskins," April 21, 1948, folder 731, box 28 (final quote); see also Jackson to "Miss Graves," folder 731, box 28, and Jackson to "the Principals of High Schools in Virginia," April 28, 1947, folder 708, box 28, all in Jackson Papers).

37. Jackson, "Non-Voting among Teachers and Workers," *Norfolk Journal and Guide*, March 20, 1943; Jackson to "the Summer School Students and Members of the Staffs of Virginia State College, Virginia Union University, and Hampton Institute," July 24, 1945, folder 707, box 28; Jackson to "the High School Principals and certain Jeanes Supervisors," March 1, 1945, folder 707, box 28; Jackson to "the High School Principals in Virginia," November 1, 1949, folder 709, box 28, Jackson Papers; Buni, *The Negro in Virginia Politics*, 138–41. For one of several appeals to teachers to register and vote, see Jackson to "the Teachers in the Schools of Virginia," April 30, 1946, folder 708, box 28, Jackson Papers.

38. Jackson to "the Principals of High Schools in Virginia," April 28, 1947, folder 708, box 28, Jackson Papers.

39. Jackson, untitled report on teacher voting behavior, 1948, folder 529, box 18, Jackson Papers; see also "The Drive to Get the Teachers Qualified to Vote Moves Ahead," *Norfolk Journal and Guide*, May 22, 1948.

40. Jackson to Wesley, October 14, 1941, folder 140, box 6, Jackson Papers (emphasis added).

41. Jackson, untitled report on teacher voting behavior, 1948, folder 529, box 18; Jackson, "Race and Suffrage in the South since 1940," 17; Annual Report, secretary of civic education, Virginia Teachers Association, 1947–48, folder 719, box 28, Jackson Papers.

Chapter 7. Years of Opportunity: Jackson and the Political Resurgence of the South

1. Egerton, *Speak Now Against the Day*, 348.
2. Jackson, "War and the Negro," *Norfolk Journal and Guide*, July 24, 1943.
3. Sullivan, *Days of Hope*, 141.
4. Egerton, *Speak Now Against the Day*, 409–16, Truman quote on 414.
5. The conventional interpretation of Truman the political calculator can be found in Kelley and Lewis, eds., *To Make Our World Anew: A History of African-Americans*, 449. For an analysis of how the President's Committee on Civil Rights and the Truman administration sought to the foreign policy implications of American racial discrimination, see Dudziak, *Cold War Civil Rights*, chap. 3.
6. Tuck, "Black Protest During the 1940s," 63.
7. Carey E. Haigler to Lucy R. Mason, May 22, 1945, Reel 63, Series 5:1, CIO Organizing Committee Papers, Operation Dixie, 1946–53.
8. Jackson, "Balance Sheet in Race Relations for 1944," *Norfolk Journal and Guide*, January 6, 1945.

9. Lucy Randolph Mason to Ralph McGill, July 19, 1945, folder "July 1945–July 1946," box 4, Mason Papers.

10. Mason to Philip Murray, October 30, 1944, folder "October 1944–June 1945," box 4, Mason Papers.

11. Sullivan, *Days of Hope,* 172, 189, 218–19; Reed, *Simple Decency and Common Sense,* 95–96; Mason to Murray, October 30, 1944, Mason Papers; Salmond, *Miss Lucy of the CIO,* 124–25; Korstad and Lichtenstein, "Opportunities Found and Lost," 787; Zieger, *The CIO,* 234, 227–41.

12. Robert Johnson to James Dombrowski, May 3, 1945, box 328 (including quotes); Dombrowksi to Johnson, April 20, 1945; Dombrowski to Johnson, June 7, 1945, folder titled "SCHW"; Boyd E. Payton to Virginia CIO Local Unions, May 7, 1945, folder titled "Letters to State CIO Local Unions," box 327, Virginia Citizens Political Action Committee (VCPAC) Papers.

13. Payton to CIO Local Unions, May 7, 1945, VCPAC Papers.

14. Johnson to Jackson, June 13, 1945; Johnson to Jackson, October 2, 1945; Johnson to Jackson, November 12, 1945, folder titled "L. P. Jackson," box 327; Johnson to Payton, October 4, 1945, folder titled "VCPAC Executive Board," box 328, VCPAC Papers.

15. Johnson to Jackson, October 20, 1945; Johnson to Jackson, November 12, 1945, folder titled "L. P. Jackson," box 327, VCPAC Papers.

16. Minutes of VCPAC Executive Board Meeting, November 27, 1945, folder titled "Minutes of Meetings," box 327, VCPAC Papers; Jackson, "Roosevelt, Dewey, and the Negro Voting Issue," *Norfolk Journal and Guide,* October 21, 1944. Looking at labor union activity in Winston-Salem, Korstad and Lichenstein conclude that "mass unionization transformed the character of the black community's traditional race advancement organizations." NAACP and Urban League leaders became increasingly militant and willing to experiment with "new forms of mass militancy" (Korstad and Lichenstein, "Opportunities Found and Lost," 797). Although Jackson took no part in direct action, he and others throughout the ranks of the Virginia Voters League, the NAACP, and the Elks began to identify with working-class concerns, recognizing that their hopes lay in mass movement, which they believed should take the form of an assault on the ballot box. Other African Americans did experiment with direct action, most notably NAACP activist Irene Morgan, who successfully challenged segregation on interstate transportation.

17. Minutes of VCPAC Executive Board Meeting, November 27, 1945, VCPAC Papers.

18. Ibid., 2–3.

19. Key, *Southern Politics in State and Nation,* 27.

20. Johnson to CIO Local Unions in Virginia, June 23, 1945; Johnson to Local Union PAC Members, June 27, 1945; Boyd Payton and Robert Johnson to presidents of CIO International Unions with membership in Virginia, July 19, 1945; Johnson to Local Unions and Political Action Committees, July 31, 1945; Johnson form letter, n.d., 1945, folder titled "Letters to State CIO Local Unions, box 327,; Robert L. Nase, campaign assistant, to "Dear Friend," June 7, 1945; Plunkett for Governor Club, "For Governor: Moss A. Plunkett of Roanoke County," n.d. (quote from platform), folder titled "Plunkett for Governor," box 328, VCPAC Papers; Key, *Southern Politics,* 28–31.

21. Minutes of VCPAC Executive Board Meeting, November 27, 1945, VCPAC Papers.

22. Jackson to Foreman, June 6, 1945; Dombrowski to Jackson, June 25, 1945, folder 1314, box 47, Jackson Papers.

23. Jackson to Foreman, December 24, 1945, folder 1276, box 44, Jackson Papers.

24. Organization Committee for the Committee For Virginia form letter, January 5, 1946, folder 1314, box 47; Committee for Virginia form letter, March 1946, folder 1315, box 47; Beecher to Jackson, March 26, 1946, folder 1315, box 47, Jackson Papers; Sullivan, *Days of Hope,* 203, 205.

25. Larissa Smith, "Where the South Begins," 239.

26. Jackson to Beecher, June 18, 1946; Jackson to Beecher, July 4, 1946 (including quote), folder 1317, box 47, Jackson Papers.

27. Jackson to Beecher, March 26, 1946, folder 1315, box 47, Jackson Papers.

28. Jackson, "Meeting with Success in Suffolk, Va.," *Norfolk Journal and Guide,* May 18, 1946.

29. Jackson to Beecher, March 26, 1946; Jackson, "Meeting with Success in Suffolk, Va.," *Norfolk Journal and Guide,* May 18, 1946.

30. Jackson, "Meeting with Success in Suffolk, Va.," *Norfolk Journal and Guide,* May 18, 1946; on Jackson's optimism about black political activity throughout the South as well as the contributions of local voting leagues and the NAACP to black voter registration, see Jackson, "Signs of an Awakening for Voting in the Deep South," *Norfolk Journal and Guide,* April 5, 1947.

31. Larissa Smith, "Where the South Begins," 233.

32. Virginia Beecher to "Citizen of Virginia," July 30, 1946, folder 1318, box 47; Beecher to E. F. Hewins, August 12, 1946, folder 1318, box 47, Jackson Papers.

33. Parke Rouse Jr. to Jackson, folder 246, box 12, Jackson Papers. For Dabney as a racial liberal determined to maintain white dominance, see J. Douglas Smith, *Managing White Supremacy,* 274–84; Dabney, *Across the Years,* 162–65.

34. O. E. McKaine to Jackson, April 26, 1946, folder 1316, box 47; Jackson, "Southern Whites Rallying to the Negro," *Norfolk Journal and Guide,* August 18, 1945; "19469–The Year of Opportunity for the Negro Voter," *Norfolk Journal and Guide,* May 11, 1946. For examples of Jackson's efforts to solicit support from white elites, particularly white ministers and academics, see Jackson to Eugene Witherspoon, February 5, 1944, folder 171, box 7, and Jackson to Louis Gottschalk, November 20, 1943, folder 166, box 7, Jackson Papers.

35. "CIO-PAC 'Descent on South' Likened to 'Carpetbaggers' by Abbitt As He Extols Byrd," *Richmond Times-Dispatch,* July 9, 1946; "Senator Byrd and the CIO," *Richmond Times-Dispatch,* July 21, 1946; "Nazis in the South," *Richmond Times-Dispatch,* July 24, 1946.

36. McKaine to Jackson, August 12, 1946, folder 1318, box 47, Jackson Papers.

37. Beecher to Jackson, August 12, 1946, folder 1318, box 47, Jackson Papers.

38. For more on the Committee for Virginia incident and the efforts of the Byrd organization to have Jackson dismissed, see Larissa Smith, "Where the South Begins," 241.

39. Jackson, "Byrd's Anti-Lynch Law," *Richmond Times- Dispatch,* August 4, 1946; L. L.

Bean, "Break Up the Machine," *Richmond Times-Dispatch*; Egerton, *Speak Now Against the Day*, 365.

40. Jackson to Durr, September 21, 1947, folder 1321, box 47, Jackson Papers.

41. Durr to Jackson, n.d., folder 1328, box 47, Jackson Papers.

42. McKaine to Jackson, August 12, 1946, folder 1318, box 47, Jackson Papers.

43. Anonymous source, interview by Alexander Heard, May 6, 1947, Southern Politics Collection.

44. Jackson, "Heavy Voting in Suffolk and Nansemond County, Virginia," *Norfolk Journal and Guide,* September 21, 1946; Jackson to O. E. McKaine, August 25, 1946, folder 1318, box 47, Jackson Papers.

45. Jackson, *Seventh Annual Report on the Voting Status of the Negroes in Virginia* (Petersburg: Virginia Voters League, 1946); *Eighth Annual Report,* (1947–48); Key, *Southern Politics,* 519.

46. O. E. McKaine, "The Third Revolution," folder 1316, box 46, Jackson Papers. McKaine reported a 150 percent voter registration increase among blacks in Birmingham, an increase from 8,000 to 20,000 voters in Savannah after a seventeen-day initiative, a dramatic improvement in Augusta from 1,200 to 4,900 registered black voters, and the addition of 2,500 voters in Durham after a twelve-day voter registration drive. Jackson believed that the Southern Conference for Human Welfare and the Southern Regional Council had inherited the mantle of the "Silent South," that group of white liberals who favored a more humane racial order than the one that had crystallized after Reconstruction. For Jackson, the emergence of these groups signaled the opportunity for authentic democratic reform (see "Southern Whites Rallying to Negro," *Norfolk Journal and Guide,* August 18, 1945; "The Cracking of the Solid South," *Norfolk Journal and Guide,* April 16, 1946). For Jackson's emphasis on the NAACP as the leading agent of political change in the South, see "1946–The Year of the Rebirth of the Negro in Southern Elections," *Norfolk Journal and Guide,* January 4, 1947.

47. Larissa Smith, "Where the South Begins," 220, 254–62, including Jackson quote on 261–62; Jackson, "The Election of Oliver W. Hill to the City Council of Richmond, Virginia," *Norfolk Journal and Guide,* June 26, 1948.

48. Jones to Jackson, October 13, 1948, folder 1359, box 48, Jackson Papers.

49. Brownie Lee Jones to Jackson, June 14, 1944, folder 1357, box 48, Jackson Papers. The school was one of several organizations that sought to bind African Americans, workers, women, religious leaders, and social reformers together in a challenge to southern bigotry and political intransigence. As Jones reported in 1946, "The richest rewards of the year have been in our cooperative relationships with such groups as: The Fellowship of Southern Churchmen, the Committee for Virginia, the local Y.W.C.A.'s in the area, the League of Women Voters, the Richmond Child Labor Committee, the N.A.A.C.P., the American Veterans' Committee, and with liberal ministers of both races" ("Report of the Director for the Year 1946," CIO Organizing Committee Papers, Operation Dixie, Reel 58, Series 4: 170).

50. Jones to Jackson, July 5, 1946; Jackson to Jones, July 7, 1946; Jones to Jackson, March 3, 1947; Jones to Jackson, July 2, 1947, folder 1357, box 48; Jones to Jackson, March

12, 1948, folder 1358, box 48; Jones to Jackson, April 14, 1948, folder 1359, box 48; Jones to Jackson, December 9, 1947, folder 1357, box 48; Jackson form letter for Southern School for Workers, September 16, 1948, folder 1359, box 48, Jackson Papers.

51. Jones to Jackson, July 26, 1948; Jones to Jackson, July 30, 1948, folder 1359, box 48; Jackson to Jones, September 14, 1948 (including quote); Jones to Jackson, folder 1360, box 48, Jackson Papers.

52. Jackson to Jones, June 8, 1947; Jones to Jackson, June 11, 1947; Jackson to Jones, August 4, 1947; Jackson to Jones, August 6, 1947 (first quote); Jackson to Jones, June 8, 1947 (second quote); Jones to Jackson, June 11, 1947 (third quote), folder 1357, box 48,, Jackson Papers; "Southern School for Workers Meeting Need Which Other Schools Neglect: Helps without Race Bias," *Norfolk Journal and Guide,* June 28, 1947. As Jackson wrote in a letter soliciting financial support for the school, the organization had "dismissed from their minds the mores of racial separation which have hampered so many other worthwhile causes and movements in the southern region in the past" (Jackson form letter, September 16, 1948, folder 1359, box 48, Jackson Papers.

53. Sullivan, *Days of Hope,* 223, 233–35.

54. Ibid., 235; Reed, *Simple Decency and Common Sense,* 128.

55. Reed, *Simple Decency and Common Sense,* 128.

56. Jackson to Durr, January 19, 1947, folder 1319, box 47 (first quote); ibid., September 21, 1947, folder 1321, box 47; Durr to Jackson, August 13, 1947, folder 1321, box 47 (second quote); Anne Gellman to Jackson, August 9, 1947, folder 1321, box 47 (third quote), Jackson Papers. Jackson had been collecting for the committee well before January 1947 (see Jackson to Beecher, December 6, 1946, folder 1318, box 47; Beecher to Jackson, October 16, 1946, folder 1318, box 47, Jackson Papers).

57. Jackson to Dombrowski, September 23, 1947, folder 1321, box 47 (first quote); Jason to Dombrowski, March 20, 1947, folder 1319, box 47 (second quote); Jason to Dombrowski, August 7, 1947, folder 1321, box 47; Jason to Dombrowski, November 28, 1948, folder 1324, box 47; Jason to Dombrowski, March 6, 1949, folder 1326, box 47, Jackson Papers.

58. Zinn, *A People's History of the United States,* 432.

59. Minutes of the Executive Board Meeting, Committee for Virginia, April 12, 1947, pp. 2–3, 6, folder 1320, box 47, Jackson Papers.

60. Ibid., 2, 5–6; Durr to Jackson, n.d., folder 1328, box 47, Jackson Papers.

61. Jackson to Durr, May 11, 1947, folder 1320, box 47; Durr to Jackson, June 30, 1947, folder 1320, box 47, Jackson Papers.

62. Report of Executive Board Meeting to Committee for Virginia, February 17, 1948, folder 1324, box 47, Jackson Papers. The committee's discussion followed the policy of the Southern Conference for Human Welfare, which recommended that state committees "determine their political course in the 1948 elections" according to local political conditions. The committee itself did not dictate any political endorsement (see "Resolutions," SCHW National Board Meeting, January 31, 1948, folder 1314, box 47, Jackson Papers).

63. Jackson to Durr, March 12, 1948, folder 1324, box 47, Jackson Papers.

64. Gellman to Jackson, March 14, 1948, folder 1324, box 47, Jackson Papers. Linda

Reed emphasizes the financial troubles and administrative disorganization caused by the separation of SCEF from SCHW in *Simple Decency and Common Sense,* 126–28, while Patricia Sullivan notes that following Clark Foreman's departure, SCHW state chapters began dissolving, often providing office space for local Progressive Party activists (see Sullivan, *Days of Hope,* 250).

65. Durr to Jackson, n.d., folder 1322, box 47,; Jackson to Gellman, December 3, 1947, folder 1322, box 47; Durr to Jackson, March 12, 1948, folder 1324, box 47, Jackson Papers.

66. Durr to Jackson, March 12, 1948, folder 1324, box 47, Jackson Papers.

67. Jackson to Dombrowski, April 21, 1948, folder 1324, box 47; Jackson to Dombrowski, May 24, 1948, folder 1324, box 47, Jackson Papers; Klibaner, "The Travail of Southern Radicals," 182–83.

68. Jackson to Harry T. Penn, November 3, 1948, folder 241, box 12, Jackson Papers. By July, the V-CRO was operating as a political action committee by endorsing the candidacy of liberal Francis Pickens Miller for the governorship. Despite the developments of the postwar period, the organization still labored under the pressure of white antipathy for black voting. As Chairman Leon A. Reid explained to members: "Wisdom demands that Negroes avoid publicity as to which way their support will go. Deplorable as it may be, the fact remains that many reactionary voters will vote against a man simply because they think Negroes are for him." Lacking the common front provided by the CIO and the Committee for Virginia, the V-CRO struggled to become a mass movement. Reid's injunction to "GET SOLIDLY BUT QUIETLY BEHIND MR. MILLER was probably not very encouraging to those who were striving to spark a grassroots movement (see Reid form letter, July 28, 1949, folder 248, box 12, Jackson Papers).

69. Houston quoted in Sullivan, *Days of Hope,* 272.

70. Dombrowski to Paul Christopher, October 20, 1947; Dombrowski to Paul Christopher, September 30, 1948, Series 565, Reel 44, Operation Dixie, CIO Organizing Committee Papers, 1946–1953; "Southern Professors Voted to End Segregation in Professional Schools," *Southern Patriot* 6 (November 1948): 1–2, box 23, "Printed Material 1948," Mason Papers.

71. Jackson to Reverend T. J. Jemison, November 14, 1948, folder 241, box 12, Jackson Papers; "A Declaration on Civil Rights," folder titled "Printed Material 1948," box 23, Mason Papers; "Report of the Director," SCEF, November 21, 1948, folder 1331, box 47, Jackson Papers.

72. "Southerners Adopt Declaration of Civil Rights; Call for End of Discrimination and Segregation," *The Southern Patriot* 6 (December 1948): 1, 4, folder 1335, box 47; Jackson to Aubrey Williams, December 22, 1948, folder 242, box 12, Jackson Papers.

Chapter 8. The Clock of Time Will Not Be Turned Back

1. Dorothy Johnson, interview, July 8, 2002.

2. Thomas S. Sellers, "Dr. Luther P. Jackson Remembered," n.d., manuscript in author's possession.

3. Jackson, "Virginia and the Civil Rights Program," folder 1689, box 66, Jackson Papers.

4. Ibid., 3; India Taylor Johnson, interview.

5. Jackson, "Virginia and the Civil Rights Program," 4.

6. Ibid., 5.

7. Ibid., 6; Jackson, "The Virginia Organization for Civil Rights Striving to Wipe Out Segregation," *Norfolk Journal and Guide,* December 27, 1947. Jackson took the lead in mobilizing the Virginia Voters League for an attack on segregation. At a meeting in 1948, he suggested that the time was ripe to press the General Assembly to end segregation. With an enlivened black electorate, desegregation could become the price for political support in the state elections of 1949 (see Minutes of the Virginia Voters' League, November 28, 1948, folder 522, box 18, Jackson Papers).

8. Jackson, "Virginia and the Civil Rights Program," 7; "The Doctrine of State's Rights —A Truth or a Fancy, Is the Question," *Norfolk Journal and Guide,* July 24, 1948. Two years later, liberal delegate Armistead Boothe introduced a bill for the desegregation of transportation on common carriers. The bill never got past the committee stage, but it revitalized the V-CRO after the defeat of the desegregation measures of 1948. Under the leadership of Jackson, Picott, Tinsley, Hill, and others, the V-CRO mobilized thousands of blacks and whites to sign petitions in favor of the measures, which V-CRO delegates presented to the bill's sponsors the day that it was read in the House of Delegates (see J. Douglas Smith, "When Reason Collides with Prejudice," 5–46; V-CRO form letter, February 13, 1950, folder 252, box 12,; Moss Plunkett to Jackson, January 23, 1950, folder 251, box 12, Jackson Papers).

9. Jackson, "Murray Bills Meet Same Fate As Other First Progressive Measures," *Norfolk Journal and Guide,* March 13, 1948; see also "Watching the Virginia Fight on Certain of Her Racial Segregation Laws," *Norfolk Journal and Guide,* March 6, 1948.

10. Jackson, "The Case of Irene Morgan—Victory for Negro Lawyers," *Norfolk Journal and Guide,* June 22, 1946; Jackson, "Virginia and Civil Rights," 7. The salary and school facility equalization cases were part of a larger assault on segregated education in the South. As Jackson explained confidentially to Aubrey Williams in December 1948, the state was "in for a number of suits yet," since the NAACP was using it as a "testing ground for future suits in all the Southern states" (Jackson to Williams, December 22, 1948, folder 242, box 12, Jackson Papers). The legal strategy proved remarkably successful at pressuring school authorities into fulfilling their public obligation to maintain equal facilities. As he explained to Charles Johnson in November 1949, "It would take years to file suits in every political subdivision of Virginia, yet this is hardly necessary since everywhere now superintendents and school boards are bending over backwards to give the colored teachers and patrons what they want in short order" (Jackson to Johnson, November 1, 1949, folder 250, box 12, Jackson Papers).

11. Jackson to Armistead Boothe, January 19, 1950, folder 251, box 12, Jackson Papers.

12. J. M. Tinsley, address at Virginia State Convention, October 23, 1949, Reel 25, Selected Branch Files, 1940–1955, NAACP Papers.

13. Jackson, "Segregation—Will it Last Always?" *Norfolk Journal and Guide,* July 20, 1946.

14. Jackson to the "Contributors to the Southern Conference for Human Welfare," December 21, 1948, box 47; Du Bois to Jackson, August 4, 1948, folder 238, box 12; Jackson to W. C. Hueston, December 7, 1948, folder 242, box 12; Jackson form letter, March 23, 1950, folder 1325, box 47; Jackson to Picott, August 6, 1949, folder 248, box 12, Jackson Papers; George S. Schuyler, "Communist Activities among the Colored People," Matthews Papers; on the variety of social and political organizations to which Jackson belonged and which were playing a critical role in mobilizing black voters, see Jackson, "The Campaign in Virginia for Registered Voters Must Not Lag," *Norfolk Journal and Guide*, April 12, 1947.

15. Jackson, "The Call for the Highly Educated." This was certainly the case with Jackson's involvement in the Committee for Virginia and, according to one source, may well have been behind Jackson's departure from the *Journal and Guide* (Madden, interview).

16. Jackson, "Arousing a Voting Consciousness," *Norfolk Journal and Guide*, May 15, 1943.

17. "Luther Porter Jackson," 195.

18. Patterson, *A Civil Rights Milestone*, 27–29; Kluger, *Simple Justice*, 466–78.

19. Johnston, "Luther Porter Jackson," 195.

Bibliography

Manuscript Collections

CIO Organizing Committee Papers. Operation Dixie. Perkins Library, Duke University, Durham, North Carolina (microfilm).

Foster, Luther. Papers. Special Collections. Virginia State University, Petersburg, Virginia.

Gandy, John M. Papers. Special Collections. Virginia State University, Petersburg, Virginia.

Hancock, Gordon B. Papers. Special Collections. Perkins Library, Duke University, Durham, North Carolina.

Jackson, Luther P. Papers. Special Collections. Virginia State University, Petersburg, Virginia.

Mason, Lucy Randolph. Papers. Special Collections. Perkins Library, Duke University, Durham, North Carolina.

Matthews, J. B. Papers. Special Collections. Perkins Library, Duke University, Durham, North Carolina.

National Association for the Advancement of Colored People (NAACP) Papers (microfilm, National Library of Congress, Washington, D.C.).

Southern Politics Collection. Special Collections. Alexander and Jean Heard Library, Vanderbilt University, Nashville, Tennessee.

Virginia Citizens Political Action Committee Papers, Special Collections. Perkins Library, Duke University, Durham, North Carolina.

Virginia Teachers Association Papers. Special Collections. Virginia State University, Petersburg, Virginia.

Interviews by Author

Flowers, Stafford. July 16, 2002, telephone interview.

Jackson, Edward. July 7, 2002, telephone interview.

Johnson, India Taylor. July 14, 2002, telephone interview.

Lucas, Louise Jeeter. July 15, 2002, telephone interview.

Lee, John. July 15, 2002, telephone interview.

Madden, Sam. July 7, 2002, telephone interview.

Spaights, Evelyn. July 16, 2002, telephone interview.

Wilkerson, Matie. July 13, 2002, telephone interview.

Interviews by Others

Jackson, Luther P. Jr. Interviewed by Luther P. Jackson III. December 9, 10, and 13, 2001, transcript of tape interview.

Johnson, Dorothy Hodge Hanson. Interviewed by Judy Hodge Dunmore. July 8, 2002, transcript of tape interview.

Newspapers

Norfolk Journal and Guide 1942–48
Petersburg Progress-Index 1938–40
Richmond Times-Dispatch 1940–48

Books, Articles, Dissertations

Anderson, James D. *The Education of Blacks in the South, 1860–1935.* Chapel Hill: University of North Carolina Press, 1988.

Barnard, Hollinger F., ed. *Outside the Magic Circle: The Autobiography of Virginia Foster.* Tuscaloosa: University of Alabama Press, 1985.

Bartley, Numan. *The New South, 1945–1980.* Baton Rouge: Louisiana State University Press, 1995.

Bass, Jack, and Walter Devries. *The Transformation of Southern Politics: Social Change and Political Consequence since 1945.* New York: Basic, 1976.

Bloom, Jack. *Class, Race, and the Civil Rights Movement.* Bloomington: Indiana University Press, 1987.

Brown, Elsa Barkley. "Negotiating and Transforming the Public Sphere: African American Life in the Transition from Slavery to Freedom." *Public Culture* 7 (1994): 107–27.

Bullock, Henry Allan. *A History of Negro Education in the South: From 1619 to the Present.* Cambridge: Harvard University Press, 1967.

Buni, Andrew. *The Negro in Virginia Politics, 1902–1965.* Charlottesville: University of Virginia Press, 1967.

Captain, Gwendolyn. "Enter Ladies and Gentlemen of Color: Gender, Sport, and the Ideal of African American Manhood and Womanhood during the Late Nineteenth and Early Twentieth Century South." *Journal of Sport History* 18 (1991): 81–102.

Chafe, William. "The Gods Bring Threads to Webs Begun." *Journal of American History* 86 (March 2000): 1531–51.

Colson, Edna M. "The Teachers' College and Normal School." *Journal of Negro Education* 2 (July 1933): 284–98.

Curtis, Marva. "Luther P. Jackson and the Virginia Voters' League." Master's thesis, Virginia State University, 1979.

Dabney, Virginius. *Across the Years: Memories of a Virginian.* New York: Doubleday, 1978.

———. *Virginia: The New Dominion.* New York: Doubleday, 1971.

Dailey, Jane, Glenda Elizabeth Gilmore, and Bryant Simon, eds. *Jumpin' Jim Crow: Southern Politics from Civil War to Civil Rights.* Princeton: Princeton University Press, 2000.

Dalfiume, Richard. "The 'Forgotten Years' of the Negro Revolution." In *The Negro in De-*

pression and War: Prelude to Revolution, 1930–1945, edited by Bernard Sternsher. Chicago: Quadrangle, 1969.

Dittmer, John. *Local People: The Struggle for Civil Rights in Mississippi.* Urbana: University of Illinois Press, 1994.

Dudziak, Mary L. *Cold War Civil Rights: Race and the Image of American Democracy.* Princeton: Princeton University Press, 2000.

Dunne, Matthew William. "Next Steps: Charles S. Johnson and Southern Liberalism." *Journal of Negro History* 83 (winter 1998): 1–34.

Eagles, Charles. "Toward New Histories of the Civil Rights Era." *Journal of Southern History* 66 (November 2000): 815–48.

Egerton, John. *Speak Now Against the Day: The Generation before the Civil Rights Movement.* Chapel Hill: University of North Carolina Press, 1994.

Fairclough, Adam. "'Being in the Field of Education and Also Being a Negro . . . Seems . . . Tragic': Black Teachers in the Jim Crow South." *Journal of American History* 87 (June 2000): 65–91.

———. *Better Day Coming: Blacks and Equality, 1890–2000.* New York: Viking, 2001.

———. *Race and Democracy: The Civil Rights Struggle in Louisiana, 1915–1972.* Athens: University of Georgia Press, 1995.

Foner, Eric. *The Story of American Freedom.* New York: Norton, 1998.

Franklin, John Hope. *From Slavery to Freedom: A History of Negro Americans.* 5th ed. New York: Knopf, 1980.

Frazier, E. Franklin. *Black Bourgeoisie: The Rise of a New Middle Class.* New York: Free Press, 1957.

Fulz , Michael. African American Teachers in the South, 1890–1940: Growth, Feminization, and Salary Discrimination." *Teachers College Record* 96 (spring 1995): 544–68.

———. "African American Teachers in the South: Powerlessness and the Ironies of Expectation and Protest." *History of Education Quarterly* 35 (winter 1995): 401–22.

———. "Teacher Training and African American Education in the South, 1900–1940." *Journal of Negro Education* 64 (spring 1995): 196–210.

Gaines, Kevin. *Uplifting the Race: Black Leadership, Politics, and Culture in the Twentieth Century.* Chapel Hill: University of North Carolina Press, 1996.

Gatewood, William B. *Aristocrats of Color: The Black Elite, 1880–1920.* Fayetteville: University of Arkansas Press, 2000.

Gavins, Raymond. *The Perils and Prospects of Southern Black Leadership: Gordon Blaine Hancock, 1884–1970.* Durham: Duke University Press, 1977.

———. "Hancock, Jackson, and Young: Virginia's Black Triumvirate, 1930–1945," *Virginia Magazine of History and Biography* 85 (autumn 1977): 470–86.

———. "Urbanization and Segregation: Black Leadership Patterns in Richmond, Virginia, 1900–1920." *South Atlantic Quarterly* 79 (summer 1980): 257–73.

Gilmore, Glenda Elizabeth. *Gender and Jim Crow: Women and the Politics of White Supremacy in North Carolina, 1896–1920.* Chapel Hill: University of North Carolina Press, 1996.

Goggin, Jacqueline. *Carter G. Woodson: A Life in Black History.* Baton Rouge: Louisiana State University Press, 1993.

————. "Countering White Racist Scholarship: Carter G. Woodson and *The Journal of Negro History*." *Journal of Negro History* 68 (autumn 1983): 355–75.

Goldfield, David R. *Black, White, and Southern: Race Relations and Southern Culture, 1940 to the Present.* Baton Rouge: Louisiana State University, 1990.

Green, Ben. *Before His Time: The Untold Story of Harry T. Moore, America's First Civil Rights Martyr.* New York: Free Press, 1999.

Grossman, James R. "A Chance to Make Good, 1900–1929." In *To Make Our World Anew: A History of African Americans,* edited by Robin D. G. Kelley and Earl Lewis, 345–408. New York: Oxford University Press, 2000.

Hale, Grace Elizabeth. "'For Colored' and 'For White': Segregating Consumption in the South." In *Jumpin' Jim Crow: Southern Politics from Civil War to Civil Rights,* edited by Jane Dailey et al., 162–82. Princeton: Princeton University Press, 2000.

————. *Making Whiteness: The Culture of Segregation in the South, 1890–1940.* New York: Vintage, 1998.

Harris, Sonette Hoston. "Woodson and Wesley: A Partnership in Building the Association For the Study of Afro-American Life and History." *Journal of Negro History* 83 (spring 1998): 109–119.

Heinemann, Ronald L. *Depression and New Deal in Virginia: The Enduring Dominion.* Charlottesville: University of Virginia Press, 1983.

————. "Virginia in the Twentieth Century: Recent Interpretations." *Virginia Magazine of History and Biography* 94 (April 1986): 131–60.

Jackson, Luther P. "The Annual History Drive in Virginia." *Virginia Teachers Bulletin* 16 (April 1939): 13, 20.

————. *Annual Report on the Voting Status of the Negroes in Virginia.* Petersburg: Virginia Voters League, 1945, 1946, 1947–48, 1949–50.

————. "The Call for the Highly Educated." *Virginia State College Gazette* 44 (December 1939): 34–40.

————. "Citizenship and Government Participation." *Virginia State College Gazette* 43 (November 1937): 10–15.

————. "Citizenship Training—A Neglected Area in Adult Education." *Journal of Negro Education* 14 (summer 1945): 477–87.

————. "The Deadline for All Citizens." *Norfolk Journal and Guide* (April 17, 1943).

————. "Free Negro Labor and Property Holding in Virginia." *Virginia State College Gazette* 43 (March 1938): 43–48.

————. *Free Negro Labor and Property Holding in Virginia, 1830–1860.* New York: D. Appleton Century, 1942.

————. *A History of the Virginia State Teachers Association.* Norfolk: Guide, 1937.

————. "Improving the Economic Status of the Negro through Governmental Participation." *Virginia Teachers Bulletin* 16 (January 1939): 15:42–43.

————. *Negro Office-Holders in Virginia, 1865–1895.* Norfolk: Guide Quality Press, 1946.

————. "Race and Suffrage in the South since 1940." *New South* (June–July, 1948): 1–26.

————. "Report of the Interest Groups on Citizenship with Emphasis on Negroes As Voters." *Virginia Teachers Bulletin* 19 (January 1942): 7–11.

————. "Unexplored Fields in the History of the Negro in the United States." *Negro History Bulletin* 8 (December 1944): 57–67.

———. "The Virginia State Teachers Association." *Virginia Teachers Bulletin* 21 (November 1944): 10, 33.

———. "The Voteless School Teachers of Virginia." *Virginia Teachers Bulletin* 18 (November 1941): 12–13.

———. "The Work of the Association and the People." *Journal of Negro History* 20 (October 1935): 385–96.

Janken, Kenneth Robert. *Rayford W. Logan and the Dilemma of the African American Intellectual.* Amherst: University of Massachusetts Press, 1993.

Johnson, Charles, et al. 1943. *To Stem This Tide: A Survey of Racial Tension Areas in the United States.* Boston: Pilgrim Press, 1943. Reprint, New York: AMS Press, 1969.

Johnson, Grace Hays. "Phases of Cultural History of Significance for Negro Students." *Journal of Negro History* 22 (January 1937): 29–37.

Johnston, James Hugo. "The History Teacher and the Changing Curriculum." *Journal of Negro History* 22 (January 1937): 44–49.

———. "Luther Porter Jackson, 1892–1950." *Negro History Bulletin* 13 (June 1950): 195–97.

Jordan, Elizabeth Cobb. "The Impact of the Negro Organization Society on Public Support for Education in Virginia, 1912–1950," Ph.D. diss., University of Virginia, 1978.

Kelley, Robin D. G. "'But a Local Phase of a World Problem': Black History's Global Vision, 1883–1950." *Journal of American History* 86 (December 1999): 1045–77.

———. "'We Are Not What We Seem': Rethinking Black Working-Class Opposition in the Jim Crow South." *Journal of American History* 80 (June 1993): 75–112.

Kelley, Robin D. G., and Earl Lewis, eds. *To Make Our World Anew: A History of African Americans.* New York: Oxford University Press, 2000.

Kennedy, David M. *Freedom from Fear: The American People in Depression and War, 1929–1945.* New York: Oxford University Press, 1999.

Key, V. O. *Southern Politics in State and Nation.* New York: Knopf, 1949.

Kirby, John B. *Black Americans in the Roosevelt Era: Liberalism and Race.* Knoxville: University of Tennessee Press, 1980.

Klibaner, Irwin. "The Travail of Southern Radicals: The Southern Conference Education Fund, 1946–1976." *Journal of Southern History* 49 (May 1983): 179–202.

Klinker, Philip A., with Rogers M. Smith. *The Unsteady March: The Rise and Decline of Racial Equality in America.* Chicago: University of Chicago Press, 1999.

Kluger, Richard. *Simple Justice: The History of* Brown v. Board of Education *and Black America's Struggle for Equality.* 1975. Reprint, New York: Vintage, 1977.

Korstad, Robert, and Nelson Lichtenstein, "Opportunities Found and Lost: Labor, Radicals, and the Early Civil Rights Movement." *Journal of American History* 75 (December 1988): 786–811.

Lamon, Lester. "Black Public Education in the South: By Whom, For Whom, and Under Whose Control?" *Journal of Thought* 18 (fall 1983): 76–89.

Lawson, Steven F. *Black Ballots: Voting Rights in the South.* New York: Columbia University Press, 1976.

———. "Freedom Then, Freedom Now: The Historiography of the Civil Rights Movement." *American Historical Review* 96 (April 1991): 456–71.

———. "From Boycotts to Ballots: The Reshaping of National Politics." In *New Directions in Civil Rights Studies,* edited by Armstead L. Robinson and Patricia Sullivan. Charlottesville: University of Virginia Press, 1991.

———. *Running for Freedom: Civil Rights and Black Politics in America since 1941.* New York: McGraw Hill, 1991. Reprint, New York: McGraw Hill.

Levine, Lawrence. *The Unpredictable Past: Explorations in American Cultural History.* New York: Oxford University Press, 1993.

Lewis, Earl. *In Their Own Interests: Race, Class, and Power in Twentieth-Century Norfolk, Virginia.* Berkeley and Los Angeles: University of California Press, 1991.

———. "'To Turn as on a Pivot': Writing African Americans into a History of Overlapping Diasporas." *American Historical Review* 100 (June 1995): 765–87.

Litwack, Leon F. *Trouble in Mind: Black Southerners in the Age of Jim Crow.* New York: Vintage, 1998.

McAdam, Doug. *Political Process and the Development of Black Insurgency, 1930–1970.* 2d ed. Chicago: University of Chicago Press, 1982.

Meier, August. *Negro Thought in America, 1880–1915: Racial Ideologies in the Era of Booker T. Washington.* Ann Arbor: University of Michigan Press, 1966.

Meier, August, and John H. Bracey. "The NAACP As a Reform Movement, 1900–1965: 'To Reach the Conscience of America.'" *Journal of Southern History* 59 (February 1993): 3–30.

Meier, August, and Elliot Rudwick. *Black History and the Historical Profession, 1915–1980.* Urbana and Champaign: University of Illinois Press, 1986.

———. "J. Franklin Jameson, Carter G. Woodson, and the Foundations of Black Historiography." *American Historical Review* 89 (October 1984): 1005–15.

Miller, Patrick. "To 'Bring the Race along Rapidly': Sport, Student Culture, and Educational Mission at Historically Black Colleges during the Interwar Years." *History of Education Quarterly* 35 (summer 1995): 111–33.

Mitchell, Eva C. "The Economic Status of the Negro in Virginia: Educational Implications." *Virginia Teachers Bulletin* 16 (January 1939): 10–12.

———. "The Milieu of the Negro Educable in Virginia." *Virginia Teachers Bulletin* 17 (January 1940): 6–9.

Moon, Henry Lee. *Balance of Power: The Negro Vote.* New York: Doubleday, 1949.

Moses, Wilson Jeremiah. *The Golden Age of Black Nationalism, 1850–1925.* New York: Oxford University Press, 1978.

Myrdal, Gunner. *An American Dilemma.* 2 vols. New York: McGraw Hill, 1964.

Palmer, L. F. "He Left a Lonesome Place." *Negro History Bulletin* 13 (June 1950): 198.

Patterson, James T. *Brown v. Board of Education: A Civil Rights Milestone and Its Troubled Legacy.* New York: Oxford University Press, 2001.

Perlstein, Daniel. "Teaching Freedom: SNCC and the Creation of the Mississippi Freedom Schools." *History of Education Quarterly* 30 (fall 1990): 297–324.

Picott, J. Rupert. *History of the Virginia Teachers Association.* Washington: National Education Association, 1975.

Polenberg, Richard. "The Good War? A Reappraisal of How World War II Affected American Society." *Virginia Magazine of History and Biography* 100 (July 1992): 295–322.

Pratt, Robert. "New Directions in Virginia's Civil Rights History." *Virginia Magazine of History and Biography* 104 (winter 1996): 149–54.

Radano, Ronald. "Soul Texts and the Blackness of Folk." *Modernism/Modernity* 2 (1995): 71–95.

Randolph, Lewis. "The Civil Rights Movement in Richmond, 1940–1977: Race, Class, and Gender in the Structuring of Protest Activity." *Proteus: A Journal of Ideas* 15 (spring 1998): 63–72.

Reddick, Lawrence. "Racial Attitudes in American History Textbooks of the South." *Journal of Negro History* 19 (July 1934): 225–65.

Reed, Linda. *Simple Decency and Common Sense: The Southern Conference Movement, 1938–1963.* Bloomington: Indiana University Press, 1991.

Roberts, Harry. "Some Background Factors in the Education of Virginia's Rural Negro Population," *Virginia Teachers Bulletin* 22 (January 1945): 14–18.

Rubin, Louis D. Jr. *Virginia: A Bicentennial History.* New York: Norton, 1977.

Salmond, John A. *Miss Lucy of the CIO: The Life and Times of Lucy Randolph Mason, 1882–1959.* Athens: University of Georgia Press, 1988.

Savoy, W. F. "The Negro in the Curricula of the Schools." *Negro History Bulletin* 8 (December 1944): 55–56.

Schneider, Mark Robert. *"We Return Fighting": The Civil Rights Movement in the Jazz Age.* Boston: Northeastern University Press, 2002.

Sherman, Richard. "'The Last Stand': The Fight for Racial Integrity in Virginia in the 1920s." *Journal of Southern History* 54 (February 1988): 69–92.

———. "The 'Teachings at Hampton Institute': Social Equality, Racial Integrity, and the Virginia Public Assemblage Act of 1926." *Virginia Magazine of History and Biography* 95 (July 1987): 275–300.

Sitkoff, Harvard. "African American Militancy in the World War II South: Another Perspective." In *Remaking Dixie: The Impact of World War II on the American South,* edited by Neil R. McMillen. Jackson: University of Mississippi Press, 1997.

———. *The Struggle for Black Equality, 1954–1980.* New York: Hill and Wang, 1981.

Smith, Gerald L. *A Black Educator in the Segregated South: Kentucky's Rufus B. Atwood.* Lexington: University Press of Kentucky, 1994.

Smith, J. Douglas. "Managing White Supremacy: Politics and Culture in Virginia, 1919–1939." Ph.D. diss., University of Virginia, 1998.

———. *Managing White Supremacy: Race, Politics, and Citizenship in Jim Crow Virginia.* Chapel Hill: University of North Carolina Press, 2002.

———. "When Reason Collides with Prejudice: Armistead Lloyd Boothe and the Politics of Desegregation in Virginia, 1948–1963." *Virginia Magazine of History and Biography* 102 (January 1994): 5–46.

Smith, Larissa. "Where the South Begins: Black Politics and Civil Rights Activism in Virginia, 1930–51." Ph.D. diss., Emory University, 2001.

Suggs, Henry Lewis. "Black Strategy and Ideology in the Segregation Era: P. B. Young and the *Norfolk Journal and Guide,* 1910–1954." Virginia Magazine of History and Biography 91 (April 1983): 161–90.

————. *P. B. Young, Newspaperman: Race, Politics, and Journalism in the New South, 1910–1962*. Charlottesville: University of Virginia Press, 1988.

————. "P. B. Young of the *Norfolk Journal and Guide*: Booker T. Washington Militant, 1904–1928." *Journal of Negro History* 64 (autumn 1979): 365–76.

Sullivan, Patricia. *Days of Hope: Race and Democracy in the New Deal Era*. Chapel Hill: University of North Carolina Press, 1996.

Talbot, Alfred Kenneth. "History of the Virginia Teachers Association, 1940–1965." Ph.D. diss., College of William and Mary, 1981.

Tindall, George Brown. *The Emergence of the New South, 1913–1945*. Baton Rouge: Louisiana State University Press, 1967.

Toppin, Edgar. *Loyal Sons and Daughters: Virginia State University, 182–1992*. Norfolk: Pictorial Heritage, 1992.

Trotter, Joe William Jr. "From a Raw Deal to a New Deal: 1929–1945." In *To Make Our World Anew: A History of African Americans*, edited by Vincent Harding, Robin D. G. Kelley, and Earl Lewis, 409–44. New York: Oxford University Press, 2000.

Tuck, Stephen. "Black Protest in the 1940s: The NAACP in Georgia." In *The Civil Rights Movement Revisited: Critical Perspectives on the Struggle for Racial Equality in the United States*, edited by Patrick B. Miller et al. Vol. 5. N.p: Lit Verlag, 2001.

Tushnet, Mark. *The NAACP's Legal Strategy against Segregated Education, 1929–1950*. Chapel Hill: University of North Carolina Press, 1987.

Walker, Vanessa Siddle. *Their Highest Potential: An African American School Community in the Segregated South*. Chapel Hill: University of North Carolina Press, 1996.

Weisbrot, Robert. *Freedom Bound: A History of America's Civil Rights Movement*. New York: Norton, 1990.

Wilkerson, Docey A. "The Negro School Movement in Virginia: From 'Equalization' to 'Integration.'" *Journal of Negro Education* 29 (winter 1960): 17–29.

Wilson, Anna Victoria. "African American Teachers and Black History in the Curriculum before Desegregation." *Journal of the Midwest History of Education Society* 24 (1997): 172–74.

Woodson, Carter G. "An Accounting for Twenty-Five Years." *Journal of Negro History* 25 (October 1940): 422–31.

————. "Negro History Week—The Eighth Year." *Journal of Negro History* 18 (April 1933): 107–13.

————. "Negro History Week—The Twelfth Year." *Journal of Negro History* 22 (April, 1937): 141–47.

Zieger, Robert H. *The CIO, 1935–1955*. Chapel Hill: University of North Carolina Press, 1994.

Zimmerman, Jonathan. "Each 'Race' Could Have Its Heroes Sung: Ethnicity and the History Wars in the 1920s." *Journal of American History* 87 (June 2000): 92–111.

Zinn, Howard. *A People's History of the United States*. 1980. New York: Harper Collins, 2001.

Index

Michael Dennis is assistant professor of history at Acadia University, Wolfville, Nova Scotia. He is the author of *Lessons in Progress: State Universities and Progressivism in the New South, 1880–1920.*